Communication, Love, and Death
in Homer and Virgil

Oklahoma Series in Classical Culture

Communication, Love, and Death in Homer and Virgil
An Introduction

Stephen Ridd

UNIVERSITY OF OKLAHOMA PRESS : NORMAN

All passages from Homer's *Iliad* and *Odyssey* and from Virgil's *Aeneid* have been translated by the author into English from their original-language editions as presented by Oxford Classical Texts: T. W. Allen and D. B. Monro, eds., *Homeri Opera Tomi I–IV*, Oxford Classical Texts (Oxford: Oxford University Press, 1902–1917); and R. Mynors, *P. Vergili Maronis Opera*, Oxford Classical Texts (Oxford: Oxford University Press, 1972).

Library of Congress Cataloging-in-Publication Data

Name: Ridd, Stephen, author.
Title: Communication, love, and death in Homer and Virgil : an introduction / Stephen Ridd.
Other titles: Oklahoma series in classical culture ; v. 54.
Description: Norman : University of Oklahoma Press, 2017. | Series: Oklahoma series in classical culture ; volume 54 | Includes bibliographical references and index.
Identifiers: LCCN 2016051440 | ISBN 978-0-8061-5729-0 (pbk. : alk. paper)
Subjects: LCSH: Homer. Iliad. | Homer. Odyssey. | Virgil. Aeneis.
Classification: LCC PA4037 .R526 2017 | DDC 881/.01—dc23
LC record available at https://lccn.loc.gov/2016051440

Communication, Love, and Death in Homer and Virgil: An Introduction is Volume 54 in the Oklahoma Series in Classical Culture.

The paper in this book meets the guidelines for permanence and durability of the Committee on Production Guidelines for Book Longevity of the Council on Library Resources, Inc. ∞

For Barbara

Contents

Acknowledgments

I am very grateful to Professor P. E. Easterling for her generous support and advice. I dedicate this book and, more specifically, the reference in chapter 6 to *Odyssey* 6.182–84, to my wife, Barbara.

Communication, Love, and Death
in Homer and Virgil

Introduction

The *Iliad,* the *Odyssey,* and the *Aeneid* tell of "the deeds both of men and of gods" (*Odyssey* 1.338), of war and of its aftermath, and of the lives and deaths of those caught up in the conflict (and of course, of much else). They present a world of the imagination, created and developed long ago. In this book I aim to make accessible to the English reader of the twenty-first century—as faithfully as possible through translation, comparison, and an awareness of cultural difference across the centuries—aspects of *communication, love, and death* within that world, and thus to share something of the richness of these three central texts of classical epic poetry. The book presents a series of readings of passages from these texts, chosen to illustrate its three subjects, and invites the reader to compare how these subjects are treated. It is based on close study of the wording of the original Greek and Latin texts as they appear in the Oxford Classical Texts, but I have translated all quotations into English. In the translations, I attempt as close a correspondence to the words and lines of the original texts as possible while conveying their sense in reasonably natural, twenty-first century English. Inevitably much is lost in translation, but the book rests on the belief that enough lives on to justify detailed, comparative study of this nature.

At the outset, it is important to make clear the limits set to this study and to give an idea of the methodology I have followed. In each chapter I focus mainly on the quotations from the three texts, though the discussion ranges widely across all three. After first establishing the context of the passages selected for discussion, I explore their wording and the ideas conveyed by this wording. The readings make use both of the traditional, word-by-word, line-by-line commentaries and the more recent, narratological approach, which looks at the recurrence of ideas and situations across a whole text. Beyond this, I attempt in the book to do something else: to give the reader a sense of ideas developing, rather than just recurring, within each of the three texts, and to look at comparable sequences of ideas in each of the two remaining texts.

Each of the book's eight chapters is divided into three parts, and these three parts focus either on the three texts, one by one, or on a single aspect of the discussion presented within the chapter. Chapter notes carry the development or comparison of ideas beyond the limits set for the main discussion and offer suggestions for further reading. I limit these suggestions to a selection of works written in English and appearing in book form. The discussion itself does not go beyond the *Iliad*, the *Odyssey*, and the *Aeneid*. However, occasional, brief reference is made to Virgil's poems the *Eclogues* and the *Georgics*, which precede the *Aeneid*. The aim of the book is to take the reader, selectively and in detail, through the three texts a number of times and in a number of different ways, and to suggest both resemblances and differences between them in their handling of the three subjects: communication, love, and death.

Four principles underlie the approach adopted and together help shape the book. The first is that the three texts should be treated on an equal basis. This contrasts with an approach often found in commentaries of the *Aeneid*, in which Homeric passages are cited as sources for the text. Virgil's debt to Homer is not to be doubted, but I do not make it a part of this book's concern.[1] Nor do I draw attention to the traditional distinction between so-called primary, Homeric epic, the product of an age-old, oral tradition, and so-called secondary, Virgilian epic, a highly self-conscious and allusive work of writing, composed in a different age and in a different language.[2] It is important to bear this distinction in mind, but instead of using such terms as "primary" and "secondary" with their suggestion of an ordering and evaluation of the three texts, I invite the reader to take a close look at individual passages within the three texts. Setting them side by side, the reader may more profitably consider similarities and differences between them. Often this process will lead to a

---

1. Knauer (1990) gives the reader a summary of this subject, while W. R. Johnson (1976) provides both a sensitive analysis of the difference between Homer's and Virgil's narrative styles and a detailed comparative reading of pairs of passages from Homer and Virgil (including translations of the passages).

2. Williams, in his introduction to the Roman ethos of the *Aeneid*, discusses how "the values of the heroic world compared and contrasted with those of Augustan Rome" (1990a, 27).

comparison between one Virgilian passage and two or more Homeric passages, and all are given equal weight in the discussion, since the book's main focus is on ideas and their potential for development, modification, and regrouping.[3]

These thoughts lead to my second and third principles, which exclude from consideration certain approaches to the texts. Whereas an appreciation of either of the Homeric poems does not require knowledge of the other, I assume that such knowledge does greatly enhance that appreciation, and particularly with regard to Homer's second poem.[4] I do not address the so-called Homeric Question[5] and thus have nothing to say in this book about how these texts may have been created. Likewise, I do not ask what might or might not have been in Virgil's conscious or subconscious mind as the *Aeneid* was taking shape. Nor do I attempt to explore the difference between what, in a broad sense, may be seen as traditional elements and what may be seen as original elements in the poem's composition. The *Aeneid* was not quite finished at the time of Virgil's death, and one feature of this incompleteness is the number of half-lines that the poem contains. These half-lines are often highly effective, and on occasion this effectiveness within the unfolding text forms part of the discussion, whatever may have been Virgil's own ideas about these half-lines.

My third principle is that the reader is able both to read through a text, line by line, and also to range back and forth across all three texts (and of course beyond, though this is outside the scope of the book). As a consequence of this principle, I do not focus on attempting to reconstruct the reception of these three texts within the classical world. Thus, while the importance of the reception of the two Homeric texts as oral works may be borne in mind, I make no attempt to decide what may be considered a listener's reasonable recall of a word or an idea from an earlier point, or number of earlier points, within the text. Instead, I address the reader of the three texts from the start. This is fundamental to the book's aim. Here, however, a complication arises in the form of a difference between the *Aeneid* and the two Homeric texts. The *Aeneid*, unlike the other two texts, presents a grand narrative: the story of the birth of a nation and the glory of that nation's great leader at the time of the *Aeneid*'s composition, the emperor Augustus. It thus engages directly and comprehensively with a historical world, which is beyond the confines

---

3. Rutherford (2013) gives a survey of Homeric studies. Hardie (1998, 53–116) surveys the study of the *Aeneid*.

4. Rutherford (2001) discusses the relationship between the *Iliad* and the *Odyssey*.

5. R. Fowler (2004) gives a concise introduction to this subject.

of the world created within the text. Although this aspect of the *Aeneid* is not a central focus in this book, details of this long-dead historical world need to be brought to the reader's attention, and I do this in a number of places in the second half of the book (chapters 6.3, 7.2, 8.2, and 8.3).

The last of my four principles concerns the main consideration influencing my selection of passages from the three texts: comparison. In each chapter, I examine passages from all three texts and invite the reader to compare them. Clearly there is an element of subjectivity here, both in selecting some passages and excluding others and also in deciding what constitutes an interesting point of resemblance or difference. The book presents a wide-ranging, and essentially open-ended, series of personal readings, and I invite the reader to share in the discussion. Also there is no set formula for the way comparison is employed in the book. My aim is to look for both similarity and diversity through this intertextual approach, and so to enrich the reader's enjoyment of these three classical texts. As Laird writes, "Intertextuality highlights the reader's role in attributing qualities to a text" (1997, 288).

The book's subjects—communication, love, and death—respond to three, deeply ingrained human needs: the need to create and share a narrative, the need to love and be loved by another, and the need to come to terms with the death of loved ones and ultimately with one's own death. My focus moves across these three subjects, but they remain integrally connected with one another. The order of the eight chapters also reflects, in a broad sense, the gradual unfolding of the three texts. My concern with communication is twofold: I examine not only how the three texts communicate with the reader but also how communication occurs between the characters within the text. I explore communication in this double sense in the first three chapters, taking the idea of singing as my starting point and looking at the various ideas associated with it. The middle three chapters give three contexts for the discussion of love: sons and mothers, Helen and the men in her life in each of the three texts, and parting. In the final two chapters I consider, respectively, communication with the dead and deaths and endings.

It is hard, if not impossible, to find an acceptable, consistent way of rendering proper names in English. Faithfulness to the original spelling pulls the translator in one direction, and familiarity with common usage pulls in another. In this book I settle for a compromise somewhere between the two. This difficulty begins with the spelling of the *Aeneid*'s author—Vergil/Virgil. I opt for the second of these. Proper names, however, raise more issues than that of their spelling in English. Where different names are given in Greek and Latin to certain immortal figures, such as Zeus/Jupiter and Aphrodite/Venus, the discussion focuses on the sense of continuing identity here rather than change, though this does not mean that the ideas associated with such pairs remain the same when the name changes. When an individual's name suggests that it carries a sense or allows the possibility of a word-play in the original language, this has been commented on only when it is taken to be central to the discussion, as in the case of Astyanax (Lord of the City), or Calypso (Concealer), or the divinely appointed change in the name of Aeneas's son from Ilus, with its association with Ilium (Troy), to Iulus, with its association with the Julian family in Rome. I will occasionally transliterate a Greek word or give a Latin word when two different senses, conveyed by separate words in English, can be felt to be present in the original word and when these different senses, including the possibility of a word-play between them, are treated as part of the discussion.

In constructing a study of this nature, I have found it virtually impossible not to express some sense of comparative evaluation of the passages selected, but I have as far as possible avoided any sense of creating a hierarchy. I leave it to the reader to make any such judgments. My aim throughout is to begin by focusing on specific passages, then to broaden the discussion by examining both the place of these passages within their unfolding text and their relation to the other two texts investigated. In doing so, I hope to show something new about these works' enduring place in the twenty-first century.

1

Singing with the
Aid of the Muse(s)

1.1 🖋 Three Openings and a Reopening

The *Iliad* and the *Odyssey* each open with an invocation:

> Sing, goddess, of the anger of Achilleus, the son of Peleus,
> an accursed anger. (*Iliad* 1.1–2)

> Tell me, Muse, of a man of many ways, who wandered
> far and wide, when he had sacked the sacred city of Troy.
> (*Odyssey* 1.1–2)

These opening invocations subordinate the narrator's voice to that of a higher authority—in the first case, the "goddess," and in the second case and more specifically, the "Muse."[1] This subordination gives the narrator's voice, as the vehicle for that authority, an unassailable authority of its own. The two openings differ in the way in which the invocation is linked to the first unfolding of the subject of the narrative. The seven-line opening of the *Iliad* unfolds with a strong sense of order and brevity. The subject, "the anger of Achilleus," is at

---

1. The Muses are goddesses who sing and dance to entertain the Olympian gods. At the start of his work, the narrator addresses the "goddess" or the "Muse" in the singular, but elsewhere the Muses also appear in the plural, both in invocations addressed to them by the narrator and within the narrative itself. Over time, nine came to be the canonical figure for the number of Muses and they appear with individual names. In the *Aeneid*, two of them are named in contexts that suggest a degree of specialization for the poetic genre over which they preside.

once presented by the narrator to the Muse, characterized as "accursed," and set in context. First its consequences are shown: pain, death, and mutilation for the Achaeans, and the working out of the plan of Zeus (*Iliad* 1.2–5). Then a fixed starting point comes: the moment when Achilleus and Agamemnon first quarreled (*Iliad* 1.6–7). No mention is made of the narrator or the reader.

The opening of the *Odyssey* is couched more in terms of a personal conversation: "Tell me, Muse." The word "me" can be felt to embrace both the narrator, as he begins his task, and also the reader, as the reader shares in this process. The ten-line opening presents the story of "a man of many ways," a man as yet unnamed: his versatility, his many wanderings, many experiences, and many sufferings on the way home. Here is a story with many strands to it, a story of human resilience, but a story also of failure and of divine punishment for wrongdoing. The introduction already gives a taste of this material in the specific fate of Odysseus's companions, who, despite their leader's best intentions, lose their homecoming through their own wicked folly (*Odyssey* 1.6–9). At the outset, a context is set for the narrative. The events about to be unfolded are a sequel to events earlier in the man's life, "when he had sacked the sacred city of Troy." This point is discussed in chapter 8.3. Within the vast field of human experience opened in the first nine lines, it is now the Muse who is presented by the narrator with the choice of a starting point: "Start at some point in this, goddess, daughter of Zeus, and tell it to us too" (*Odyssey* 1.10). The word "too" can be felt to contribute to the sense of a shared story, a story that is, in some sense, already "there," already known to the Muse, even before the start of its telling involves "us too" in it.[2]

The opening of the *Aeneid* is expressed in still more personal terms, and it reverts to the idea of singing. Now the narrator begins, not with an invocation to the Muse, but with a confident declaration in the first person: "I sing of arms and the man, who from the shores of Troy / was the first to come to Italy, an exile by fate" (*Aeneid* 1.1–2). The eleven-line introduction of the *Aeneid* begins by presenting the subject of its narrative in two halves: "arms" and the travels of an as-yet unnamed "man." With the lightest of touches, this opening suggests comparison both with the *Iliad* and with the *Odyssey*. The *Aeneid*, like the *Iliad*, will be concerned with "arms," and its starting point will

---

2. Goldhill (1991) gives a wide-ranging discussion of the *Odyssey*. Its main focus is on "the relation between representation in language . . . and the construction of (social) identity." Pucci (1995) takes the opening description of a man "of many ways/turns" (*polutropos*) as a starting point for a detailed comparative reading of the two poems.

be "Troy." But, as with the opening of the *Odyssey*, the mention of Troy acts as a point of departure, a starting point for a further sequence of events. The "man" of whom the *Aeneid*'s narrator sings is, in some ways, like the "man" presented at the start of the *Odyssey*: he has far to wander, and in the course of his wanderings he suffers much from a god's (in his case, Juno's) divine anger. Unlike Odysseus, however, he is not traveling back home but is in search of a new home for himself and his people. His journey, aided by fate, takes him from "Troy," from defeat, destruction, and exile, through renewed suffering in war, to the founding of a new city and ultimately a great new nation, the narrator's own nation, "Italy" with its capital, "Rome" (*Aeneid* 1.1–7).[3] Here, as in the opening of the *Odyssey*, is a narrative that draws attention to the size of its subject, but now it does so, not in the context of the many-sided nature of individual, human experience, but rather in the context of a grand narrative: the story of the birth of a nation (*Aeneid* 1.33).

After the initial, seven-line outline, which discreetly offers the reader a simultaneous comparison with the *Iliad* and the *Odyssey* and confidently stakes out its own territory, the narrator turns to make an invocation to the Muse:

> Muse, relate the causes to me; from what damage to her divinity,
> from what sense of pain the queen of the gods impelled a man
> of outstanding duty to endure such misfortunes, to enter upon
> so many labors. Do such fits of anger belong to the celestial spirits?
>   (*Aeneid* 1.8–11)

Whereas the *Iliad* tells of the working out of Zeus' plan, and the *Odyssey* tells of divine punishment for wrongdoing, divine involvement in the narrative of the *Aeneid* is of a more problematic nature. Here is a story of undeserved human suffering and, at first sight, of inexplicable divine anger. A further comparison can now be made between the three openings. After Achilleus and Agamemnon have been introduced in the opening seven lines of the *Iliad*, the narrative uses a question-and-answer technique as an opening gambit: "Which of the gods brought them to fight in this quarrel? / Leto's and Zeus's son" (*Iliad* 1.8–9). And at once the narrative is launched. The *Aeneid*'s opening eleven lines, by contrast, end by posing a sad, unanswered question in which the address to the Muse allows the narrator to share with the reader

---

3. Camps (1969) gives a concise introduction to "Fate and the Gods" in the *Aeneid*. Gransden (2004) discusses "Fate and Free Will."

an editorial response to the subject of his narrative. Unlike the narrator of the *Odyssey* ("Tell me . . . tell it to us too"), however, the narrator here does not share his narrative so directly with the reader. Instead, he introduces into the narrative his own voice in dialogue with the Muse. In doing so, he introduces a sense of openness, the sense of an important question raised but left unanswered, before giving the starting point of his narrative by turning aside to introduce another ancient city, Carthage, and by explaining Juno's love for that city and the reasons for her deep-seated hatred of the Trojans and their future descendants. The reasons for Juno's hatred belong partly in the world of history (*Aeneid* 1.12–22) and partly in the mythological world inherited from her Homeric counterpart, Hera (*Aeneid* 1.23–28). This combination of motives helps immediately locate the narrative of the *Aeneid* midway between these two worlds.[4]

Neither the *Iliad* nor the *Odyssey* has a clearly marked halfway point in its narrative, but the *Aeneid*, devised from the start in the form of twelve, distinct books, does contain such a structural break: a reopening. This fresh start does not come with mathematical precision at exactly the halfway point. The narrative extends across the end of *Aeneid* 6 and into the start of *Aeneid* 7 before coming to a pause at line 36, as Aeneas and his companions reach the mouth of the Tiber. At this point there is a substantial invocation specifically to Erato, the Muse associated with love:

> Come now, Erato, I will set out who were the kings,
> what the state of affairs and what the condition of ancient Latium,
> when a foreign army first brought a fleet to the shores of Ausonia,
> and I will recall the origins of the first fighting.
> You, goddess, you advise your bard.[5] I will tell of bristling wars,
> I will tell of battle lines, of kings driven to death by their proud
> > spirits,
> of the Tyrrhenian contingent and of all Hesperia forced to take up[6]
> arms. A greater order of events is born to me,
> a greater work I set in motion. (*Aeneid* 7.37–45)

4. On the role of the gods in the *Aeneid*, see Feeney (1991, 129–87) and Lyne (1987, 61–99).

5. The word in line 41 translated as "bard" combines the senses of "prophet" or "inspired speaker" and "poet."

6. Ausonia and Hesperia (The Western Land) are names for Italy. "The Tyrrhenian contingent" refers to the Etruscans, whose help Aeneas gains for the war in Italy.

Now that the wanderings of Aeneas and his companions in search of their promised land are over, the narrative makes a fresh start. The narrator devotes eight and a half lines to this reopening before setting out the background for this second, Italian phase of his story and introducing a new set of characters and circumstances (*Aeneid* 7.45–106). Central to these new circumstances are the advent and spread of war between the Trojans, now presented from a fresh viewpoint as "a foreign army," and the local Italian population. The move to the second part of the *Aeneid* thus marks, in broad terms, a change of emphasis—from wanderings to the "arms" heralded at its opening—and hence a heightening of its subject matter to a full, epic grandeur reminiscent of the *Iliad,* the pinnacle of the epic genre. By her presence at this carefully controlled turning point in the narrative, Erato suggests a different nuance in the presentation of what is the traditional, Iliadic subject matter of "kings, fighting, death and proud spirits." She even creates a slight but effective dissonance, as this new material is given its introductory fanfare. The narrator, who now styles himself "bard," confidently sets out his coming subject matter and proclaims a new and greater creation on his part. In the midst of this confidence, however, a call comes to the Muse Erato for advice and, by implication, for help to stop the narrative from becoming too historical and military, and thus too heavy. Instead, a hint is given that even the traditionally elevated, epic subject matter of the second half of the *Aeneid* will, like its more widely ranging first half, incorporate narrative involving the subjects of love and marriage, and almost at once this is borne out. King Latinus is introduced in midline (*Aeneid* 7.45), followed by his daughter, Lavinia, together with the complications surrounding the family's wedding plans for her (*Aeneid* 7.52–80). And so the narrative of the second half of the *Aeneid* is launched.[7]

1.2 ✒ Lists of Fighting Forces

Communication between the narrator and his Muse enables him, in different ways in the three poems, to introduce the subject of his narrative and, in the second and third of them, to make contact with the reader. Renewed invocations occur both in the *Iliad* and in closely similar contexts in the *Aeneid*; they do not occur in the *Odyssey*. The first and most substantial of them, in

---

7. For the broad division of the *Aeneid* into an Odyssean first half and an Iliadic second half, see Gransden (2004, 26–33). Gransden (1984) focuses the reader's attention on the second half of the *Aeneid*.

the second book of the *Iliad*, takes up ten lines and introduces the great list of Achaean leaders and the contingents brought in their ships to fight at Troy:

> Tell me now, you Muses whose dwelling is on Olympos—
> for you are goddesses, you are both present and know everything,
> while we hear only its fame and do not know anything—
> who the leaders and the captains of the Danaans were.[8]
> As for the host of men, I could not speak of it or name it,
> not if I had ten tongues and ten mouths,
> a voice that never stopped and a heart of bronze,
> unless the Olympian Muses, daughters of aegis-bearing Zeus,
> were to give me the memory of how many came to Troy.
> Now I will tell of the leaders of the ships and of all their ships.
>   (*Iliad* 2.484–93)

Here the narrator of the *Iliad* makes the first of his rare appearances ("Tell me. . . . Now I will tell"). In doing so, he places himself firmly in the same, limited, human world as the reader ("we hear . . . and do not know"). The human world has no direct access to the relevant, detailed knowledge of the past needed at this point, and so the narrator must rely on tradition ("fame"). The Muses, on the other hand, in their omnipresence and omniscience, transcend human limitation. Through their communication with the narrator, they make possible for him a task otherwise far beyond human power, namely, the recording of the vast numbers involved in the expedition to Troy. They do this by their gift of "memory."[9] As at the opening of the *Iliad*, the invocation authorizes the narrator to speak, but now it goes beyond that and guarantees that the great detail he is about to go into cannot be challenged. At the same time, the tone of gently self-mocking hyperbole ("not if I had ten tongues") prevents this rare focus on the narrator himself from becoming too serious an intervention within his narrative.

Passages combining a strong sense of movement and colorful description surround the lists of Achaean and Trojan forces (*Iliad* 2.441–83, 780–815;

---

8. Homer uses the words "Achaeans," "Argives," and "Danaans" to refer to the Greek forces. In addition to using these terms, Virgil uses various forms of the word "Greek."

9. For further discussion of the relationship between the singer and the Muse(s), see Graziosi and Haubold (2005, 44–48). In post-Homeric times, the Muses were regarded as the daughters of Zeus and Memory. Osborne (2004) gives a concise introduction to the relationship between the historical world in which the Homeric poems were created and the world that the Homeric poems create.

3.1–14), and these passages set the two lists in context as the moment of encounter between the two armies approaches. Whereas *Iliad* 1 plunges the reader into the middle of the Trojan War, *Iliad* 2–4, as Griffin (1980) notes, take the reader back to the early stages of the war, though with no suggestion of a break. The placing of the two lists, particularly the huge list of Achaean forces, creates an effective hiatus as the tension in the narrative mounts. As the two great armies deploy and prepare to confront each other, they are not presented as anonymous, undifferentiated masses; instead, each of the regional contingents, each of their leaders, and the places from which the men under their command have come, are closely identified. The result is a vast and powerful collection of proper names. Part of this power lies in a fundamental aspect of communication: naming. Presented on this scale, a list of proper names of people and places, together with supporting, statistical details and some element of description, shows a world endowed with order and significance. The small-scale, local level and the whole, vast picture complement one another. Here is something fixed and lasting: a timeless commemoration that brings individuals, their followers, and their homes to life. The sense of shared existence and shared endeavor is carefully set between, on the one hand, the preliminary scene of disastrous discord among the Achaean high command and the near collapse of the campaign and, on the other hand, the relentless killing and destruction once the fighting begins. Within the overall architecture of the *Iliad,* the list of Achaean forces, placed toward its beginning, is complemented toward its end by the involvement of the whole surviving Achaean army in the funeral games, arranged in honor of Patroklos by Achilleus (*Iliad* 23.257–24.2). Also created here is a sense of broad, geographical space and diversity, which contrasts with the insistent concentration of focus on the war zone: the shore, the camp, the battlefield, and the enemy city. In this context of commemoration, with its wide-ranging associations, the proper names are endowed with their own resonance. They are, with the aid of the Muses and metaphorically speaking, given the power to sing.

A further, brief invocation comes immediately following the line that signals the end of the list:

These then were the leaders and captains of the Danaans.
Which one stood out as the best, you tell me, Muse,
among the warriors and horses who followed the sons of Atreus.
(*Iliad* 2.760–62)

The answers to these two related questions are at once given by the narrator (*Iliad* 2.763–68). These winners, however, owe their place of honor to the absence of Achilleus, (*Iliad* 2.769–73). Were it not for his angry withdrawal from the fighting, Achilleus would have been the outright winner in both fields. After the account of the massive, collective military presence, given with amazing attention to detail, the focus switches to the one, crucially absent figure, who, together with his contingent of men and horses, is now idling his time away, out of the fighting (*Iliad* 2.771–79). After the great list, the reader is thus led back with gentle irony to recall the starting point of the *Iliad*, the anger of Achilleus and its consequences.

As well as celebrating the Muses' power to aid the narrator through the gift of memory, the list also contains a striking instance of their power to do the reverse: to bring a singer to an abrupt and devastating halt and to take away his divine gift and the memory of his skill. This stands out as the only instance within the list of an elaboration of details that have no direct connection with the fighting. A series of place names (*Iliad* 2.591–94) comes to an end with Dorion:

> and Dorion, where the Muses,
> meeting Thamyris, the Thracian, stopped his singing,
> as he came from Oichalia, from Eurytos of Oichalia.
> For he boasted and declared that he would win, even if
> the Muses themselves, the daughters of Zeus, who holds
>   the aegis,[10]
> were to sing, and they became angry and paralyzed him
> and took from him the divine voice and made him forget his lyre
>   playing. (*Iliad* 2.594–600)

The singer may sing of boastfulness on the part of the epic heroes on the battlefield, but he must not emulate it himself in the exercise of his divinely given art. As the mention of the event at Dorion reminds the narrator, the punishment for such a transgression is terrible and complete.

In the *Aeneid*, the two lists of opposing forces are set well apart (*Aeneid* 7.641–817 and 10.163–214), and neither is on such an extended scale as the list of Achaean forces in the *Iliad*. First to be listed are the Italian leaders and

---

10. The aegis appears to have been imagined as a tasseled goatskin covered with terrifying images and worn over the shoulders. It was used by Zeus, Athene, and Apollo. Cf. *Iliad* 2.446–51; 5.738–42; 15.229–30, 307–11; 21.400–401.

their forces, who answer the call to arms to protect their land against the "foreign army" (*Aeneid* 7.38–39) brought by a fleet to its shores. The narrator introduces this list with an address to the Muses:

> Throw wide now Helicon,[11] goddesses, and set song in motion,
> of what kings were roused to war, what battle lines followed them
> and filled the plains, with what warriors even then
> the bountiful land of Italy flourished, with what a blaze of weapons.
> For you, goddesses, both remember and can relate it,
> but to us barely does a thin breeze of its fame glide down.
>   (*Aeneid* 7.641–46)

The narrator calls on the Muses to sing and gives them their subject. How the traditional epic requirement of a list of fighting forces is presented here offers scope in itself for colorful description, as can be seen by comparing the sense of human limitation expressed in the *Iliad*'s "while we hear only its fame and do not know anything" (*Iliad* 2.486) with the *Aeneid*'s similar expression, "but to us barely does a thin breeze of its fame glide down" (*Aeneid* 7.646). Such a "thin breeze" is in no danger of producing anything too heavy for the reader, by way of a list of names and numbers.

The list of Italian forces takes the form of a sequence of colorful descriptions of individuals, and this results in a sense of diversity rather than of collective identity. They are shown on the move, one after the other, rather than as part of a static review. The reader is thus presented with a succession of vignettes that create a kaleidoscopic sense of movement, variety, and color. Here is an opportunity to tell a wealth of diverse, miniature stories of memorable individuals and places, many of them given an additional sense of immediacy by being addressed by name by the narrator. As the conflict is about to begin in earnest, the names of people and places are given. For the most part, these have a strong, local, Italian resonance, but the names also maintain links with the older, epic world of the Greeks. Taken collectively, these stories give the narrator the opportunity within this epic context to sing in praise of his own land of Italy (cf. the so-called "praises of Italy" at *Georgics* 2.136–76), a land of varied peoples and places, founded and defended by brave and exotic warriors of a bygone age, with equally diverse manners of fighting. Hardie writes that "in the *Aeneid* Virgil's attachment to Italy, already displayed

---

11. A mountain in central Greece, on the summit of which there was a sanctuary of the Muses.

in the *Eclogues* and *Georgics,* engages with Augustus' policy of national unity"
(1998, 66). Together with this diversity and pride in Italy's past, however, there
is also a sense of ambivalence. King Latinus is horrified by the consequences
of this unjust war, which his people, under the influence of the hot-headed
Turnus, are bringing on themselves, but he is powerless to stop the rush to war
created by Juno and her servant, the Fury Allecto. This sense of disapproval
colors the first entry in the list of Italian forces. Mezentius, the leader from
Etruria, is the antithesis of "dutiful" Aeneas. Mezentius is "a despiser of the
gods" (*Aeneid* 7.648), and yet his handsome son, Lausus, who fights by his
side and who deserves to have had a better father, will be an example of filial
piety taken to its ultimate limit when he selflessly gives his life to protect his
father from the wrath of Aeneas on the battlefield (*Aeneid* 10.789–820). Once
again, as at its opening, the *Aeneid* presents its reader with a morally complex
and problematic narrative.

The widening of the traditional, epic subject matter, hinted at in the
appeal to Erato for guidance, becomes apparent toward the end of the list in
the two descriptions that frame that of Turnus. Before him comes Virbius,
the handsome son of Hippolytus, and the story is given of how his father,
"called back with the aid of Paeonian[12] herbs and the love of Diana" (*Aeneid*
7.769), was miraculously brought back to life. At the end of the list and at
the head of her cavalry comes Camilla, the Amazon-like maiden warrior. She
has supernatural powers of flight, and as she passes by, all eyes are turned
on her to gape at her royal costume of purple and gold, complemented by
a Lycian quiver: "and a shepherd's myrtle-stick with a spear-tip fixed to its
end" (*Aeneid* 7.817, the last line in the list and the last line of *Aeneid* 7). Not
only are Greek and Italian elements blended in these two entries, but there
is also a hint of a poetic genre other than epic, a hint of a world of love and
magic, of shepherds and shepherdesses. A comparison with the *Georgics* has
earlier been suggested; here, for a moment or two, are details reminiscent of
the world of the *Eclogues.* Virgil's Muses fulfill comprehensively the prayer
made to them at the start of the list to "set song in motion."

At *Aeneid* 10.147–62, Aeneas sails back at night towards the Trojan camp
with his new ally by his side, Pallas, the young son of King Evander. They
come with sea-borne reinforcements sent to aid the Trojans by Tarchon, the
Etruscan king. At this moment of comparative peace, before the renewal

---

12. Paeon is the title of Apollo in his role as healer.

of battle, the second list comes, detailing the contingents that make up the thirty-strong Etruscan fleet (*Aeneid* 10.166–214). This second list opens with the same, introductory invocation as the first: "Throw wide now Helicon, goddesses, and set song in motion" (*Aeneid* 10.163), but the second list is on a much smaller scale than the first, and its geographical focus is restricted. Etruria, keen to fight against the hated Mezentius, and the area to the north, including Mantua, are commemorated for the timely contribution they make to Aeneas in a land that has, for the most part, turned against the Trojans. Virgil gives prominence here to his own birthplace, Mantua (*Aeneid* 10.198–203). Jenkyns (1998) compares the anonymity of the narrators of the *Iliad* and the *Odyssey* with the individual seal that Virgil subtly gives to his work.[13]

Once again this list of fighting forces contains plenty of colorful description and a sense of movement, as the ships sail in line. As in the first list, the traditional subject matter is extended, and as before (*Aeneid* 7.761–82), mention of a son leads to a story about his father:

> I would not pass over you, Cunarus, leader of the Ligurians,
> most brave in war, and Cupavo with your handful of followers,
> whose swan feathers rise from the crest of your helmet
> (a reproach against you and your mother, god of Love) and the
>   mark of his father's transformation.
> For they say that while Cycnus was singing in grief for his
>   beloved Phaethon,
> amid the poplar leaves, in the shade from his sisters,
> and was consoling himself with the Muse for the sorrow of love,
> he drew round himself, with soft plumage, the whiteness of
>   old age,
> leaving the earth and seeking the stars with his voice. (*Aeneid*
>   10.185–93)

Already in the first list, Turnus's shield is decorated with the story of a metamorphosis: Io turned into a heifer (*Aeneid* 7.789–92). Now another story of metamorphosis is given in the description of an item of military equipment, in this case Cupavo's plumed helmet. Phaethon's sisters, grieving for their brother's death, have already been transformed into trees, which provide the

---

13. For Etruria's place alongside the future Roman state, cf. *Georgics* 2.533–34. For earlier references to Mantua, cf. *Eclogue* 9.27–28, *Georgics* 2.198–99 and 3.10–12, where the narrator promises to bring the Muses to his home town in triumph.

shade in which Cupavo's father Cycnus (Swan) sings his lament. And now "the Muse" appears with a new task, to console a lover for the loss of his beloved, rather than singing of armed forces in unison with her sisters. S. J. Harrison writes that "the use . . . of the themes of singing in the shade and songs of unhappy love irresistibly recalls . . . the *Eclogues*: the story of Cycnus is thus a 'pastoral' digression from the epic world of the catalogue" (1991, 121). As he sings, Cycnus is metamorphosed into a swan. His supernatural covering in downy feathers resembles a sudden, instantaneous aging from an adult lover into "the whiteness of old age." Then, as he takes to the air, his lament becomes a swansong, and there is the suggestion of an impending further transformation from a swan into a constellation among the stars. Once again a list of fighting forces provides Virgil's Muses with a richly imaginative opportunity "to set song in motion."

1.3 ✍ Battles and Burning Ships

There are three further invocations of the Muses in the *Iliad*. All reuse the line that opens the invocation at the start of the list of Achaean forces and their ships: "Tell me now you Muses, whose dwelling is on Olympos" (*Iliad* 11.218, 14.508, 16.112). In each case, the word "first" occurs in the line that follows. These subsequent invocations within the central section of the poem bring a brief pause in the onward flow of the narrative, for a moment drawing attention back to the narrator and his authority and creating the sense of a starting point for a fresh sequence of events within the developing narrative. The first two invocations occur in the context of battles. At *Iliad* 11.216–17, Agamemnon himself leads the attack and is keen to fight far ahead of his fellow warriors. At this point comes the invocation:

> Tell me now you Muses, whose dwelling is on Olympos,
> who the first was to come out against Agamemnon
> of the Trojans themselves or of their renowned allies.
> (*Iliad* 11.218–20)

The answer is at once given by the narrator, who describes in detail the Thracian champion Iphidamas's encounter with Agamemnon and his death at Agamemnon's hands. The invocation honors the enemy warrior, who is the first to brave the field against the storming figure of the Achaeans' commander-in-chief, and whose death in that encounter sets in motion a sequence of events that leads to a change of fortune on the battlefield, which has already been heralded (*Iliad* 11.181–209).

In the second half of *Iliad* 14, Poseidon turns the tide of battle in favor of the Achaeans. The fighting intensifies, with horrific details. Fear grips the Trojan army, and the one thought in the minds of the soldiers is self-preservation. At this point, a renewed invocation comes:

> Tell me now you Muses, whose dwelling is on Olympos,
> who the first was of the Achaeans to raise the bloody spoils of war,
> when the famous earth-shaker inclined the battle their way.
> (*Iliad* 14.508–10)

This time the question prompts more than an immediate answer: Aias, son of Telamon, was the first to inflict a wound on an enemy leader, and he is followed by a short list of further victors and their victims (*Iliad* 14.511–22).[14] Here the invocation heralds the commemoration of current Achaean triumphs on the battlefield, and in particular the first of them, before Zeus wakes up at the start of *Iliad* 15 and the narrative moves off in a fresh direction.

In *Iliad* 15, the narrator looks forward to the unfolding sequence of events in the remaining third of his narrative, first through Zeus's speech to Hera (*Iliad* 15.49–77) and later through a brief recall of Zeus's plan (*Iliad* 15.593–602). In this second passage, attention is drawn to what will be the final turning point in the fortunes of war and the catalyst for the final sequence of events: when the results of Zeus's promise to Thetis to bring honor to her son by helping the Trojans (*Iliad* 1.508–10, 523–30) reach a climax, and Hektor succeeds in setting fire to one of the Achaean ships. The long-acknowledged threat to the Achaean ships comes ever closer, and just as Patroklos persuades Achilleus to let him go into battle wearing Achilleus's arms, Aias falters in his defense of the Achaean ships. At this point comes the final invocation: "Tell me now you Muses, whose dwelling is on Olympos, / how fire first fell upon the ships of the Achaeans" (*Iliad* 16.112–13). The narrative returns for a further eight and a half lines to the forced retreat of Aias before the crucial moment arrives. A ship is set alight. Achilleus slaps his thighs and, sensing the danger, rouses Patroklos and his men to battle (*Iliad* 16.122–29), beginning the critical sequence of events. This final invocation is thus the one most deeply embedded into the unfolding narrative.

14. Elsewhere the posing of a direct question in the form "Who was the first . . . ?" or "Who was the first and who was the last, whom a particular warrior killed?" is used to introduce lists of victims, at *Iliad* 5.703–4; 8.273; 11.299–300; 16.692–93; *Aeneid* 11.664–65.

The *Aeneid* contains two further invocations of the Muses, the first in the context of an attempt to set ships on fire and the second in the thick of the fighting. Both occur in *Aeneid* 9. At the start of the book, Turnus launches an attack on the Trojan camp in Aeneas's absence. He tries to draw the Trojans out into open battle by setting fire to the fleet, which lies moored alongside the camp. As his men are on the point of setting fire to the ships, the narrative is interrupted with these words:

> Which god, O Muses, turned aside such a savage conflagration
> from the Trojans? Who drove back such great fire from the ships?
> Speak: in olden days it was believed as fact but the fame of it lives
>   forever. (*Aeneid* 9.77–79)

There follows a flashback to an earlier conversation that Cybele, the mother of the gods, is said to have had with Jupiter (*Aeneid* 9.80–103). From time to time the *Aeneid*'s narrator sets himself a little apart from his narrative and suggests that he is following a tradition. He does this by saying that something is said to be the case, or "the story goes that," or by using a similar formulation.[15] The time has now arrived for the fulfilment of Jupiter's promise to Cybele to turn into sea-nymphs the Trojan ships that have survived to the end of their journey. Turnus's attempt to set fire to them prompts a spectacular intervention by the mother of the gods and the promised metamorphosis (*Aeneid* 9.107–22). Williams writes, "Virgil snatches us away from the awful inevitability of unopposed military might into the pastoral world . . . where at the moment of death there is intervention, escape, transformation from the mortal world." (1990a, 35).

Both the successful fire-attack on the Achaean ship in *Iliad* 16 and this unsuccessful attempt to set fire to the Trojan ships in *Aeneid* 9 are richly significant moments of heightened intensity within the narrative. The metamorphosis of the ships in *Aeneid* 9, heralded by the invocation to the Muses, signals the end of an era. Juno has done her best to stop the Trojans from sailing to their promised land, but now that the surviving ships have reached it, an older, benign goddess, fortified with Jupiter's overriding authority,

---

15. This occurs for the first time at *Aeneid* 1.15–16. A slightly different, more skeptical nuance is given by the words "if the story is true" (*Aeneid* 3.551) and "if the story merits belief" (*Georgics* 3.391; *Aeneid* 6.173). From time to time the narrators in the *Iliad* and the *Odyssey* use the words "they say that" to preface a statement. A memorable example of this occurs at *Odyssey* 6.42–46, where the narrator gives a description of the gods' home on Olympos.

guarantees their safety from further attack. The Trojan ships have been storm-tossed, and one of them has been lost at sea (*Aeneid* 1.113–19, 584–85). Some have been threatened with fire by initially hostile Carthaginian forces (*Aeneid* 1.525), and some have been set on fire and destroyed by the demoralized Trojan women (*Aeneid* 5.654–99). But now those that remain have completed their work. They become divine, and before long they reappear with supernatural power to bring news and advice to their former captain and his followers (*Aeneid* 10.219–48).

As before, at *Aeneid* 1.8–11 and 7.37–45, an invocation to the Muse(s) leads the narrator to pass an editorial comment on his narrative. A change of emphasis can be felt here when line 79 is compared with the call upon the Muses in *Iliad* 2:

> Tell me now you Muses, whose dwelling is on Olympos,
> for you are goddesses, you are both present and know everything,
> while we hear only the fame of it and do not know anything.
> (*Iliad* 2.484–86)

The *Iliad*'s Muses are omniscient. They bring to the narrator's task a sense of the absolute, as they communicate information to him from their store of universal knowledge. This contrasts with a fallible, human reliance on "fame," mediated by an oral tradition. In *Aeneid* 9, a different contrast is suggested. "Fact" is acknowledged to be a matter of "belief" rather than of divinely guaranteed knowledge. It is a belief located in the past and something that can be contrasted with a sense of the absolute. Now that absolute is applied to the tradition itself rather than to the guarantee of its authenticity: "but the fame of it lives forever."

At *Aeneid* 9.503–4 the war trumpet sounds after the ill-fated nighttime sortie of Nisus and Euryalus. The siege of the Trojan camp begins and is vigorously countered by the defending Trojans (*Aeneid* 9. 505–24). A renewed invocation to the Muses comes a short way into this description of battle:

> You Muses, O Calliope, I beg, breathe into me as I sing
> what slaughter Turnus brought there and then with his sword,
> what deaths
> he dealt out, who it was that each man sent down to the
> Underworld,
> and unroll with me the vast realm of war. (*Aeneid* 9.525–28)

The narrative resumes at once with the description of a Trojan watchtower, the intense fighting around it, and its collapse when set on fire by the enemy.

The call to the Muses, addressed to Calliope, particularly associated with epic poetry and the most senior Muse, empowers the narrator to take his narrative in the traditional epic direction: the exploits of a leading warrior on the battlefield, time-honored similes from the world of nature, and a list of victors and their victims (*Aeneid* 9.530–89). The presentation of such material is now conceived by the narrator as a collaboration with the Muses both in oral terms ("breathe into me as I sing") and in written terms, as a process of unrolling a vast record of war.[16]

Despite the aid that the two narrators receive from the Muse(s), both at the start and in the course of their task, there come moments both in the *Iliad* and in the *Aeneid* when each expresses a sense of his own, human limitation when confronted by the enormity of attempting a complete narrative of events. Such a point occurs twice in the *Iliad*. The first occasion comes halfway through the narrative, when the Trojans are storming the Achaean camp:

> Others were fighting in battle around other gates.
> It would be hard for me to tell it all, as though I were a god.
> For all around the stone wall there arose the terrible blaze
> of fire. (*Iliad* 12.175–78)

The second occasion comes three-quarters of the way through, when Menelaos calls for united support to defend the body of Patroklos from the enemy. Three warriors who respond to this call are named, and the passage continues: "But of the others, whose mind could give the names / of those who came after them and roused the Achaean battle?" (*Iliad* 17.260–61). In each of these two passages, the narrator acknowledges the existence of "others" beyond the individuals on whom he focuses, and in each he explains why his narrative must stop short of completeness. In the first passage, the blaze of fire "all around" blocks the others from his view. In a spirit similar to his more extended intervention at *Iliad* 2.488–92, he reminds the reader that he is, after all, only human. In the second passage, a plight similar to that of the narrator has already been expressed shortly before by Menelaos himself: "It is hard for me to distinguish clearly each / of the leaders, for so great is the blaze of conflict on the battlefield" (*Iliad* 17.252–53). The rhetorical question raised by the narrator in the second passage also draws to an end the description of Menelaos's call for help, suggesting the possibility of a further list of fighters without the need for the elaboration of detail.

---

16. Books in classical times were formed of sheets glued together to form a roll, which would be unrolled to be read.

In the *Aeneid,* a single comparable moment comes toward the end of the narrative and is explored in more detail. At *Aeneid* 12.494–99, in the thick of battle, Aeneas's anger rises as he is frustrated in his pursuit of Turnus and embarks on an indiscriminate slaughter of enemy forces. However, before the narrator gives an interlaced account of the killings carried out by the two commanders of the warring forces, he expresses his difficulty in a rhetorical question:

> What god could now unfold for me in song so many bitter
>   sufferings,
> such varied slaughter and the deaths of leaders,
> which now Turnus, now the Trojan hero, deals out in turn,
> all over the plain? (*Aeneid* 12.500–503)

Here the narrator's difficulty is not only that posed by the impossibility of achieving completeness for his narrative, but also includes an emotional nuance, which draws attention to the scale of human suffering: "so many bitter sufferings." As the passage continues, the questioning tone becomes more insistent: "Was it your will, Jupiter, that nations destined to be / forever at peace should clash with such force?" (*Aeneid* 12.503–4). While the opening of the *Iliad* confidently asserts, "and the will of Zeus was being accomplished" (*Iliad* 1.5), the tone adopted by the narrator of the *Aeneid* as the narrative moves towards its final phase is characteristically more questioning. It now takes the form of an anguished paradox presented no longer to the Muse but to Jupiter himself. At the start of his narrative (*Aeneid* 1.11), the narrator, addressing the Muse, shares with the reader a troubled question about the imponderable nature of the divine involvement in his narrative about "a man distinguished for his sense of duty." Here, toward the end, as the carnage wrought by the leaders of the two sides reaches a climax, the sense of the incomprehensible nature of the divine will is extended to take in the fate of both warring sides. At the same time, the confident prediction of an everlasting harmony to come between the two currently warring nations ("nations destined to be forever at peace") looks forward to the concessions finally made by Juno in her reply to the expression of Jupiter's will (*Aeneid* 12.808–28). I discuss in chapter 8.3 how the reader may respond to the narrator's raising troubled questions of this nature at either end of his narrative.

2

Singing and Celebration

2.1 🖉 Singing and Celebrating the Deeds of the Gods

At *Iliad* 1.430–71, Odysseus and his crew carry out Agamemnon's orders to take Chryseis back home to her father, the priest of Apollo at Chryse, and make a lavish sacrifice to the god to appease his anger. The return of the girl to her father at the altar and the sacrifice to Apollo take place with due ritual. Apollo hears the father's prayer to remove the plague from the Achaean army, all take part in the sacrifice and attendant feasting and drinking, and the rest of the day is given over to singing and dancing in praise of Apollo:

> And all day long the Achaean young men appeased the god
> with song and dance, with beautiful singing of a paean of praise,
> making music to the god who acts from afar, and it delighted his
>   heart to hear them. (*Iliad* 1.472–74)[1]

Here in Chryse, watched over by Apollo (*Iliad* 1.37), the world of conflict between individuals and between armies is left behind. All share equally in the feasting and drinking, confirming and celebrating the rediscovered sense of harmony between man and god. With the relaxing of tension comes a relaxation to the sense of time: all day can now be spent in appeasing the god, in the rhythmical movements of the dance and the "beautiful singing"

---

1. Kearns (2004) gives a concise introduction to the subject of the gods in the Homeric epics. For further discussion, see Graziosi and Haubold (2005, 65–93). For the wider religious background, see Gould (1985).

of a hymn in his praise, a thanksgiving for relief from trouble. Apollo's heart is delighted and his anger appeased. This sense of well-being, however, is not sustained for long since Odysseus and his companions must leave Chryse's holy music making, delightful to the distant god, and be wafted back to the war-torn plain of Troy by a wind sent by Apollo. Here once again he will take the side of their enemies.

In the first half of the *Aeneid*, the refugees from the sack of Troy, hounded by the relentless anger of Juno, have no cause to express a sense of harmony between man and god through singing and music making. Indeed, when such activity is recalled by Aeneas, it is associated with the terrible memory of the Wooden Horse and its central part in the destruction of Troy:

> the fatal machine climbs the walls,
> its womb full of arms. Around it boys and unmarried girls
> sing sacred songs and delight to put their hands on the rope,
> and she makes her way in, a threatening presence gliding into the
>   midst of the city.
> O my country! O Troy, home of the gods, and walls of the people of
>   Dardanus,[2]
> famed in war! (*Aeneid* 2.237–42)

The Trojans' deluded belief that they are taking part in a holy ritual gives a bitter irony to this anguished memory of deception and imminent destruction.

By the start of the second half of the *Aeneid*, the sacked city of Troy lies far behind, and Aeneas and his Trojan survivors are assured of a new home in their promised land of Italy. Juno's anger, however, still pursues them, and now a new war with the local Italian tribes is about to break out. Once again, as in *Iliad* 1, the world of conflict is for a time left behind, and the scene changes to one of harmonious celebration of the gods. Now, however, the change of scene and its timing are more deeply embedded within the unfolding narrative. At *Aeneid* 8.97–104, Aeneas sails up the river Tiber and reaches Evander's humble settlement of Pallanteum, the site of the future city of Rome.[3] His arrival coincides with the celebrations being held there in honor of Hercules. Aeneas is given a warm welcome and is invited to share in these annual celebrations and learn the story that lies behind them (*Aeneid* 8.184–279). As evening falls, the religious celebrations take on a new form:

---

2. For Dardanos, the son of Zeus, as a founding father of the Trojans, cf. *Iliad* 20.215–18.

3. Gransden discusses the role of Evander in the *Aeneid* (1976, 24–29).

> Then, with music playing, the Dancing Priests appear around the
>   flaming altars,
> their foreheads bound with boughs from the poplar tree.
> On one side stands a chorus of young men, on the other a chorus
>   of old men,
> who sing praises to Hercules and tell of his deeds. (*Aeneid*
>   8.285–88)

There follows a brief account of Hercules' labors, the first part told in indirect speech, the second in words addressed directly to Hercules himself. This leads to a call upon the god:

> "Hail, true offspring of Jupiter, new glory added to the gods,
> come and favor us, and with auspicious step attend your sacred
>   rites."
> Such are the words they sing in celebration. (*Aeneid* 8.301–3)

The reader is encouraged to see these celebrations as Aeneas sees them, but with an extended sense of their significance. Here is an account of no "empty superstition" (*Aeneid* 8.187) but a well-established ritual, one celebrated in the Rome of Virgil's day on a specific day and at a specific site. The Roman state's adoption of the Greek cult of Herakles (Hercules) is here given its roots in the Pallanteum of the Greek émigré Evander. The "Dancing Priests," familiar elsewhere in Roman religious ritual, appear in this context and help give the occasion its festive quality. At the center of all this, Hercules stands as a model both for Aeneas and for the reader to consider: a hero who triumphs over the forces of evil and disorder to make the world a safer place to live in, a place where civilization can develop, and who ultimately receives that rare and greatest of rewards, deification. Here too is a story that fits snugly alongside the official, Augustan narrative of a savior-leader who rids civilization of its enemies and gives it a new-found sense of security and purpose, whose recent triumphal celebrations coincide in the calendar with this festival of Hercules, and who, like Hercules, traces his origin back to the gods and can ultimately look forward to his own place among them.[4]

Odysseus too, in the course of his long journey home, witnesses singing and dancing in celebration of the deeds of the gods. But this celebration is of a

---

4. For further discussion, see Galinsky (1990) and Feeney (1991, 156–62), who notes that Hercules bridges the divide between gods and mortals, both in terms of his power and in terms of his perspective within the narrative.

light-hearted kind and is introduced as an opportunity to celebrate the talents of the performers. At *Odyssey* 8.241–55, King Alkinöos calls for a display of dancing and singing in honor of his guest, and a runner is dispatched to the palace to fetch the lyre for Demodokos. The sports marshals make a smooth, wide area for the dancing display, and the blind singer steps into the middle of it to complete the transformation of the scene. Demodokos's song, framed by two virtuoso performances of dancing, is the centerpiece of an exuberant, outdoor entertainment. Its subject is the illicit love affair of Ares and Aphrodite and the trick devised to trap them by Hephaistos, the outraged husband. The song is allowed to run its full course without interruption, and it brings universal delight to its audience (*Odyssey* 8.266–369). The antagonism that has arisen on the sports field between the visitor and a member of the home team is quickly laid aside, and admiration of the wonderful dancing brings a return of good spirits and a sense of harmony between hosts and their guest.

Before and after this, in the traditional, indoor setting of entertainment to accompany the feast, Demodokos sings of the war at Troy. But the song he now sings out in the open, framed by the two displays of dancing, makes a sharp contrast with the world of war and human suffering. In this song, Ares makes love, not war:

> But he struck up a prelude on his lyre for his beautiful singing
> about the love affair of Ares and Aphrodite with the beautiful
>   crown,
> how first they made love together in Hephaistos's house,
> in secret. (*Odyssey* 8.266–69)[5]

Rather than arousing men's anger toward each other on the battlefield, Ares is now the focus of another's anger, and rather than being a figure of fear, he is now the butt of comedy as the other gods laugh at him for letting himself get caught by the lame Hephaistos. He is last seen speeding off to the distant land of Thrace (*Odyssey* 8.361). Aphrodite's relationship with Ares differs from that found in the *Iliad*. There it is that of brother and sister (*Iliad* 5.355–63; 21.416–17), whereas here in Demodokos's song her role is similar to that of her protégée Helen in the *Iliad*: she willingly commits adultery with her handsome lover. But whereas in the *Iliad* the consequences of Paris's

---

5. Burkert (2009) uses the song of Demodokos as a means of exploring the different religious worlds of the two poems. Graziosi and Haubold (2005, 83–84) also set Demodokos's song in its wider context. They write, "The very language of epic is shaped by the project of describing the gods to mortals."

elopement with Menelaos's wife are death and destruction on a vast scale, in Demodokos's song, the sight of Ares and Aphrodite caught in bed together by the net devised by her lame husband Hephaistos provokes uncontrollable laughter from the gods (*Odyssey* 8.326–27).[6]

The comedy continues in the crosstalk between Apollo and Hermes as they stand at the doorway and look at the two lovers trapped in bed together:

> Then lord Apollo, son of Zeus, spoke to Hermes:
> "Hermes, son of Zeus, guide and giver of good things,
> would you be willing to go to bed with golden Aphrodite and sleep
>   with her,
> even if you were held down with mighty chains?"
> And the guide and slayer of Argos answered him then:
> "If only I had the chance, far-shooting lord Apollo!
> If I had three times this many chains round me, ones that could
>   not be broken,
> and you gods and goddesses looking on,
> I would still sleep with golden Aphrodite."
> Those were his words and laughter went up from the immortal
>   gods. (*Odyssey* 8.334–43)

The humor pulls in the opposite direction from the moral of the story, celebrating rather than curbing the power of Aphrodite and turning into a joke the cuckolded husband's scheme to punish the lovers by chaining them down and making them a public spectacle.

At the end of the song, Aphrodite too is restored to one of her natural, earthly habitats, Paphos in Cyprus, at the opposite end of the world from Ares.[7] Here she is in a world where she can once again wear a smiling face, a world of hot fragrant baths and lovely new clothes to put on, a world that reflects the one Demodokos's home audience itself enjoys and that it extends to its guest from overseas (*Odyssey* 8.364–66, 248–49, 424–42).

After the moment of bad temper on the sports field, the outcome of Demodokos's story can be felt to have a special relish for Odysseus. Shown here is the victory of cunning (*Odyssey* 8.276, 281–82, 317) over speed of foot (*Odyssey*

---

6. For a scene showing Zeus and Hera making love (the so-called Deception of Zeus), cf. *Iliad* 14.153–353. For a scene showing Venus and her "dearest husband" Vulcan making love, cf. *Aeneid* 8.370–406.

7. For Ares' association with Thrace, cf. *Iliad* 13.298–302, and for the association of Venus with Paphos, cf. *Aeneid* 1.415–17.

8.329–32), the victory of the defining characteristic of Odysseus himself (*Odyssey* 9.19–20) over that of the other superhero, swift-footed Achilleus, with whom Demodokos earlier couples him (*Odyssey* 8.75). Below the humor and playfulness, however, run deeper currents. In the mortal world, adultery is no laughing matter, as the insistent example of Aegisthos and Clytaemnestra makes clear to the reader,[8] nor is it something to be settled lightly by the guarantee of compensation by a third party (*Odyssey* 8.344–58). As the gods laugh to see the two lovers trapped in each other's arms, one of them comments ironically to his neighbor that "bad deeds do not do well" (*Odyssey* 8.329). Later Odysseus himself propounds a similar, though now deadly serious, moral concerning the fate of the slaughtered suitors for the terrified herald Medon to think about and pass on to others: "doing good is a great deal better than doing evil" (*Odyssey* 22.374). How the song is presented strengthens this ironic interplay between the comic atmosphere at the conclusion of the song of Ares and Aphrodite, sung in faraway Scherie for Odysseus's entertainment, and the bloody climax of the main narrative once Odysseus returns home to Ithaca. A seamless transition at *Odyssey* 8.268–69 takes the narrative from Demodokos's prelude into the full account of his song given in indirect form by the narrator. Although frequent use of direct speech given to the characters in the song enlivens this indirect form of presentation, Demodokos himself recedes from view until the end of the song (*Odyssey* 8.367), so that the unseen narrator of the *Odyssey* and the blind poet of the Phaeacian court become, for a time, one and the same voice.

2.2 ✥ Singing and Celebrating the Deeds of Men

At *Iliad* 9. 182–85, a delegation from Agamemnon sets out with a package of proposals aimed at persuading Achilleus to reenter the fighting. On their arrival, they find him occupied:

> They found him delighting his heart with the clear-sounding lyre,
> a beautiful, intricate instrument with a silver crossbar,
> which he took from the spoils when he destroyed the city of Eëtion.
> It was with this that he was delighting his heart and he was sing-
>   ing the famous deeds of men.
> Patroklos alone sat opposite him in silence,
> waiting until Achilleus should stop singing. (*Iliad* 9.186–91)

8. Cf. *Odyssey* 1.32–43, 298–300; 3.193–98, 248–75, 303–10; 4.518–37; 11.387–466; 24.191–202.

In his anger against Agamemnon, Achilleus has isolated himself from his fellow warriors, but he is pining for the heat of battle (*Iliad* 1.488–92). Now he has found a way of taking his mind off his all-consuming anger, a way of "delighting his heart." He may no longer be able to win glory for himself in the public context of war, but he can gain comfort from singing about such activity to himself and his closest friend and celebrating the fame that it confers. As in the choral singing to Apollo in *Iliad* 1, singing is here associated with a sense of harmony in contrast to discord. But now the singing brings about that effect reflexively and privately. The great-hearted warrior finds temporary escape from his anger in his own singing.[9]

The lyre in Achilleus's hands, to which attention is drawn in lines 186–88, acts as a bridge between the world that Achilleus creates through his singing and the world of warfare itself since it is part of the spoils he has taken in war.[10] It also acts as a bridge in another way, helping span the potentially awkward moment of the arrival of the delegation from Agamemnon. When the newcomers stand before him, Achilleus is surprised by the interruption, and he and Patroklos both rise to their feet, the lyre still firmly in Achilleus's hand (*Iliad* 9.192–95). But these are friends, not enemies. Despite his anger (*Iliad* 9.197–98), Achilleus gives them an appropriately warm welcome, and they are feasted in style. Now the lyre acts as a reassuring symbol of conviviality (*Odyssey* 17.269–71) before discord returns again with the passionate argument that follows the meal.

Later, as he stands over the body of the fallen Hektor, Achilleus addresses his fellow commanders (*Iliad* 22.377–94). His mind is in turmoil. After this crucial enemy loss, he first looks forward to the next move in the war, but then he falters in his ability to see significance in this next stage of concerted activity and reverts to his own inconsolable grief for the loss of his beloved friend. Finally, he turns back abruptly to call for a song of triumph and thanksgiving for what he and his fellow warriors have achieved:

"Come now, sons of the Achaeans, let us sing a paean
as we go back to the hollow ships and take this body with us.
We have won great glory. We have killed godlike Hektor,
whom the Trojans throughout their city glorified like a god."
  (*Iliad* 22.391–94)

---

9. Cf. *Iliad* 13. 730–31 for the uniqueness of this combination of military and musical talents.

10. Cf. *Iliad* 6. 414–19 for Andromache's account of how Achilleus killed her father Eëtion but took care to give him a heroic burial.

As in *Iliad* 1, the singing of a paean expresses thanksgiving for relief from trouble, but now, in this context of victory celebration, things are more complex, more problematic. In *Iliad* 1, the singing of a paean brought closure to a period of conflict and delight to the attentive god. Now Achilleus's call to sing a paean brings a momentary sense of wellbeing through the sharing of an achievement of fundamental importance to the Achaean war effort. After Achilleus's painful refusal to support his comrades at the front, here is the expression of a much-needed sense of togetherness and success. But instantly the narrative undermines this sense of wellbeing by focusing attention on the corpse of his fallen adversary: "So he spoke, and devised shameful deeds upon godlike Hektor" (*Iliad* 22.395).[11]

The interpretation of the evaluative phrase "shameful deeds," which occurs both here and at *Iliad* 23.24, raises a longstanding question. Is the viewpoint that of the passive figure of Hektor's corpse (i.e., bringing shame on him and his surviving forces), or is it that of the narrator, passing comment on the actions of Achilleus? Richardson (1993) explores the wider context in which this and related words are used in the last three books of the *Iliad*. He notes that Achilleus uses the word "shamefully" to describe to the fatally wounded Hektor how dogs and birds will pull his body apart (*Iliad* 22.335–36). He also notes that Achilleus cannot be imagined as passing adverse comment on himself here. He writes, "at 22.395 there has not as yet been any explicit condemnation of Akhilleus' acts, however much they are portrayed as brutal and degrading" (1993, 147). Later, however, as Achilleus persists in his "enraged shameful treatment" of godlike Hektor, Apollo thwarts his efforts (*Iliad* 24.14–22) and criticizes the gods for allowing the continuation of such "shameful treatment" (*Iliad* 24.33–54), and Zeus brings it to an end (*Iliad* 24.64–76). Richardson concludes, "So in the end the gods uphold the principle that Hektor's body should not have been so treated" (1993, 147). Here then it seems to be not so much a case of the reader's needing to be aware of the cultural difference that I mention in the introduction. Rather, the reader is offered a carefully controlled investigation and reassessment of a cultural norm that in the end is shown to be at variance with the values the *Iliad* upholds. In the violence toward the dead enemy that

---

11. For an examination of the central place of "shame" in the value system of the Homeric heroes, see Dodds (1951). Hooker (1998, 18) notes that the concept includes the ideas "shame before others," "respect for others," and "awe before the gods." He further notes that the last of these "represents the earliest meaning." For further examination of Homeric society and its values as the depiction of "a world in transition," see Graziosi and Haubold (2005, 95–119).

erupts from the grief-stricken Achilleus, the body of the "godlike Hektor" (*Iliad* 22.393, 394, 395) is mutilated and defiled (*Iliad* 22.396–404). As the Achaeans prepare to sing a paean in celebration and thanks for their "great glory," and as Achilleus's victory secures for him a place among the "famous deeds of men," the narrative at once shows a deed that encapsulates the ugly reprisals of war.

In the *Odyssey*, singing in celebration of the deeds of men takes place not in the immediacy of the battlefield but in the more relaxed context of entertainment to accompany the feast. Here is a subject that has attracted a great deal of critical attention.[12] At *Odyssey* 8.62–70, King Alkinöos gives instructions to call the godlike singer Demodokos to the feast to be held in honor of the as-yet unidentified guest. Care is taken to see that the blind singer is made comfortable in their midst. Within this world apart, the singer has a special isolation and "otherness" by virtue of his blindness. His world is dominated by the divine gift of song and the special love of the Muse (*Odyssey* 8.44, 63). But there is a price to be paid in human terms for being singled out to receive this divine favor. The divine dispensation requires, at best, a balance,[13] a compensatory loss of a much-prized human faculty: Demodokos is blind.

When the guests have had enough to eat and drink, the singer begins:

> The Muse set the singer forth to sing the famous deeds of men,
> on a course of song whose fame then reached the broad heaven:
> the quarrel of Odysseus and Peleus's son, Achilleus,
> how once they quarreled at the rich feast of the gods
> with violent words, and Agamemnon, lord of men,
> rejoiced in his mind that the best of the Achaeans were quarreling,
> for thus had Phoibos Apollo spoken to him in an oracle,
> at holy Pytho, when he crossed the stone threshold
> to consult the oracle. For then came rolling round the start of the
>   trouble
> for Trojans and Danaans alike, through the plans of great Zeus.
>   (*Odyssey* 8.73–82)

Demodokos's choice of subject makes Odysseus cry, but he is anxious not to be seen crying by his hosts on this festive occasion and hides his face. Each time the singer pauses, Odysseus wipes away the tears, removes the cloak from his

---

12. See Segal (1994), Nagy (1999, 15–25), Macleod (2001), and Doherty (2009).
13. Cf. *Iliad* 24.527–33 for a vivid image of this divine dispensation.

head, and makes a libation to the gods. The Phaeacian nobles, by contrast, are delighted by Demodokos's song and urge him to continue. Once again Odysseus conceals his head and cries. Only Alkinöos notices that Odysseus is crying and tactfully brings the feasting and its accompaniment to an end (*Odyssey* 8.83–103).

The narrator's account of Demodokos's song, which describes events leading to the outbreak of the Trojan War, gives a prominent place to Odysseus. His quarrel with Achilleus is ranked among "the famous deeds of men" and is already accorded great fame at the time of its singing (*Odyssey* 8.73–74). In Demodokos's song, Odysseus is presented at an earlier time in his life, before "the start of the trouble" caused by the war. In this flashback, he shares with Achilleus the title of being "the best of the Achaeans," and the conflict recorded between them hints at the difference between these two superheroes. The sudden bringing to life of his earlier, heroic self in this public context, coupled with a reminder of the troubles that the war was about to cause for both sides, brings tears to Odysseus's eyes. However, the pain of these memories is not as yet something that Odysseus can share with the pleasure-loving Phaeacians, whose lives have been untouched by such "trouble" and who are eager to hear more. The blind singer and the man covering his head as he listens are drawn together by this secret bond of communication.

Later in the day and after the outdoor entertainment, the feasting resumes. The blind singer is led to his place in the middle of the banquet as an honored member of the community (*Odyssey* 8.471–73). After the admiration aroused by the Phaeacian dancers, it is the turn of their singer to be the focus of praise. As a token of the warmth of his feelings toward the singer, even though his own heart is heavy, Odysseus orders the herald to take a slice of the best cut of meat from his plate and give it to Demodokos. He then speaks these words:

> "For wherever men live upon the earth, singers
> have a share in honor and command respect, since the Muse
> has taught them the paths of song and has loved the tribe of
>   singers."
> So he spoke, and the herald, taking it, put it into the hands
> of the hero Demodokos, and he received it and it gladdened his
>   heart. (*Odyssey* 8.479–83)[14]

14. Cf. *Iliad* 7.321–22 for a gift of meat as a mark of honor paid by one hero to another.

This moment of celebration of the singer extends beyond the immediate context to singers in general and thus creates an ironic self-consciousness in the text for the reader to enjoy. The singer's subject may be a bitter one for some in his audience, one that brings tears to the eyes, but the special divine favor that he receives commands honor and respect. The singer may not be able to see his audience, but a warm appreciation of him is something that gladdens his heart, something that can for a moment even put him on a par with the heroes of whom he sings.

In his first song Demodokos sings of events on the eve of the Trojan War. The reader is not shown Demodokos singing of the war itself, a subject already treated comprehensively in the *Iliad*. Instead, reference is made to Demodokos's skill in handling this subject. Odysseus compliments the singer on his excellent sense of order in recounting the achievements and sufferings of the Achaeans. It is, he says, offering the reader the chance to enjoy the irony that comes from the concealment of his own identity: "as if you yourself had been there or had heard it from another" (*Odyssey* 8.491). Now Odysseus asks him to change direction and to sing of the wooden horse:

> "But come now, change your path and sing of the construction
> of the wooden horse, which Epeios made, with Athena's help,
> the trick that godlike Odysseus took to the acropolis,
> having filled it with men, who razed Troy to the ground.
> If you can recount this for me in a fitting manner,
> I shall proclaim at once to all the world
> that the god's gift to you of divine song was generous indeed."
> So he spoke, and Demodokos, stirred by the god, began and
>   revealed the song. (*Odyssey* 8.492–99)

The irony now becomes a game, and the special relationship between Odysseus and the blind singer takes on a new form. The singer gives prominence to the name of Odysseus, thereby conferring fame on him (*Odyssey* 8.502, 517), even though Odysseus's identity is still hidden from his hosts. Conversely, if the singer's account of his actions satisfies Odysseus, he will ensure fame for Demodokos by proclaiming to the world the abundance of his divine gift. The secret, enclosed bond of communication has now been exchanged for something that belongs potentially in the public world: the dependence of hero and singer on each other and on divine assistance for their fame.

As he listens, Odysseus once again responds with tears, but now there is no attempt at concealment. Now the narrative brings out the scale of his emotion with an elaborate simile:

> These things did the famous singer sing, but Odysseus's heart
> melted and the tears from his eyes ran down his cheeks.
> Just as a woman weeps when she clings to her dear husband,
> who has fallen in battle, out in front of his city and his people,
> while warding off from his town and the children the pitiless day,
> and she sees him quivering in the throes of death,
> and casts herself upon him, shrieking with grief, but the enemy
> come up behind her and beat her on the back and shoulders with
>   their spears,
> and carry her off into slavery, to hard labor and suffering,
> and her cheeks are hollowed with most pitiful anguish,
> just so pitiful were the tears that welled up in Odysseus's eyes.
>   (*Odyssey* 8.521–31)[15]

As before, it is the watchful king who sees Odysseus's distress. Now Alkinöos judges it time to address the matter in public, and so he makes a speech in which Demodokos is told to stop and the guest is politely but firmly asked to reveal his identity and the cause of his tears at hearing the singer tell the fate of Troy and of those who fought there (*Odyssey* 8.536–43, 548–54, 577–86).

In a number of ways this simile challenges presuppositions and suggests new correspondences. A veteran warrior, the architect of victory, responds to hearing his achievements sung in public, at his own request, not with a retrospective glow of triumph but by dissolving into tears. As he cries, his tears are like those of an innocent victim of war, a grief-stricken woman holding her dying husband in her arms, while enemy soldiers rain blows on her from behind and drag her off to a lifetime of hard labor. Remembrance of wartime experience and its constant proximity to death and suffering, aroused by the singer, unleashes tears of pain, an outpouring of human emotion that is not limited by the distinctions between winner and loser, combatant and noncombatant, male and female. Here the abiding image of war is presented from a feminine viewpoint and is one of ugly brutality and undeserved suffering. Foley writes of such similes, where for example a man is compared with a woman, that they "seem to suggest both a sense

---

15. Buxton (2004) discusses the range and effectiveness of Homeric similes.

of identity between people in different social and sexual roles and a loss of stability, an inversion of the normal" (2009, 190). The relaxed enjoyment of the after-dinner entertainment provided by the singer, something valued both by Alkinöos and by Odysseus himself (*Odyssey* 8.542–43; 9.2–11), is set into sharp contrast with Odysseus's reception of the singer, which is described with the extended image of life destroyed and blighted on the battlefield. There is also another sense in which the reader may feel that correspondences are suggested here. Odysseus praises Demodokos for the wonderful sense of order and authenticity with which he sings of the fate of the Achaeans, their achievements, and their sufferings. The stopping point for this narrative comes before he reaches an account of the wooden horse and the sack of Troy (*Odyssey* 8.489–95). Here is a description that would equally well fit the *Iliad*, and the extended simile (itself more a feature of the *Iliad* than of the *Odyssey*) might be felt to reawaken the tragic vision of the *Iliad*, as seen for example in the fate of Andromache (*Iliad* 6.405–13, 431–32, 450–65; 22.482–86; 24.723–45). In drawing victor and vanquished together through their tears, it also invites comparison with the moment when Achilleus and Priam are brought together through their tears for the fate of their loved ones (*Iliad* 24.507–12).

The description of Odysseus's tears is testimony to the power of the singer, both the singer within the narrative and the narrator himself, and the celebration of the singer continues in the graceful words with which Odysseus answers his host:

> "Lord Alkinöos, illustrious among all peoples,
> this is indeed a fine thing, to listen to a singer
> such as this, whose voice is like that of the gods.
> For I say that there is no achievement in life that brings more
>   pleasure
> than when joy reigns over the people,
> and, up and down the hall, the banqueters listen to a singer."
>   (*Odyssey* 9.1–7)

Demodokos has been entertaining the banqueters by singing about Odysseus. When Odysseus at last reveals his identity to them (*Odyssey* 9.16–21), it is as if he steps out of the singer's songs, and he does so at a moment when the singer has been placed in the center of universal wellbeing, a world away from the private sorrows that the singer has such power to conjure up.

The situation is very different for Odysseus's own singer, Phemios. When he first appears near the beginning of the *Odyssey,* Phemios is shown singing "under compulsion" for the after-dinner entertainment of the suitors (*Odyssey* 1.150–55, 325–52). Toward the end of the *Odyssey*, he almost loses his life amid the carnage in the hall. Two terrified figures plead to be spared by Odysseus: Leodes, augur to the suitors, and Phemios (*Odyssey* 22.310–19, 330–53). Leodes pleads in vain and is beheaded even as he speaks, whereas Phemios's plea for his life is successful and prompts Telemachos into thinking about the life of another innocent party, the herald Medon (*Odyssey* 22.320–29, 357–58). Kneeling in supplication and on the border between life and death, the singer puts his art of persuasion to the supreme test:

> "I beg you, Odysseus, have respect for me and pity me.
> You will be sorry for it one day, if you kill a singer
> such as I am, I who sing both to gods and to men.
> I am self-taught and a god has implanted in my mind
> all kinds of paths. And when I am by you, I seem to sing to you
> as if to a god. So do not long to cut me down." (*Odyssey* 22.344–49)

By now Odysseus, the great story teller and archer, has been shown in some senses to resemble the singer/lyre-player. Both King Alkinöos and Eumaios the swineherd liken his storytelling skill to that of a singer (*Odyssey* 11.367–69; 17.518–21), and his inspection of the great bow is likened in another of the *Odyssey*'s comparatively rare, extended similes to a singer/lyre-player's fine tuning of his lyre (*Odyssey* 21.404–11). Now, however, the singer makes clear to Odysseus his own, unique position and in consequence the reasons why his life should be spared. In a number of complementary ways, the singer bridges the world of the gods and the world of men. He has already been shown to celebrate alike "the deeds of men and of gods" (*Odyssey* 1.338). Now he reminds Odysseus that he "sings both to gods and to men" and that, while his particular skill requires his own, human efforts to train for it, the comprehensive range of his creative ability is nevertheless something god-given.[16] What is more, through his singing Phemios can extend a sense of the divine into the human world. When he is close at hand, he can create in his listener the sensation of an almost divine transformation: "I seem to sing to you as if to a god." A time must surely come when the desire to kill such a singer, if carried through, will be regretted. These abstract thoughts are complemented by a piece of incontrovertible evidence in Phemios's favor. Telemachos can support his claim that he was, as the narrator has twice made clear, acting under duress (*Odyssey*

---

16. Segal (1994, 138–39) discusses this combination of the human and the divine in the singer's art.

22.350–56, 1.154; 22.331). So Phemios is spared, and together with the herald Medon he is instructed by Odysseus to leave the slaughterhouse, though both of them still expect at any moment to be killed (*Odyssey* 22.375–80).

Aeneas shares with Odysseus the experience of being moved to tears by a representation of the Trojan War and the part he played in it, but in Aeneas's case, this is a visual experience rather than one brought to his ears by a singer. Wrapped in a cloud that makes them invisible, Aeneas and his faithful companion Achates look at the lofty temple to Juno under construction in Carthage. Aeneas's eyes are drawn to the scenes of the Trojan War depicted on it (*Aeneid* 1.446–93). He responds to this unexpected encounter with his past life as a representative not of the winning but of the losing side, and yet paradoxically the experience brings with it a note of optimism. Its effect on Aeneas is to raise his spirits, despite his tears. The basis for this emotional change is the thought, colored with a sense of moral pride, of the fame of these events, a fame that has traveled on ahead of Aeneas and his companions, even to this faraway world. Even after defeat and misfortune, the Trojans' labors and the heroic part played by Priam in those labors receive the commemoration they deserve, and this commemoration through art lifts Aeneas's spirits and somehow holds out a promise of salvation. Visual art, no less than the singer's art, has the power to give pleasure even when its subject is a bitter one. In response to these positive thoughts coming after the renewed miseries of the recent past, Aeneas's emotions can now find expression. His tears flow freely throughout the scene, and he himself draws attention to tears as a response to the human condition: "there are tears for the way things are" (the first half of *Aeneid* 1.462). And whereas the narrator of the *Odyssey* uses a powerful, extended simile to suggest the universality of human suffering evoked by an art form (*Odyssey* 8.523–31), Aeneas makes the point himself in words of great simplicity and profundity: "and our mortality touches the imagination" (the second half of *Aeneid* 1.462).

This representation of the events that form the background to the main narrative in a visual rather than an oral form affects the nature of the interplay between the two. Instead of an oral context, where the details recorded depend on the singer or his response to a request from his audience, the details selected for representation are now set down in unalterable form and in the more remote, religious context of the decoration of a temple under construction. Such a narrative does not rest on its topicality for its appeal (*Odyssey* 1.351–52) but has a timeless quality. Here is a context for Aeneas and his companion, and with them the reader, to look up and see in distilled form a commemoration of the whole tragic-heroic experience of the Trojan War. Amid the figures of that war, depicted in stone for all to see, Aeneas recognizes himself and the part he played in it (*Aeneid* 1.488).[17] This moment of optimism, however, is tinged with a double irony. The temple whose decoration celebrates these events is sacred to Juno, still the relentless enemy of the Trojans and here honored in her favorite city (*Aeneid* 1.15–16), which is destined to be the arch-enemy of the Trojans' descendants. The visual nature of this experience also makes possible a second irony. Immediately after Aeneas expresses his new-found sense of optimism, the narrator gives the reader an ironic reminder of the gulf between life and art: "So he speaks and feeds his mind on an empty picture" (*Aeneid* 1. 464). Parry and W. R. Johnson respond in very different ways to this scene. Writing of Aeneas, Parry states, "Here he can look back on his losses, and see them made beautiful and given universal meaning because human art has transfigured them" (1966, 122). W. R. Johnson writes, "He deludes himself into feeling heartened because the realities he confronts are, literally, intolerable" (1976, 104). He continues, "In part Vergil reminds us that art is illusion, that his poem is illusion" (105). It is a mark both of the profoundly paradoxical nature of these lines and of the balance they display that they can accommodate such radical disagreement.[18]

The *Aeneid* does not show within its narrative a singer celebrating the deeds of men. In its first half, in the context of after-dinner entertainment for the Carthaginians and their Trojan guests, the singer Iopas sings of scientific subjects: the sun and moon and the constellations; the origins of life, rain, and fire; and the reason for the short winter nights. Such an ambitious program is outlined in a mere five lines by the narrator (*Aeneid* 1.742–46).[19] In the second half of the *Aeneid*, Cretheus, a singer who like Demodokos enjoys the friendship of the Muses and whose epic interests resemble those of the *Aeneid*'s narrator himself, ends a list of those who fall to the sword of Turnus:

> and Cretheus, friend to the Muses,
> Cretheus, the Muses' companion, whose heart was always set on
>   songs
> and the lyre and on setting lines of verse to his strings,
> who always used to sing of horses, of men's arms and their battles.
>   (*Aeneid* 9.774–77)

---

17. The *Aeneid* has no place for questioning Aeneas's war record (*Aeneid* 2.431–34). This contrasts with the *Iliad*, cf. *Iliad* 13.459–61; 20.187–91. For the wider picture of the Homeric Aineias (Aeneas) in action, cf. *Iliad* 13.481–505; 20.158–339.

18. S. J. Harrison (1990) notes a wider division between those who take a broadly optimistic view of the *Aeneid* and those who take a more pessimistic view.

19. Hardie compares the roles of Iopas and Demodokos as singers (1986, 52–66).

Earlier in *Aeneid* 9, however, the narrator himself, now unaided by the Muse(s), intervenes in order to address a heartfelt epitaph to the two fallen Trojan warriors, Nisus and Euryalus:

> Fortunate pair! If my songs have any power,
> no day will ever remove you from an eternity of remembrance,
> as long as the house of Aeneas dwells by the immoveable rock
> of the Capitol and the Roman father holds command. (*Aeneid*
>   9.446–49)

Hardie examines the complexity of the Nisus and Euryalus episode and notes that it provides "a litmus test of varying critical approaches to the meaning of the poem as a whole" (1994, 23).[20]

Nisus and Euryalus first appear as athletes in the funeral games held to honor Anchises. Euryalus is a boy of outstanding beauty and is loved by Nisus "with a pure love" (*Aeneid* 5.294–96, 317–61). When a fall close to the finishing line robs Nisus of victory, his love of Euryalus makes him block the path of his nearest rival and so give the victory to Euryalus. The resulting dispute over who should qualify for the prizes for the race is resolved with tact and good nature by Aeneas, and Nisus himself is included in the number (*Aeneid* 5.327–61). After this comparatively light-hearted introduction, the pair are reintroduced in *Aeneid* 9 in a context of wartime crisis. Night has fallen and the Trojan camp is under siege from Turnus and his forces while Aeneas himself is away at Pallanteum. Nisus and Euryalus volunteer to carry out a dangerous mission: to break through enemy lines and bring Aeneas news of the attack on the camp. They also plan to slaughter large numbers of the sleeping enemy forces and to return laden with plunder. Their bold plan wins the admiration and gratitude of the war council and of young Ascanius, but ultimately their mission is a failure and costs them their lives. The whole of this sequence (*Aeneid* 9.176–449) forms a self-contained episode, culminating in the four-line address to the "fortunate pair" and leading to the enemy's discovery of the slaughter in their camp, the parading of the heads of Nisus and Euryalus within sight of the beleaguered Trojan camp, and the anguished response by Euryalus's mother to the news of her son's death (*Aeneid* 9.450–502).

In the somber atmosphere of the nighttime war council, Nisus, Euryalus, and Ascanius are all aware that fortune may turn against the two warriors (*Aeneid* 9.210–15, 282–83, 299–303). As the two leave, the failure of their

---

20. For further discussion, see Gransden (1984, 102–19) and W. R. Johnson (1976, 59–66).

mission is foreshadowed by the narrator. Ascanius gives them instructions to take to his father, "but the breezes / plucked them away and gave them undelivered to the clouds" (*Aeneid* 9.312–13).[21] Once unforeseen disaster has struck and the couple have been spotted by the enemy, one misfortune follows another. Euryalus suffers the nightmarish experience of getting lost at night in a dark forest, pursued by enemies who close in on him from all sides and ultimately catch him and put him to death. Nisus experiences the terrible realization that his beloved is no longer following him out of danger[22] and that he cannot save him. When Nisus sees that Euryalus has been caught, he kills two of the enemy with his javelins. But this only precipitates the execution of Euryalus before the eyes of his horrified and guilt-ridden lover, and Euryalus's death is at once followed by the death of Nisus, who gives his own life to ensure that the killer of Euryalus is himself killed in revenge.

Against such a background of anguish, violent death, and the failure of their mission, the narrator's four-line celebration of the "fortunate pair" comes as a jolt, suggesting that the criteria for passing this judgement lie more in the consideration of their inner life than in the traditional, external forms of heroic achievement on the battlefield. At the start of the episode, Nisus and Euryalus, "united in a single love" (*Aeneid* 9.182), are on guard duty together. Nisus tells Euryalus how he longs to make his mark in the war, and how the idea is forming in his mind to exploit the enemy's reduced state of watchfulness and to secure the all-important return of Aeneas. Nisus's enthusiasm for this idea is infectious, and Euryalus is "struck with a great love of heroic glory" (*Aeneid* 9.197–98) and insists that he should accompany Nisus on his mission, regardless of the danger. All Nisus's arguments to dissuade him out of concern for his safety are fruitless, and the two of them make their way together to put their plan before the young king-in-waiting (*Aeneid* 9.184–223). In this way, before being made public, Nisus's brave but dangerous plan first becomes a focus for the exploration of the selfless love and commitment of the two towards each other. Love and traditional heroic glory are here intimately bound together. The Trojan elder Aletes responds enthusiastically to Nisus's plan, and young Ascanius offers him a list of rewards if the two are successful in bringing Aeneas back (*Aeneid* 9.246–74). As in the context of the nighttime operations of *Iliad* 10 (212–17, 304–8, 319–31),

---

21. Similarly, but with less pathos, the narrator at *Iliad* 10. 332, 336–37 makes clear that the Trojan Dolon will not return from his nighttime spying mission to give his report to Hektor.

22. Cf. Aeneas's loss of Creusa at *Aeneid* 2.735–73 and Orpheus's loss of Eurydice at *Georgics* 4.485–505.

the public recognition of bravery and conspicuous, material prizes play an important part. But here the heroic value system is more complex and regards as paramount the inner sense of pride and satisfaction, which the gods and the soldiers' own character guarantee for such bravery (*Aeneid* 9.252–54).

Also prominent in this context of the Trojan war council are the emotional ties that link Nisus and Euryalus with Ascanius and his absent father Aeneas. More than anything, Ascanius needs the return of his absent father (*Aeneid* 9.257).[23] His present welfare and his hopes for the future rest on the efforts of Nisus and Euryalus to secure his father's return. This reliance on them on the part of the anxious, young king-in-waiting adds a sense of personal responsibility to their all-important mission. In the short conversation that now follows between Ascanius and Euryalus, who has not so far spoken (*Aeneid* 9.275–303), an intimate bond is at once established between the two beautiful boys (*Aeneid* 9.179–80, 293, 310). In Euryalus, Ascanius sees someone only a little older than himself, someone whom he can idolize for his bravery and embrace as his bosom friend and confidant. Euryalus rises to the occasion and promises in his reply a determination to follow the path of bravery throughout his life. His selfless concern for the welfare of his mother, who is unaware of her son's dangerous mission[24] (a concern already voiced on his behalf by Nisus a little earlier, at *Aeneid* 9.216–18), moves the whole company to tears and has a special effect on Ascanius, conjuring up in his mind the image of his own relationship of love and duty with his father (*Aeneid* 9.294). Euryalus and Nisus receive the heartfelt support of their commanders, young and old alike, as they embark on their mission, and they are assured of the personal trust put in them by Ascanius himself, who is already showing a maturity beyond his years (*Aeneid* 9.309–12).

Nisus and Euryalus make a sharp contrast with Achilleus and Patroklos, whose relationship is discussed in chapters 4.1 and 7.3. In the *Iliad,* Achilleus's behavior drives a wedge between the two men (*Iliad* 11.653–54; 16.29–35) and contributes to Patroklos's death. Achilleus's violent grief at the loss of his dear friend is accompanied by a sense of self-loathing (*Iliad* 18.97–106). The love that Nisus and Euryalus have for one another, by contrast, drives them into battle together (*Aeneid* 9.182) and remains constant to the end of their tragically short

---

23. In this his plight resembles that of Telemachos; cf. *Odyssey* 1.253–54. But Ascanius's need of his father to take control of the crisis is shared by the whole Trojan community.

24. Similarly, at *Odyssey* 2.373–76, Telemachos does not inform Penelope of his departure in order to spare her tears at the thought of the risks that he is running.

lives. After his frantic search in the labyrinth of the forest, Nisus is forced to see the death of his beloved Euryalus, but unlike Achilleus, Nisus is there at the end for his friend, desperately trying to shield him. Euryalus's fault, as Nisus testifies to the powers above and tries to make the enemy forces hear, was no more than this: "he only loved too much his unhappy friend" (*Aeneid* 9.430). And when Nisus gives his life to avenge Euryalus and falls over the body of his beloved, he finds in death the peace that eluded him at the start of the episode (*Aeneid* 9.445, 187). Oliensis writes that, paradoxically, "This dying-together is in effect the epic's most fully consummated marriage" (1997, 310).

Nisus and Euryalus play a comparatively brief part in the *Aeneid*. Nevertheless, the narrator reserves for his valediction to them his most direct reference to his own creative powers: "If my songs have any power, / no day will ever remove you from an eternity of remembrance." In the *Odyssey*, Odysseus draws attention to Demodokos's power as a singer, and the narrative then explores in depth the paradoxical emotional effect that the power of the singer has on his listener (*Odyssey* 8.487–98, 521–31). Here too at *Aeneid* 9.446–49, as the narrator turns attention for a moment to his own creative powers, the preceding narrative suggests that these powers can create a paradoxical effect, inviting the reader to see with hindsight in this nighttime episode both misfortune and good fortune. In the context of the valediction, a careful sense of balance is created. On the one hand, there is the grand narrative: the story of "the house of Aeneas" and the birth of a nation. Here is the big picture in which can be set the traditional epic prize of undying fame, "an eternity of remembrance,"[25] a fame that is now tinged with the sense of the gratitude of a nation toward its fallen heroes. On the other hand, here is a small, closely observed detail within the overall picture: the story of the selfless love and thwarted desire of two individuals to serve their commanders and win what they perceive as heroic glory. Here too is a story in which, with the aid of a sympathetic reader ("if my songs have any power"), the narrator can create an enduring celebration of the deeds of men.

2.3 ✤ Singing and Dancing, Courtship and Marriage

At *Iliad* 18.457–67, Thetis begs Hephaistos to make a new set of armor for her son since his own has been lost to the enemy with the death of Patroklos. Hephaistos gladly agrees and promises to create something that will command

---

25. Cf. the "undying fame" of which Achilleus speaks at *Iliad* 9.413.

widespread admiration, even though he has not the power to save Achilleus from his fate. *Iliad* 18.478–608 describes his creation of a great shield and the numerous scenes depicted on it by the god. Edwards gives a detailed discussion of this shield of Achilleus. He notes that "the poet clearly visualizes a round shield" (1991, 201) (rather than, for example, a figure-of-eight shield). First the god put on it the earth, sky, and sea, the sun, moon, and stars; next, two fine cities, one shown in peacetime and the other in the midst of war; then various scenes of seasonal work on the land, and a scene of dancing; and in the last band, running around the rim of the shield, he put the mighty Ocean River.

Scenes showing singing and dancing play a prominent part in the design of the shield's decoration. First to appear in the scenes showing life on earth are wedding celebrations:

> And he made on it two cities of articulate men,
> beautiful ones. In one there were weddings and feasting
> and they were leading the brides from their rooms, with blazing
>   torches,
> through the city, and the loud wedding song arose.
> Young men were whirling around, dancing and, in their midst,
> the sound of pipes and lyres rang out, and the women,
> each of them standing at their doorways, marveled at it all. (*Iliad*
>   18.490–96)

Amid the scenes of seasonal activity in the country, he put a vineyard, where grapes were being harvested to the accompaniment of youthful music and dancing:

> Girls and young men, in their innocence of heart, were carrying
> the honey-sweet fruit in woven baskets,
> and, in their midst, a child was playing lovely music
> on the clear-sounding lyre, and was singing a beautiful lament,
> in a high voice, and they were all stamping the ground and singing
> and dancing around, in time to the music. (*Iliad* 18.567–72)

The final scene, before the mighty Ocean River depicted on the rim of the shield, is a dance floor filled with young people dancing:

> And on it the famous, lame god patterned a dance floor,
> like the one that once in broad Knossos
> Daidalos fashioned for Ariadne with her lovely hair.

Here young men and girls, prized as marriage-partners,
were dancing and holding each other by the wrist. *(Iliad* 18.590–94)

These young dancers are shown in all their finery, and the movements of
their dances are carefully described and watched with delight:

And a great crowd stood around the lovely dance,
delighting in it, and two leaping dancers were whirling
among them in their midst and leading the movements. *(Iliad*
    18.603–6)²⁶

The singing and music making in these three scenes contribute much
to the picture of peaceful, cooperative, creative activity. They contrast with
the scenes shown alongside them that portray conflict between predator and
prey and in law and warfare. Here the two sexes are shown in harmony. As
the brides are led through the city in torch-lit processions, the sound of the
wedding song rings out, and the young men display their dancing skill, to
the admiration of the women standing in their doorways, as they pass by.
The celebration of bringing home the new vintage is also an opportunity to
celebrate youthful innocence. At the center of this idyllic scene, the singer and
lyre-player is now a child, and the power of music turns a ritual lament into
a happy occasion, an opportunity for the young people to dance together. In
the closing scene, as the two sexes touch each other on the dance floor, there
is universal enjoyment for the onlookers in the beauty and excitement of the
dance. No Paris here runs off with another man's Helen; no suggestion of
violence or menace lies below the surface as on the dance floor at the palace
of Ithaca. Instead, the scene suggests a bygone age: the world of Knossos,
Ariadne, and Daidalos. This comparison in lines 591–92 shows the narrator's confidence in his descriptive powers. Even the divine creation of the
representation of human life can be likened to a preexisting human model,
known to the narrator.

Apart from these three names, the only proper names to appear in the
description of the scenes on the shield are those of the constellations (lines
486–88); the two deities Ares and Pallas Athene (line 516), shown towering

---

26. The oddity of the line numbering here reflects the existence after "delighting in it" of the words
"and with them a godlike singer was making music, / playing on his lyre." These words, beginning and
ending in the middle of a line, properly belong at *Odyssey* 4.17–18. Their authenticity in *Iliad* 18 has long
been questioned, though some editions retain them. They are omitted by the Oxford Classical Text and
hence do not form part of the discussion.

above the diminutive human figures in the thick of the fighting; and the abstractions Strife, Battle-Din, and Doom (line 535). Here is an "anywhere" for the reader to imagine, in contrast both to the "here and now" of the main narrative and the massive accumulation of names, places, and numbers in the list of Achaean forces in *Iliad* 2.484–760. From the words "On it he fashioned the earth" onward (*Iliad* 18.483), with which the description of the scenes on the shield opens, the reader is shown the process of divine creation. After the initial description of the heavenly bodies with their timeless present tenses (*Iliad* 18.487–89), the numerous activities of humans and other animals are recorded in the past tense. "In one [city] there were weddings and feasting," "girls and young men, in their innocence of heart, were carrying / the honey-sweet fruit in buckets," and so on. This quickly establishes the sense of a separate linear narrative existing within the overarching narrative. Thus the reader is encouraged to imagine the divinely constructed shield not as a static lifeless object but as a medium in which is recorded a connected sequence of miniature narratives, each able to show a situation developing through time, and each having the power, when needed, to evoke sounds and to reveal the plans and thoughts of those taking part in it. But alongside this sense of linear narrative, there is also a suggestion of a different shape as an organizing principle. The roundness of the shield, on which varied scenes of life are shown, suggests a representation of the world as a disk. Taken in its entirety, the description of the shield's scenes also forms a ring, ending where it began in scenes of dancing. The reference to "Ocean" immediately before the start of the first scene and immediately after the end of the last scene (*Iliad* 18.489, 607) adds to this sense of ring composition. Here is both a world and a cycle of life, subtly ordered to bring out life's contrasts and diversity, its pleasures and pains, and its inextricable links with death. Here, closest to the surrounding waters of Ocean that are depicted on the rim of the shield, is a dance of life.

The relationship between the two narratives—the generic scenes on the shield and the vast, surrounding narrative of specific detail—can now be explored. Some features are shared and so help the reader connect the two. Both show a city under armed attack and facing an uncertain future. Both show its civilian population watching events from the battlements of the city, its armed forces making a counterattack, fierce fighting beside a river, and the corpses of the fallen being dragged away by the two sides. However, while anger, war, and violent death make up the predominant subject of the overarching narrative, on the shield this dark side of human existence is set in a wider context, with contrasting scenes of cooperative and creative human activity also depicted. In one sense, the *Iliad*'s main narrative itself can be seen to belong within this picture of the world shown on the shield. Paradoxically, it is the microcosm shown on the shield that gives the big picture through the multiplicity of cunningly wrought detail, conceived by the mind of the god (*Iliad* 18.481–82). Here the description of warfare is stripped of its glory and is shown in tragic contrast with the opportunities for cooperation and happiness afforded in peace. In another sense, the shield, in all its intricacy, can be felt to relate specifically to Achilleus and his fate. Driven by the imperative to avenge the killing in war of his closest friend, Achilleus is about to rejoin the war effort of his comrades. Here on his shield, created for him by a god, is a world for him to carry into battle, to protect him from despair and to give him a sense of his place in that world, a sense of identity based on more than mere outward appearances—the individual warrior's panoply, which can be loaned to another and subsequently lost. Here, finally, there is another paradox. Achilleus receives the cunningly wrought shield and the rest of his new armor with a fierce joy and a surge of anger, and he prepares to arm himself for battle (*Iliad* 19.15–23). But the divine gift, despite the wonderful way it comes to life, does not have the power to save the great warrior from an early death on the battlefield. Taplin (2001) gives a detailed discussion of the scenes shown on the shield and compares its place within the *Iliad* with that of its similes, drawing attention to the *Iliad*'s tragic vision.

Singing and dancing, courtship and marriage also play an important part in the narrative of the homecoming of Odysseus, though now they are surrounded with a different kind of irony, one that consists in an increasing sense of dramatic concealment. At *Odyssey* 1.150–55, the thoughts of Penelope's suitors turn to singing and dancing as after-dinner entertainment, and Phemios, accompanying himself on the lyre, sings for them, though only under compulsion. While the suitors' attention is occupied in this way, Telemachos and the newly arrived visitor Mentes (Athene in disguise) talk at some distance from the main company. Telemachos opens his bitter outburst against the suitors by drawing attention to their carefree enjoyment of Phemios's playing and singing (*Odyssey* 1.158–60). When the conversation comes to an end and Athene disappears, Telemachos goes over to join the suitors, and attention returns to the singer and his audience (*Odyssey* 1.325–27). Penelope too, in her upper room, hears his divine singing and with her two maids comes downstairs to ask Phemios tearfully to stop and to sing of some other subject (*Odyssey* 1.328–44). Penelope's sudden, highly emotional appearance and equally sudden withdrawal a few moments later provoke a noisy expression of the suitors' desire to go to bed with her (*Odyssey* 1.365–66), but Telemachos takes control of the situation and steers their thoughts back to the delights of the feast and the singer:

> "Suitors of my mother, with your overwhelming arrogance,
> now let us enjoy the feast. Stop shouting,
> for it is a fine thing indeed to listen to a singer
> such as this one, with a voice like the gods." (*Odyssey* 1.368–71)

Telemachos's changed attitude toward Phemios's singing is a measure of the change that has been brought about in him by his conversation with Athene-Mentes. Now he can recognize the singer's godlike quality and enjoy that recognition as part of the sense of superiority and control that it gives him over the rowdy and arrogant suitors. Before long, the description of the suitors returns to the point reached at *Odyssey* 1.151–52:

> And they turned to enjoy themselves with dancing
> and lovely singing, and waited for the night to come down.
> And black night came down on them, as they were enjoying them-
>   selves. (*Odyssey* 1.421–23)

Singing, dancing, and concealment create an ironic atmosphere for the reader to enjoy, as "black night" duly falls on the suitors' revels.

As the disguised Odysseus approaches his old home for the first time, he hears the sounds of Phemios's lyre as Phemios prepares to sing. Together with the smell of cooking meat, this shows him that there are "many men" inside, feasting and being entertained (*Odyssey* 17.260–71). Twice more after Odysseus's return in disguise, the suitors are shown enjoying the delights of singing and dancing, unaware of his identity, as evening draws on (*Odyssey* 17.605–6; 18.304–6, this second passage repeated from 1.421–23). Tension mounts as the necessity for Penelope to choose a new husband seems to be drawing nearer and the reader waits to see when Odysseus will reveal his identity and get his revenge on his wife's wicked suitors. Singing and dancing, courtship rituals, and the aggrieved husband's concealed observation of the scene deepen the sense of irony as the climax approaches.

In the aftermath of the killings, the irony takes on a complex, new form as Odysseus explains to Telemachos his plan to gain time before having to deal with the backlash from the victims' relatives. The men are to take a bath and put on fresh clothes, and the serving women too are to put on clean clothes.

Then Phemios with his lyre will provide music for them all to enjoy and dance to, and so convey to the outside world the impression that a wedding is taking place. This will give them the opportunity to work out their strategy with Zeus's help (*Odyssey* 23.133–36). Odysseus's orders are carried out, and everything goes according to plan:

> The godlike singer took
> the hollow lyre and aroused in them the desire
> for sweet music and blameless dancing,
> and the great hall echoed around to the sound of their feet,
> as the men danced with the women wearing their lovely girdles.
> And when anyone outside the hall heard them, they would say;
> "Certainly someone has married the much-wooed queen.
> Hard woman! She could not bring herself to preserve the great house
> of her wedded husband, until the time should come for him to return."
> That is what they would say, but they did not know what had happened. (*Odyssey* 23.143–52)

Phemios's services are recruited here by his master in the interests of disinformation: for the concealment rather than the celebration of the deeds achieved. Segal discusses the ironies in this scene and writes, "Thus even when Odysseus accomplishes his great exploit, the usual terms of heroic *kleos* (fame) are inverted" (1997, 108). In this way, for those outside and unaware of events in the palace, the story of Penelope and her suitors appears to have an ending different from the one in the process of unfolding. But in another sense and for those in the know, the story presented to the outside world through the medium of Phemios's music does contain an important element of truth. A wedding is in a sense taking place, reenacted as the culmination of the overthrow of the wicked suitors. After twenty years and much suffering, Odysseus has returned to his wife and home. After so long a separation and after the frenzied killing of their enemies, husband and wife need time and privacy to adapt to the massive change of circumstances in their lives and to be fully reunited. This is a process that has begun but that is as yet far from complete. In the meantime, the great hall has been cleaned and fumigated, and so transformed from a slaughterhouse back into a dance hall. The household, clean and smart and purged of its enemy occupation, celebrates its new-found sense of unity with "sweet music and blameless dancing." As the men and women dance together, they provide a background tableau for the return to intimacy between husband and wife. At the same time, below the surface of this time of well-earned peace and harmony, the reader is reminded of the unfinished business with the forces of Odysseus's enemies, who will be intent on revenge when they hear the news of the killing of the suitors.

3

Supernatural Singing

3.1 🖋 Siren Voices

The Muses themselves are heard singing near the start of the *Iliad*, and their singing is also recalled near the end of the *Odyssey*. When Zeus and Hera quarrel over Thetis's supplication to Zeus on behalf of her son, there is uproar among the gods, and it takes the adroit words of Hephaistos and his timely bustling around and replenishing of the gods' cups to avert a brawl and restore them to good humor (*Iliad* 1.488–600). The gods' feasting, in which all have an equal share, can now go on all day until sunset: "And they did not lack the lyre of great beauty, which Apollo held, / nor the Muses, who sang antiphonally in beautiful voice" (*Iliad* 1.603–4). At *Odyssey* 24.35–97, the ghost of Agamemnon in the Underworld contrasts Achilleus's fortune with his own. Achilleus died a glorious death in action and was accorded a hero's funeral with full honors. Thetis came out of the sea with her fellow Nereids to stand by her son's body and to dress it in an immortal shroud, and the Muses attended:

> The Muses, nine in all, singing antiphonally in beautiful voice,
> sang a dirge. Then you would not have seen a single Argive
> without tears. So greatly did the sweet-singing Muse rouse them.
> (*Odyssey* 24.60–62)[1]

---

1. Elsewhere in the *Odyssey* there is reference only to a Muse in the singular. The switch from plural to singular in this passage is surprising.

The antiphonal singing of the Muses, accompanied by Apollo, brings beauty and a sense of order to the gods as they feast on Mount Olympos, and in the Underworld it is recorded that their singing at the funeral of Achilleus brought a universal outpouring of human grief.[2] Immortals and mortals, the living and the dead, banqueters and mourners all respond to the singing of the Muses.

In the *Odyssey* the sound of the singing of supernatural feminine voices comes also from other sources. First Calypso and then Circe are shown singing alone over their work. Calypso's unearthly singing poses no threat to a male god. After flying far out to sea, Hermes finds her cave, with Calypso herself inside:

> And she was inside, singing with a lovely voice,
> as she moved along the loom and wove with her golden shuttle.
>   (*Odyssey* 5.61–62)

As she sings over her work, her "lovely voice," her beautiful hair, the pervasive scent of aromatic wood burning in the hearth, and the beauties of the natural and the cultivated world that surround her cave entrance, mingle to arouse the senses. The male figure about to enter this enclosed feminine space, in this case the god Hermes, is filled with wonder and pleasure, and he pauses before entering (*Odyssey* 5.55–77). Circe, too, in her home in a clearing of the mountain forest, sings over her work as the reconnaissance party sent out by Odysseus comes within earshot of her, "and they heard Circe singing with a lovely voice, / as she moved along the great, immortal loom" (*Odyssey* 10.221–22). Her singing, however, has lethal consequences for her human, male visitors since it begins the process by which they are lured into her magic world and turned in their outward form into pigs. Writing of the traditional story patterns and folktales of the Odyssey, Schein states that they "tend to represent what is 'human' as male and most of the 'pleasures' and 'dangers'—or what a male imagination fantasizes as such—as female" (1995, 19).

But feminine magic can be countered. With Hermes' help, Odysseus transforms Circe from a wicked sorceress into a safe, sexual partner and helpful ally from the supernatural world, and when he returns from his visit to the world of the dead, Circe herself tells him how to deal with the next threat from supernatural feminine singers once he resumes his homeward journey:

---

2. For human singing giving shape to the outpouring of lamentation, cf. *Iliad* 24.720–22.

"First you will come to the Sirens, who cast
their spell on all men who approach them.
Whoever in his ignorance comes near to them and hears the voice
of the Sirens will never see his wife and darling children
standing beside him on his return home, with beaming faces,
but the Sirens, with their sweet singing, cast their spell on him,
as they sit in the meadow, and bones and a great heap
of rotting corpses lie around and skin shriveling up." (*Odyssey*
    12.39–46)

As they sail past, Odysseus must seal the ears of his crew with wax. If he wishes to enjoy hearing the voice of the pair of Sirens,[3] he must let himself be tied, hand and foot, to the mast of his ship, and if he tells the crew to untie him, they must tie him up more securely until they have gone past (*Odyssey* 12.47–54). Odysseus's ship is sped by the wind toward the island of the Sirens, but all of a sudden the wind drops. The crew furl the sail and take to the oars. Odysseus seals their ears with melted wax and is tied to the mast (*Odyssey* 12.166–80). Now Odysseus tells what happened as the ship came within sound of the Sirens' island:

"They did not miss our swift ship
coming close by them, but produced their sweet song:
'Come here, Odysseus of many stories, great glory of the
    Achaeans,
beach your ship, so that you may hear our voice.
For never has anyone sailed past here in his black ship,
before he has heard the honey-sweet voice that pours from
    our lips.
It delights him and he goes on his way, knowing more than
    he knew.
For we know everything that the Argives and the Trojans suffered
on the broad plain of Troy, at the will of the gods,
and we know whatever happens on the bountiful earth.'
These were the words that came from their lovely voices, but my
    heart
longed to listen, and I ordered my companions to set me free,
with many a nod and a frown." (*Odyssey* 12.182–94)

---

3. At *Odyssey* 12.52 and 12.167, the Sirens are characterized as a pair; elsewhere in the *Odyssey* they are referred to not in the specific dual form but in the plural.

His crew do as they have been told, devoting their energies to their rowing, and Odysseus is tied more tightly to the mast until they have sailed past and the sound of the Sirens' singing can be heard no more. Only then do his companions take the wax out of their ears and untie Odysseus (*Odyssey* 12.194–200).

Both Calypso and Circe attempt to use their supernatural feminine power to trap the male and to divert him from his path (*Odyssey* 1.55–57; 10.235–36). This process reaches a climax with the description of the Sirens. The Sirens, however, are altogether more elusive and mysterious. They belong, not in an enclosed feminine world with its loom to keep them busy, but in the outside world, the world of adventure on the high seas, of close encounters with death in various, terrifying guises, and they are indistinguishable from one another, their whole existence focused on their magical singing. The devastation that surrounds them suggests an image of the aftermath of war, where no attempt has been made to collect the remains of the fallen and to give them due burial. Such a terrifying image of death and decay hangs over those who are lured by the beauty of the Sirens' singing into beaching their ship in order to stay and listen to them. Segal writes of them, "They are the first adventure of Odysseus after Hades . . . and they stand in close proximity to that dead world of purely retrospective heroism, where the only existence is in song" (1994, 100).

The reader can only imagine the unearthly beauty of the sound, but the words of their invitation are reproduced by Odysseus. Both in the manner in which they address him and in their promise to delight him with their singing, the Sirens pull Odysseus back toward the past, toward the heroic part he played in the Trojan War. But the pull of the past war is now shown as a destructive force, a lethal threat to the completion of the homeward journey. Just as Odysseus in some sense stepped out of Demodokos's accounts of his wartime exploits when he revealed his identity to the Phaeacians, so now he recalls how he was enticed by the beauty of the Sirens' singing to step back into that past world and to lose himself in it. Now the recall of this earlier world is both more precise and more complex than the general reference to Odysseus's status as a great war hero, which appeared when Demodokos sang of his exploits. Now the Sirens coaxingly address him as "Odysseus of many stories," a description that in the *Iliad* is applied uniquely to him (*Iliad* 9.673; 10.544; 11.430) and that now plays on the two senses of knowing many stories and of being the subject of many stories. Now he fulfills both senses of this description of him, telling a series of stories about his own adventures, in one of which he recalls being tempted to become no more than a listener, oblivious to the call of home and family, his power to act surrendered voluntarily, and even his ability to communicate in words with his crew taken from him by the temporary deafness he has inflicted on them.

A comparison of the Sirens with the Muses suggests a number of contrasts and inversions. As the human singer begins, he calls on the Muse to sing or to speak and presents her with the subject of the song. The Muse sets him forth on his path of song, or provides the divine starting point that enables him to reveal the song (*Iliad* 1.1–7; *Odyssey* 1.1–10, 8.73–74, 499). A creative partnership is thus initiated. The Sirens, by contrast, call on the approaching sailors to listen and, in doing so, to surrender complete control to them. The human singer calls on the Muses to provide him with the memory that he needs to tell the details of his story *(Iliad* 2.484–93). By their charmed singing, the Sirens bring oblivion and decay. Both Muses and Sirens have divine omniscience, but whereas the singer carefully acknowledges his own limitation, the Sirens hold out the tempting prize of increasing knowledge and ultimately knowledge without limit (*Odyssey* 12.188–91). Even the Muse may require a forfeit from the human she has chosen to love and to whom she has given the gift of sweet song (*Odyssey* 8.63–64). But the forfeit demanded by the Sirens from their listeners is entire absorption in their singing, something which, in the human world, can lead only to death. Different views of the relationship between the Sirens and the Muses of the *Iliad* are taken by Pucci (1996) and Doherty (1995). In Pucci's view, "the implication is obviously that the poet of the *Odyssey* considers the divine inspirers of the *Iliad* to possess the attributes of the Sirens rather than the attributes generally granted to the Muses. . . . In this way, by incorporating their Iliadic song into the poem, the Odyssey appropriates the *Iliad* with a gesture of disavowal" (1996, 196–97). Doherty is more persuasive here. She sees the Sirens' song as "threatening the *Odyssey* narrative . . . not so much because the Sirens are Muses of the *Iliad* as because they are unauthorized Muses, seductive rather than dependent females who command the language of poetry for their own inscrutable purposes" (1995, 85).

The gender of the Sirens suggests two further thoughts about their singing and Odysseus's experience of its beauty. The singing of stories that confer glory, although initially requiring the voice of a goddess, is a male-oriented activity: the singer sings "the deeds of men and of the gods" (*Odyssey* 1.338). Odysseus praises Demodokos for his ability to sing with a proper sense of order: "what the Achaeans achieved and suffered and what troubles they had" (*Odyssey* 8.490). The Sirens give a different focus to their outline of the Trojan War: "For we know everything that the Argives and Trojans suffered / on the broad plain of Troy, at the will of the gods" (*Odyssey* 12.189–90). The suffering of both sides in the war is of equal concern now; the fighting sides are pictured as the playthings of the gods and no sense of achievement is conferred. A feminine viewpoint on the experience of war has already been allowed to emerge by the narrator in the lengthy simile at *Odyssey* 8.523–31. Now that feminine viewpoint is repositioned in a supernatural world and enlarged to show, not the deeds of men, but a picture of indiscriminate suffering inflicted on the warring sides at the whim of the gods. It is enlarged still further to embrace the whole world: "and we know whatever happens on the bountiful earth" (*Odyssey* 12.191).

Regardless of the danger, Odysseus struggles to get a closer hearing, but thanks to the measures Circe has told him to take, he struggles in vain. Odysseus must temporarily surrender the outward features of his human life, the outward signs of his masculinity. He must give up the power of movement and the control of his crew, and he must be reduced to an adjunct to the ship's wooden mast, standing bound to it. Thus the male figure can, magically, have safe access into the dangerous, feminine world, in this case a sound world, and temporarily bring it under his control. But the strong countermagic can last only as long as his desire to break it is ignored. Odysseus stands erect, enraptured, straining to make contact while beneath him water is made to move by the regular thrust of the oars. For a moment, before the ship passes on and the Sirens' singing can be heard no more, the most beautiful and enticing sound of feminine voices singing and bringing the offer of knowledge beyond human limit and a terrifying reminder of human mortality is one with the subliminal suggestion of the sexual act.

3.2 ⚰ Singing and Dancing in Elysium

As Aeneas and his Trojan fleet approach the coast of Italy, they too pass by the Sirens' rocks, which are white from the bones littered on them. But the only sound to be heard now is the crashing of the waves (*Aeneid* 5.864–66). The beautiful sound of supernatural singing in the *Aeneid* comes not from mythical monsters but within the mystical vision of Elysium that unfolds as Aeneas and the Sibyl near the end of their journey through the Underworld. After the claustrophobic darkness of the early part of this journey and the dizzying horror of the glimpse down into the pit of Tartarus, Elysium opens up before them as a beautiful, airy, dazzling landscape, "a blessed dwelling-place" (*Aeneid* 6.637–41). At *Odyssey*

4.561–69 the Elysian plain is situated, not in the Underworld, but "at the ends of the world," and it gives its inhabitants a life of ease and a gently refreshing climate. Williams writes, "Homer's Elysian plain was exclusively for those of divine birth; Virgil's groves of the blessed are open to all human beings who by their virtue have deserved to be in paradise" (1990b, 199). Various groups can be seen here. Some are exercising and wrestling, some are dancing and singing:

> Part stamp out dances with their feet and sing songs,
> and the Thracian priest too is there, with his long robe,
> and responds in time to the music, with the seven distinct notes of
> his lyre,
> plucking the strings now with his fingers and now with an ivory
> plectrum. (*Aeneid* 6.644–47)

Here too are Trojan heroes from days gone by, still attending to their armor and their horses. To the right and left of the scene, spread over the grass, Aeneas sees others "feasting and singing in a chorus a joyful paean / amid a glade of sweet-smelling laurel" (*Aeneid* 6.657–58), while from high up a mighty river rolls down through the forest. Here are those wounded while fighting for their country, those who led a pure life as priests or were inspired to speak words worthy of Apollo, those who improved life by their discoveries or ensured that they would be remembered for their services (*Aeneid* 6.660–64).[4] In the midst of this crowd of garlanded figures stands Musaeus,[5] head and shoulders above the rest, and he replies to the Sibyl's enquiry about Anchises and guides them to a hill-top. Below them is a green valley, and down in this valley is Anchises (*Aeneid* 6.665–81).

The singing and dancing of the blessed spirits in Elysium differ from the singing and dancing in the human world shown in the *Iliad* and the *Odyssey*. Now there is no association between the two sexes. Now dancing and singing are set amid a series of sporting and military scenes, and before attention switches to those, figures who have performed outstanding service to their community in various fields of human life are commemorated. In this supernatural context, musical accompaniment on the lyre is provided by Orpheus, but gone now is any connection between his music and the loss

---

4. Nisus and Euryalus qualify on two counts for entry into this company of blessed spirits: they suffered wounds fighting for the rebirth of their country, and the narrator ensures at *Aeneid* 9. 446–49 that they are remembered by others for their services.

5. A shadowy figure associated with Orpheus.

of his beloved Eurydice (*Aeneid* 6.119–20; cf. *Georgics* 4.453–527). Now he is the unnamed lyre player, dressed in his characteristic long robe and referred to as "the Thracian priest." Now the music he provides is associated with the mysteries of Orphic initiation,[6] and the more traditional form of religious expression through music also appears. The sounds of supernatural singing in *Aeneid* 6 are associated with initiation and religious inspiration, and the mortal travelers' experience of the beauty of these supernatural sounds is a part of their journey rather than an obstacle to its completion.

3.3 Singing and Seeing into the Future

In Latin "singing" is a term often found in contexts of prophetic utterance. Thus the association between singing and seeing into the future forms an important thread of ideas in the *Aeneid*. This is explored by O'Hara, who writes, "The idea that the future is generally less bright than is predicted in prophecies is quintessentially Vergilian" (1990, 164). This ironic gap between prediction and outcome is established from the start since prophetic singing occurs first in the context of Sinon's deception of the unsuspecting Trojans (*Aeneid* 2.124–25, 176). Later, as Aeneas describes the Trojans' search for a new home after the fall of Troy, prophetic singing keeps them suspended between hope and fear. Central in human terms now is the figure of Anchises.[7] When Apollo at Delos tells the Trojans that the original land of their ancestors will receive them back, Anchises wrongly interprets Apollo to mean Crete. A plague soon falls on the Trojans when they try to make Crete their new home, and Anchises now orders a return to Delos (Ortygia) to ask Apollo once again for help (*Aeneid* 3.94–146). At this point, however, the reassuring figures of the household gods, carefully preserved from the ruins of Troy by Aeneas, appear to him in a dream and act as the mouthpiece of Apollo himself: "What Apollo is going to say to you, when you land in Ortygia, / he sings here and, look, he sends us of his own accord to your threshold" (*Aeneid* 3.154–55). They explain that the recent journey to Crete was a mistake, a misunderstanding of Apollo's command, and they point the way to Hesperia (The Western Land), which the ghost of Creusa first predicted that Aeneas would reach (*Aeneid* 2.781–82), and which they now identify as Italy (*Aeneid* 3.161–71). Anchises is prompted to recall the prophecies of Cassandra:

---

6. Dodds (1951, 147–49) gives a concise introduction to the subject of Orpheus and Orphism.

7. On father figures in the *Aeneid* see Lee (1979) and Gransden (2004, 79–83).

> "Son, hard-pressed by the fate of Troy,
> to me alone Cassandra used to sing of such things befalling us.
> Now I recall her foretelling that this was something destined for
>   our people,
> and often she would call out 'Hesperia' and 'the kingdom of Italy.'
> But who could believe that the Trojans would come to the shores
> of Hesperia? Who was moved then by the prophetess, Cassandra?"
>   (*Aeneid* 3.182–87)

The Trojans are in good spirits as they set to sea once again, but the next leg of their journey brings them a return to nightmarish experiences in their encounter with the monstrous Harpies, who attack the Trojans from the air.[8] When the Trojans attempt to defend themselves against these monsters, the leader of the Harpies, Celaeno, prophesies a dreadful revenge on the Trojans: once they have reached Italy, dire famine will force them to gnaw round their own tables for food before they can build their city. The Trojans are terrified by these threats, and as soon as Anchises has led them in prayer to avert such an undeserved fate, the Trojans set sail once again (*Aeneid* 3.209–67). These threats find fulfilment in a light-hearted way (*Aeneid* 7.107–29), but in the light of all the trials and sufferings that lie ahead for the Trojans in Italy, this itself is unduly optimistic. When they reach Buthrotum, however, on the northwest mainland of Greece, they are given the chance to reestablish a reassuring link with their past since incredible news comes to them: Priam's son Helenus is now ruling over nearby Greek cities and is married to Andromache. After a tearful reunion with these dear friends from the past, Aeneas takes his dilemma to Helenus, who like his sister Cassandra had the power of prophecy, but who unlike her did not suffer the curse never to be believed.[9] The divine powers, Aeneas tells Helenus, have spoken to him in unanimously favorable terms of the Trojans' search for the distant land of Italy:

> "Only the Harpy Celaeno sings a strange, new prodigy,
> words terrible to utter, and threatens dire anger upon us
> and obscene famine." (*Aeneid* 3.365–67)

These words lead Aeneas to ask the prophet about the dangers that lie ahead and the means to overcome them, and when the religious ritual has been duly

---

8. In the *Odyssey* "harpies" are storm-wind spirits that snatch their victims away never to be seen again, rather than winged monsters; cf. *Odyssey* 1.241; 20.63–66, 77–78.

9. For Helenus's (Helenos) credentials as a prophet, cf. *Iliad* 6.6; 7.44–53.

observed, Helenus takes the expectant Aeneas by the hand to Apollo's threshold: "And this then is what the priest sings from his divine mouth" (*Aeneid* 3.373).

At this point in their wanderings Aeneas and his followers are poised to leave the old Greek world and travel across the sea to the new Italian world, where they will find the home promised to them by divine fate. They finally come ashore on the coast of Italy at the start of *Aeneid* 6. Helenus's lengthy prophecy in the middle of *Aeneid* 3 is thus placed at the mid-point in the account of their wanderings, which is shared by the narrator and by Aeneas himself and takes up the first five books of the *Aeneid*. In outline, the first three-quarters of the prophecy (*Aeneid* 3.374–440) give the big picture: a reassuring, divine confirmation that Aeneas and his followers are on the right path, and an urgent reminder of the need to overcome the hostility of Juno. In detail, the prophecy up to this point takes the form of a number of vignettes and pieces of advice. It is no more than "a few of many things" (*Aeneid* 3.377), and much that is still to come receives no mention. In this way it arouses the reader's interest without giving too much away and helps tie together past, present, and future.

In the final quarter of his prophecy (*Aeneid* 3.441–62), Helenus focuses on the time when Aeneas will come ashore in Italy and visit Cumae and the divine lake Avernus. At this point he gives a detailed vision of a further stage of prophetic singing:

> "You will see a crazed prophetess, who deep in a rocky cave
> sings the fates and puts marks and names on leaves.
> Whatever songs the maiden has written on the leaves
> she arranges in sequence and shuts them away in the cave,
> and they remain unmoved in their place and do not lose their
>   order.
> But when the hinge turns and a light wind blows on them,
> when the open door has thrown into confusion the insubstantial
>   leaves,
> never then does she care to catch them, as they fly around in the
>   hollow cave,
> or call them back into place or join up the songs.
> People consult her but go away unanswered and they hate the seat
>   of the Sibyl." (*Aeneid* 3.443–52)[10]

---

10. Williams (1962) gives a concise introduction to the Sibyl of Cumae and her collection of oracles known as the Sibylline books. For a more wide-ranging discussion, see Guillermo (2013).

Helenus continues: "You must approach the prophetess and entreat her through your prayers / to sing her oracles herself, and graciously to open her mouth and give voice" (*Aeneid* 3.456–57). The Sibyl, he says, will explain to Aeneas about the peoples of Italy and the coming wars, guide him through the labors that lie ahead, and, given due reverence, crown his path with success. With these encouraging words contrasting with the eerie vision that precedes them, Helenus's own prophecy draws to an end (*Aeneid* 3.458–65).

Helenus's vision of the Sibyl's prophetic singing is itself delivered with an oracular sense of mystery. In a faraway land Aeneas will come to a sacred lake, where the only sounds are the wind in the trees and the singing of a "crazed prophetess" whose songs of fate come up from the depth of a rocky cave. In particular, an aura of mystery surrounds the reference to the prophetess' writing. Only one, allusive reference to writing occurs within the two Homeric epics (*Iliad* 6.168–70), and within the epic world it recreates, the *Aeneid* itself makes only occasional allusions to writing (*Aeneid* 1.262; 3.286–88; 6.71–74; 9.528). The leaves fall from the trees, but this apparently dead material carries the imprint of the future since the virgin prophetess has the mysterious power to transcribe her songs of fate onto the leaves in the form of "marks" and "names" and to arrange these leaves into the right order. Preserved in this way, her songs are hidden away by her in the cave, where they remain undisturbed and in their right sequence until the door of her cave opens. The imagery in this arresting vision suggests wide-ranging thoughts about communication, life, and death. On one side of a door is the motionless eternity of the depths of the earth. It is here where the lifecycle ends and where it mysteriously begins afresh. But this all lies far from human sight or understanding, behind a door.[11] On the other side of the door, the wind blows and provides the air for life. The Sibyl has the power to cross between these two worlds, but the permanent record of her songs of fate belongs within the first of the two worlds. The stillness of eternity has no dealings with the chaotic movement that comes with the breath of life. The songs of fate at once disintegrate when the wind blows the door open, and the sense they once carried is now of no concern to the Sibyl. Here the image of writing on leaves becomes a powerfully ambivalent one. On the one hand, it suggests a process of establishing order and significance, a means to "join up" her songs in the form of a papyrus scroll (or, in a modern sense, in the form

11. For the image of a door standing between life and death, cf. *Aeneid* 6.106–7.

of the leaves of a book). On the other hand, it can also suggest the opposite: something insubstantial and quick to disintegrate, the plaything of a mere puff of wind. The flesh and blood figure of Aeneas is permitted access to the Sibyl's otherworldly songs, but he must beg her to sing them to him in person and not entrust them to the leaves (*Aeneid* 3.456–57; 6.74–76).

When Aeneas comes ashore at Cumae at the start of *Aeneid* 6, his first thought is to find the temple of Apollo and the vast cave of the Sibyl, where, under possession by the god, she has the power to reveal the secrets of the future (*Aeneid* 6.9–13). Human communication with the Sibyl now experiences the opposite conditions of those conceived in Helenus's vision. In place of one door forever separating the two worlds, the cave in the rock is now approached by one hundred entrances, and the Sibyl's prophetic responses come rushing out of these entrances in the form of one hundred voices (*Aeneid* 6.42–44). The due sacrifices are made, and the priestess calls the Trojans into the lofty temple. Her transformation under possession by the god is now beginning. Cold fear grips his companions, but Aeneas makes an impassioned series of prayers and vows to Apollo, to all the gods who once opposed Troy, and to the prophetess (*Aeneid* 6.45–76). The Sibyl is now within the cave and struggles violently but ineffectually to free herself from the god's possession. The hundred entrances open of their own accord and bear the responses of the prophetess out on the air (*Aeneid* 6.79–82).

Her words are riddling, at one moment offering hope and at the next fearful forebodings: the great dangers to Aeneas from the sea now lie in the past, but worse perils remain by land. The Trojans will come into a kingdom in Lavinium, but they will wish they had not come, for the Sibyl has a vision of wars and bloodshed:

> "I see wars, bristling wars,
> and the Tiber foaming with streams of blood.
> The Simoïs and the Xanthus Rivers will be there for you
> and the camp of the Greeks. Another Achilles is already brought to
>   life in Latium,
> he too born of a goddess." (*Aeneid* 6.86–90)

Juno will not leave the Trojans alone, and they will be forced to beg for help from communities in Italy. The reason for these troubles is expressed emphatically: "The cause of so much suffering for the Trojans once again a foreign wife, / once again a marriage into a different nation" (*Aeneid* 6. 93–94). Aeneas must

not give in but must go all the more boldly where Fortune allows him. The
first path to safety will open up where it is least expected, from a Greek city.

> With such words from her inner sanctuary the Cumaean Sibyl
> sings horrifying, tortuous paths and booms out from the cave,
> wrapping the truth in obscurity. (*Aeneid* 6.98–100)

Here at the start of *Aeneid* 6, Aeneas and his followers are once again at
a moment of transition between two worlds: the world they have left behind
and their promised new world. Like the earlier, much longer prophecy of
Helenus, the Sibyl's vision of the future for the Trojans (*Aeneid* 6.83–97) is
deeply embedded within the developing narrative. Looking back, the Sibyl's
words recall the program set out initially by the narrator (*Aeneid* 1.1–7) and
help mark the transition to the second part of it. The Trojans' journey from
Troy to a new world is not only a geographical one, with all its attendant risks,
dangers, and conflict, but also a complex, emotional one in which the past will
continue to haunt the future. A key feature of visions of the Trojans' promised
new home is its river, the Tiber. The ghost of Creusa is the first to speak of
this, and it is a recurring component of this vision (*Aeneid* 2.780–83; 3.500;
5.83, 797). But now the Sibyl, as she sees into the future, gives an opposite
vision of the Tiber, reawakening the horrors of a massacre such as that of
the Trojans driven by Achilleus into the river Xanthus, where "the water
grew red with the blood" (*Iliad* 21.21). The sense of the coming of a new war
resembling the past war gathers strength: in the Sibyl's vision the two rivers
of Troy reappear, the Simoïs and the Xanthus, between which the Achaeans
and the Trojans met in battle (*Iliad* 6.1–4); a Greek camp and another Achilles
are there, waiting to confront the Trojans in Latium. The strongly suggestive
phrase "another Achilles" is discussed in chapter 8.2.

In the Sibyl's prophecy there is both continuity and change. The Trojans
will not be able to shake off Juno's malignant hold on them, but they must learn
to adapt to changed circumstances, however unlikely they may seem (cf. *Aeneid*
2.49, 65–66), and look now for salvation rather than treachery and destruction
from a Greek city. The closest link, however, between past and future is reserved
by the Sibyl for the role of a "foreign wife" as the cause "once again" of all the
Trojans' troubles. Here too, however, as the narrative develops, it becomes clear
that there is change, as well as a repetition, of past experience. When Lavinia,
Aeneas's future bride, is first introduced to the reader, it is clear both that she
is little more than a child, standing on the brink of adult married life and also

that it is this time in her life, rather than any action of hers, that will cause the trouble. Already there is conflict brewing between her parents over whether or not she should marry Turnus, the most eligible of her local suitors (*Aeneid* 7.45–106). In an alarming portent, Lavinia's hair starts to burn as her father lights the fire for a sacrificial offering on the altar, and this becomes the occasion for prophecy: "for they were singing that she would be marked out by fame and by fate / but that it foretold a great war for the people" (*Aeneid* 7.79–80).

King Latinus consults his divine father, the prophetic god Faunus, and is told to wait for sons-in-law to come from overseas, who will bring fame and worldwide dominion to his people (*Aeneid* 7.96–101). A little later, when news of the arrival of Aeneas and the Trojans is brought to him, Latinus is quick to identify Aeneas as the husband destined for his daughter, and in this context he speaks of prophetic singing in a tone of unalloyed confidence and pride, with no apparent thought for the second half of the prophecy:

> "that sons-in-law from foreign shores will come,
> this, they sing, is awaiting us in Latium, and with their blood they
>   will carry
> our name to the stars." (*Aeneid* 7.270–72)

Ironically, however, the word "blood," in addition to suggesting a bloodline, can also carry the ominous undertone of "bloodshed."

By the start of *Aeneid* 8, the second half of the prophecy made when Lavinia's hair catches fire has been fulfilled, and the Trojans find themselves on the brink of a "great war." *Aeneid* 8 marks a lull before the storm of full-scale war. At its start, the river-god, old Tiberinus, appears to Aeneas in his sleep as he lies on the riverbank under the night sky, and the god speaks words of reassurance. Aeneas has succeeded in his mission: he has brought Troy safely out of enemy hands and back to its true home, and he has preserved the "everlasting" heart of the city. His coming is expected, and he has here a settled home for himself and the household gods (*Aeneid* 8.36–39). He need not fear the threat of war: "All the swelling anger / of the gods has subsided" (*Aeneid* 8.40–41). A moment's pregnant silence is created by the half-line at line 41. Despite this blanket reassurance, Juno's "anger and threats" remain for the Trojans to overcome through prayer, as Tiberinus acknowledges a little later (*Aeneid* 8.60–61). Here is the big picture, delivered to an anxious Aeneas who has at long last succumbed to sleep (*Aeneid* 8.26–30), and delivered in such a way as to hint also, for a moment, at a premature sense in his sleeping mind that all is now well. The fulfilment of the omen of the white sow and its thirty-strong litter (*Aeneid* 8.43–48, 81–85; cf. 3.389–93) will prove to him, on waking, that this is no empty dream: within thirty years Ascanius will found a city with the distinguished name of "Alba" (White City). Of all this there can be no doubt: "There is no uncertainty in what I sing" (*Aeneid* 8.49).

Gone now is the Sibyl's vision of "the Tiber foaming with steams of blood," and in place of truth wrapped in obscurity, there is now "no uncertainty" in what the river-god sings. The Sibyl spoke paradoxically of the first help for the Trojans coming from a Greek city, and now the river-god explains this. Aeneas must seek help from Evander and his Arcadians at Pallanteum. In this way he will prove victorious, and the river-god himself will lead him to his destination. Aeneas must pray at dawn to Juno and conquer her hostility with supplicatory vows. With a description of himself as the river Tiber in all his glory, the river-god brings his speech, the last full-scale prophecy in the *Aeneid,* to an end and dives down deep into his own waters (*Aeneid* 8. 62–67). Nevertheless, the river-god's full-hearted support for Aeneas does not stop him later from helping Aeneas's enemy Turnus (*Aeneid* 9.815–18).

Across the first two thirds of the *Aeneid,* prophetic singing is received with a wide variety of different responses: fatal ignorance, the clearing away of an earlier misunderstanding, dismissal and disbelief, fear and the collapse of morale, confident words of prayer, an optimistic identification of prophetic singing with the listener's own thoughts and wishes, and finally a prayer upon awakening (*Aeneid* 2.195–98; 3.172–79, 186–87, 259–60; 6.54–55; 7.272–73; 8.67–70). All this creates a complex strand of communication within the narrative. The end of this sequence of prophetic singing, which extends across the Trojans' travels in search of a new home, is given from the site of the future city of Rome. As Evander shows Aeneas around, he explains how guidance from his mother the nymph Carmentis[12] and from Apollo helped bring him to this new home, and he points out an altar and a gate, which commemorate her name:

> Scarcely had he said this when he moved on from here and showed
>   an altar
> and a gate, which the Romans refer to as the Carmental Gate,
> in ancient honor of the nymph Carmentis,
> a prophetess of fate, who was the first to sing that the descendants
>   of Aeneas
> would be great and Pallanteum a noble city. (*Aeneid* 8.337–41)

---

12. The name suggests, by association, the Latin word *carmen* (song). O'Hara (1990, 21), commenting on Virgil's interest in etymology, writes, "often the name expresses the true nature of the thing."

Prophetic singing is given a firm place here within the *Aeneid*'s grand narrative, and its authenticity is guaranteed by the sudden flash forward from the Pallanteum of Evander to its successor, the "noble city" of the narrator's own day, with its well-established religious rituals and familiar landmarks, linking past and present. Here, as the narrator simultaneously looks forward and backward, the *Aeneid*'s prophetic singing is shown to have received its fulfilment.

4

Sons and Mothers

4.1 ✒ Sharing the Pain

At *Iliad* 1.348–56, Achilleus sits alone in tears at the edge of the sea, far from his companions. He stretches his hands out in prayer to his beloved mother and tells her his wrongs. The life that she, a goddess, has given to him is short, and Zeus ought to have guaranteed him honor in compensation. But he has no honor from Zeus since Agamemnon has dishonored him by taking away his war prize, Briseïs:

> So he spoke through his tears and his revered mother heard him
> as she sat in the depths of the sea, beside her old father,
> and swiftly she rose from the grey sea, like mist,
> and sat down before him, as the tears fell from him.
> She stroked him with her hand and spoke aloud to him:
> "Child, why are you crying? What pain has entered your heart?
> Tell me. Do not keep it a secret, so that we can know it together."
> (*Iliad* 1.357–63)

With a deep groan Achilleus recounts the events that have led to the removal of Briseïs and asks Thetis to pray to Zeus to grant him revenge on Agamemnon by bringing help to the Trojans (*Iliad* 1.364–412):

> Then Thetis answered him, through her tears:
> "Oh my poor child! Why did I suffer to give birth to you? Why did
>   I bring you up?

> If only you were sitting beside the ships, without tears and without
>   pain,
> since your fate is a short life, no length of time at all.
> But now you are both soon to die and wretched beyond all others.
> So it was for an evil fate that I gave birth to you in the house."
>   (*Iliad* 1.413–18)

Thetis accepts her son's request to go to Zeus as soon as possible and to beg for revenge, telling him to stay beside the ships and to persist in his anger against the Achaeans and in his refusal to fight (*Iliad* 1.419–27). Schein (1984) takes the reader systematically through the *Iliad,* concentrating on the central role and complex character of Achilleus. He writes, "The force and intensity of his anger are more than human and his daemonic power sets him apart from all other mortals" (1984, 91).[1]

In this scene the physical world, the internal world of Achilleus's emotions, and the divine world are all closely interwoven. Achilleus cries, and it is as if "the boundless sea" (*Iliad* 1.350) mirrors the extent of his pain. But the sea is also the home of his beloved mother, and she at once hears his prayer and rises up "swiftly" from the grey sea, "like mist." Through this tiny simile the narrator transforms the physical and emotional world of Achilleus. Thetis comes out of the mists of the sea, and it is as if the infinite expanse of "the grey sea" is transformed into the closeness of a mother's touch, the reassurance of her shared tears and her attentiveness to her son's troubles.

Thetis's divinity makes possible what would be impossible for a mortal mother: a visit to her warrior son far away from home on campaign, bringing him sympathy and assistance. But this intervention by a mother in her adult son's life does not threaten the son's authority or alter his outlook. It is he who calls to her and she who comes in answer. The mother's shared grief at the shortness of her son's life and his excessive suffering mirrors and confirms his own view of the situation, and she unquestioningly takes on the role of intermediary for her son's plan of revenge, supporting his strategy of angry noncooperation with his fellow Achaeans. This meeting of mother and son is set apart from the eyes and ears of the rest of the world, and as it comes to an end, the focus of Achilleus's emotion is left as it was before: anger that the

---

1. Nagy (1999) examines the place of Achilleus both within and beyond Homer. Slatkin (2001) discusses the role of Thetis both in the *Iliad* and in the wider mythological background. For further discussion of the anger of Achilleus, see chapter 8.1.

beautiful woman who was his prize in war has been taken away from him by force (*Iliad* 1.428–30).

The brief moments of communication that Achilleus has with Thetis, and the references that are made to her both by Achilleus himself and by the narrator, help create the sense of Achilleus's life stretching outside the confines of the narrative, back to a time before the war,[2] and forward to the tragically short time before he himself must die. At *Iliad* 9.410–16, Achilleus records how Thetis tells him that he has two opposite fates: either to stay fighting at Troy and lose his homecoming but win undying fame, or to return home to a long life but lose his heroic fame. For a time in the first half of the *Iliad*, Achilleus seems to be on the brink of accepting the second of these fates (*Iliad* 1.169–71; 9.356–67, 427–29), but as the pressure on the Achaean forces from the enemy mounts, the situation is reversed, and attention begins to focus on the fated deaths on the battlefield of Achilleus and his beloved companion Patroklos. Schein examines the special bond between Achilleus and Patroklos and explores this against the wider background of Achilleus's capacity for showing tenderness, friendship, and affection, as well as extreme anger (1984, 115–20, 123–24nn18–20, 126–27nn41, 43). I discuss this relationship in more detail in chapter 7.3. Information from Thetis to her son on the subject of Patroklos's fate is either withheld from him altogether or veiled in obscurity (*Iliad* 17.401–11; 18.8–13). Her emotional involvement in the mortal world is confined to her own suffering as Achilleus's mother and her sharing in the suffering of her now-adult son, who is destined soon to die.

When Achilleus learns of Patroklos's death, his mother responds at once to the expression of her son's intense grief:

> He uttered a terrible cry of pain, and his revered mother heard him,
> as she sat in the depths of the sea beside her old father,
> and she cried out too, and the goddesses gathered around her,
> all the daughters of Nereus, down in the depths of the sea. (*Iliad*
>   18.35–38)

Thirty-three of Thetis's fellow Nereids are now listed by name (*Iliad* 18.39–48), and they and all the other daughters of Nereus fill the white cave and beat their breasts as Thetis utters a divine lament for her sufferings (*Iliad* 18.50–62).

---

2. In his father's house, Achilleus has often heard Thetis tell how she helped Zeus when he was in trouble (*Iliad* 1.396–407). Thetis put on board her son's ship a chest full of warm clothes and blankets (*Iliad* 16.221–24).

Her fate is to be "the wretched mother of the best of men," doomed never to see the return of her great warrior-son, and unable to relieve his suffering. At the end of her lament, accompanied by her weeping sisters, she comes to Achilleus to hear what is causing him such pain far from the fighting. The billows of the sea part around them and her sisters come ashore in a row by the ships of the Myrmidons (*Iliad* 18.63–69).

Once again the inner, emotional world of Achilleus, the physical world, and the divine world are closely interwoven, but now the effect is to widen the response to his suffering. Attention focuses on Thetis and her sister Nereids. The list of their names, many of which reflect characteristics of the sea, creates a change of pace, temporarily arresting the momentum of human grief and suggesting a vivid sense of individualized, divine lamentation that is taking place simultaneously within the sea. This list of feminine names and the context of mourning in which it occurs make a strong contrast with the lists of masculine, fighting forces discussed in chapter 1.2. The list also shows Thetis both as belonging within this divine sisterhood and as being fundamentally detached from it in having had a mortal man as her husband and having now a mortal son, whose suffering and impending death she laments. The subject of her lament, however, differs now from that of her son, taking the reader away from the immediacy of Patroklos's death and forward in divine foresight to Achilleus's own approaching death, which is inexorably tied to it.

This foreshadowing of Achilleus's death is also conveyed by the sight of the great warrior, who has collapsed at the news of Patroklos's death and is now stretched out full-length on the ground, covered in dust and ashes, and it continues as his pitying mother holds his head (*Iliad* 18.23–27, 70–72)[3] while a chorus of female figures, both human and divine, laments in the background. Despite the physical contact, a complex irony now creates a sense of emotional distance between the two worlds of mother and son. Thetis laments that her coming to her son can bring him no comfort (*Iliad* 18.62), and this proves all too true in their first exchange of words. Having set in motion the sequence of events that Achilleus asked for when they met before, Thetis might reasonably expect her son to be pleased. But the loss of Patroklos destroys any pleasure that he might have derived from the success of his revenge plan on the Achaean leader and his forces (*Iliad* 18.73–82). Patroklos's death and its

---

3. For this gesture of mourning, cf. *Iliad* 23.136; 24.712, 724.

emotional significance for another human thus require a mortal to reveal it to a goddess, to explain the changed situation to her.

With the loss of his beloved friend comes also the loss of Achilleus's own armor, which passes into enemy hands. The fate of these awe-inspiring objects, so much part of the warrior's identity, has an added, emotional significance since they were a wedding gift to Peleus from the gods on the day when they gave Thetis to a mortal husband (*Iliad* 18.82–85).[4] This thought leads Achilleus to wish that his parents had never married:

> "If only you had stayed with the deathless sea-nymphs,
> living there, and Peleus had taken a mortal wife.
> But now immeasurable grief will come to your heart too,
> for the death of your son, whom you will never receive
> back home, for I have no will in my heart
> to live or to mix with my fellow men, unless Hektor
> is first struck down by my spear and loses his life,
> and pays the price for making Patroklos, son of Menoitios, his
>   prey." (*Iliad* 18.86–93)

Thetis's marriage to Achilleus's father Peleus has given her a double life, partly in the immortal world with her sisters and her father at the bottom of the sea, and partly in the mortal world with her aging, human husband. Within this double life, her capacity for sustained suffering on behalf of her mortal son gives her a close affinity with the mortal world. She suffers as the mother who knows that she is about to lose her beloved son, and her immortality ensures that her suffering will never end. Her ability in the past to rescue three male gods—Zeus, Dionysos, and Hephaistos (*Iliad* 1.396–406; 6.135–37; 18.394–405)—throws into sharp contrast her powerlessness in the face of the imminent death of her mortal son. Her son, in turn, sympathizes both with her fate and the fate of his father. His resolve, however, remains unwavering:

> Then Thetis answered him through her tears:
> "Indeed your fate will be swift to come, my child, from what you
>   are saying,
> for, after Hektor, then at once your doom is ready waiting."

---

4. For Thetis's account of the suffering caused to her by her marriage to the mortal Peleus, which was forced on her by Zeus, cf. *Iliad* 18.429–35.

With a great groan, swift-footed Achilleus answered her:
"At once may I die, since I was not to ward off
my companion's death, but he perished, far from his homeland,
when he needed me to defend him in battle." (*Iliad* 18.94–100)

Despite his outpouring of emotion, Achilleus speaks now with great firmness of purpose and a clear-sighted and wide-ranging vision (*Iliad* 18.97–126). He seizes on Thetis's words that he is doomed to die "at once" after Hektor dies. Elsewhere Achilleus is eloquent on the finality of death (*Iliad* 9.406–9), but this "at once" holds no terrors for him. Rather, it is embraced as something logically to be wished for since he did nothing to stop the death of his beloved companion. This thought leads him to take the first of two steps in a crucial change of outlook. There are many others among his companions besides Patroklos whom he has failed to save from death at the hands of Hektor. He now comes to see these dead companions not as expendable within the strategy imposed by his personal quarrel with Agamemnon but as an indictment on his prolonged inactivity:

"But I sit here beside the ships, a useless encumbrance upon the
    land,
I who have no like among the bronze-clad Achaeans
in war." (*Iliad* 18.104–6)

This bitter thought leads to a wish for the impossible: if only rivalry and anger could be eliminated from the world of gods and of men. Having confronted and articulated the complex and pervasive power of anger, Achilleus is able to take a second, even greater step forward and to view the anger that Agamemnon aroused in him, even though it still hurts him, as a thing of the past. Necessity has forced him to restrain the feelings of his heart. Having confronted the terrible consequences of his anger in the presence of his mother's sympathetic tears, he finds the strength to see beyond the past and to fulfill his one remaining desire: to confront the killer of his beloved friend. This renewed sense of purpose brings with it an acceptance of death, whenever the gods may bring it, and a commitment to the heroic ideal of winning glory and inflicting bitter revenge on the enemy. Schein (1984, 67–88) explores these central themes in the *Iliad*.[5] Achilleus's speech ends by returning to its starting point and by rejecting any caution implied by Thetis's warning of his impending death in

---

5. For further discussion of the heroic code, see Redfield (1994, 99–127).

battle: "Do not hold me back from battle, even though you love me. You will not persuade me" (*Iliad* 18.126).

Thetis's reply to this speech, in which her son bares his heart to her and unflinchingly embraces his imminent death, gives him her full support and brings a quickening of pace by looking forward to the coming sequence of events (*Iliad* 18.127–37). First she confirms her son's discovery of a new sense of purpose and hence the start of his reintegration into his warrior society: "Yes indeed, my son. Truly it is no bad thing, / to ward off sheer destruction from hard-pressed companions" (*Iliad* 18.128–29). The loss of his weapons must be acknowledged, but although Hektor now has Achilleus's armor on his shoulders, he will not glory in it for long since his death is close at hand. Achilleus himself should not reenter the fray until he has seen her at dawn the next morning, bringing him a fine set of armor from lord Hephaistos. With these words, she turns away from her son and instructs her fellow Nereids to return home to their father, while she goes to Olympos once again on her son's behalf. This time she will not deliver a request of his for help for the Achaeans' enemies but will ask, on her own initiative, for divine armor for her son's return to the fighting to aid his "hard-pressed companions" (*Iliad* 18.138–47).

Dawn comes and Thetis returns. As she swoops down from Olympos towards the ships, bringing the god's gift, she is like a hawk (*Iliad* 18.616–17). She finds her beloved son embracing the body of Patroklos, uttering piercing cries of grief and surrounded by his mourning companions. She stands in their midst, takes Achilleus by the hand, and speaks to him:

> "My child, we should leave this man to lie, even though we grieve,
> since first he was brought down at the will of the gods.
> But as for you, take this glorious armor from Hephaistos,
> fine armor indeed, such as no man before has borne on his
>   shoulders." (*Iliad* 19.8–11)

As she places it in front of Achilleus, the intricately designed armor rings out. His companions draw back in terror, but the sight of it intensifies Achilleus's anger, and a fierce gleam comes into his eyes. He delights in holding the god's shining gift and examining its intricate detail. Even so, his thoughts are still torn between admiration for his divine armor and anxiety about the decomposing body of his dead companion (*Iliad* 19.21–27). In reply, Thetis tells her son to have no such anxiety. She directs him to summon an assembly and publicly renounce his anger against Agamemnon, and then at once to arm himself for battle. So saying, she rouses Achilleus's fighting spirit and preserves Patroklos's body by dripping ambrosia and nectar into his nostrils. Achilleus is now seen marching along the seashore and shouting out in a terrifying voice to arouse the Achaean heroes (*Iliad* 19.28–41).

Gone now is the mother's lament for the shortness of her son's life. Death in battle "at the will of the gods" is something that must be accepted. The dead must be left to lie. They cannot be brought back to life, however hard the pain of loss. The mortal dread of physical decomposition after death, which still shares a place in Achilleus's mind with his eager acceptance of the immortal armor, is something that Thetis, in her divinity, can remove. As for Achilleus himself, first he must revisit the site of his public humiliation by Agamemnon. Just as Achilleus first took the initiative in calling an assembly (*Iliad* 1.54), so he should now call an assembly again in order publicly to revoke his anger against Agamemnon. Thus the two immediate causes of Achilleus's emotional turmoil—grief and fear in the presence of death—are addressed together by Thetis. Furthermore, the deep-seated, underlying cause—the anger toward Agamemnon, already privately renounced in his mother's presence—can after a public confirmation that it is over be rechanneled with the help of the gift of divine armor in such a way as to bring him a fierce joy, the joy of anticipated revenge. The seashore, where for so long (in narrative terms) Achilleus has been inactive, crushed by the weight of his depression, now becomes a place where he strides purposefully along, like a god, and shouts out in a terrifying voice to arouse his fellow soldiers.

By the start of *Iliad* 24, however, it is clear that revenge for the killing of Patroklos has not brought Achilleus closure. He remains sleepless with grief, and when daylight comes, he expresses the violence of his feelings by reenacting his initial disfigurement of Hektor's corpse (*Iliad* 24.3–18). In the divine world, things are similarly at an impasse (*Iliad* 24.18–73) until Zeus summons Thetis to tell her some wise words that will enable Achilleus to receive gifts from Priam in return for giving up Hektor (*Iliad* 24.74–76). Thetis is to leave her lamentation for her son's fate (*Iliad* 24.83–86) and to play the role of intermediary between Zeus and her son, just as she did in *Iliad* 1. Now, however, the communication will go in the opposite direction, and now the starting point for the message is not human but divine anger, as Zeus makes clear to Thetis. Achilleus's refusal to let go of Hektor's body shows a heart in the grip of madness. He should fear the anger of the gods and above all of Zeus and give Hektor back. Zeus will also ensure that Priam brings a ransom for the body, which will gladden Achilleus's heart (*Iliad* 24.112–19).

I discuss this scene further in chapter 8.1.

Thetis does as she is bidden and darts down to Achilleus's tent, where she finds her son crying endlessly for Patroklos. His close companions have returned to the normal routine of life and are making breakfast. Thetis sits down next to her son and strokes him once again with her hand before speaking to him:

> "My son, how much longer will you eat out your heart
> in lamentation and grief, with no thought for food
> or bed? It is a good thing to make love
> to a woman, for you have not long to live, but already
> death and harsh destiny stand close beside you." (*Iliad* 24.128–32)

Thetis gives her son the message from Zeus, adding her own voice to the call for Achilleus to give Hektor back:

> "Come now, give him back, and receive the ransom for the corpse."
> Swift-footed Achilleus replied to her and said:
> "So be it. Whoever brings the ransom may take the corpse,
> if the Olympian himself puts his whole heart behind the order."
> So they talked much together by the gathering of the ships,
> and many a winged word passed between mother and son. (*Iliad*
>   24.137–42)

Another of the *Iliad*'s great turning points comes in this final exchange between mother and son. But this one comes about, not as the result of a complex mental process, as in *Iliad* 18, but rather as a sudden moment of acceptance of divine will. With the briefest of responses from him—"So be it"[6]—Achilleus's world changes. His unabated anger and grief have driven him to the brink of madness, where nothing in his life matters but the obsessive, compulsive, and constantly thwarted punishment of one dead body at the empty tomb of another. Now, in response to his mother's words and the message she has conveyed to him from Zeus, Achilleus finds instant release from this emotional stranglehold, just as he grants release to the tangible object at the center of this fixation on death, Hektor's corpse. In place of his all-consuming human anger and grief, comes a due fear for the anger of the

---

6. The punctuation and interpretation of the words at this point in the text are uncertain. The interpretation given here follows the text in the Oxford Classical Text and the translation of W. Leaf (1898, 580). Other views are given by Macleod (1982, 101) and Richardson (1993, 289–90).

gods and, in turn, restitution to him of honor from Zeus. This honor, like the anger and grief it replaces, has a tangible manifestation in the form of the gifts the enemy king will bring to him as a ransom, which will warm his heart.

Thus Thetis, who lamented before that she was unable to help her son, has twice been the means of bringing him both great emotional release in the presence of death and the opportunity to move on, the first time through her own intervention and the second time through being the channel for conveying the wishes of Zeus. On both occasions, she has been the voice of emotional restraint, and restraint has finally prevailed. Thetis's own tears of "immeasurable grief" (*Iliad* 18.88) for her son's death may continue to flow in her watery cave. But the human world must acknowledge a return from grief and all-consuming anger to the satisfaction of other needs, such as the need for food and sleep. Making love to a woman is also something good, as Thetis reminds her son, something to set against the shortness of life and the rapid approach of death. Thetis can direct her son's thoughts to Briseïs, whose forceful removal initially caused her son such anger and led indirectly to such terrible, unforeseen consequences for him (cf. *Iliad* 24.676, where Achilleus is shown sleeping beside the beautiful Briseïs), and son and mother are finally shown together in animated conversation. Richardson (1993) notes how a sense of balance is created between Thetis's first and last communication with her son (*Iliad* 1.357–430; 24.126–42). Of the ending of the latter scene he writes, "To leave them thus together is a most unusual way of closing the scene, as normally the divine visitor would return to heaven" (Richardson 1993, 290).

4.2 ⚶ A Mother from Another World

Just as Thetis approaches Zeus on her son's behalf near the start of the *Iliad,* so Venus brings the problems of her son Aeneas to the attention of Jupiter near the start of the *Aeneid,* but the initiative for this intervention comes from Venus herself.[7] Aeneas does not know of his mother's concern for him at this point, or of Jupiter's reassuring reply to her, in which he unfolds the future destiny both of Aeneas and of his descendants (*Aeneid* 1.227–96). The feeling of unfairness that prompts this intervention comes now from the divine world,

---

7. Camps (1969, 21–30) gives a concise introduction to the characterization of Aeneas. For further discussion of characterization in the *Aeneid,* see Laird (1997, 282–93). Gransden (2004, 24–26) gives a concise introduction to the Aeneas legend.

from Venus's sense that Jupiter has broken his promise that the world-ruling Roman nation will come one day from the defeated Trojans:

> "What crime can my Aeneas have committed against you,
> or the Trojans, who have suffered so many deaths
> and who, for the sake of Italy, find the whole world closed to
>   them?" (*Aeneid* 1.231–33)

By her rhetorical questions Venus puts pressure on her all-powerful father, identifying herself closely with the fate of her son and his people and reminding Jupiter that she and they are his descendants:

> "As for us, your descendants, to whom you grant the citadel of
>   heaven,
> we have lost our ships (it is unspeakable!) and on account of the
>   anger of one individual,
> we are betrayed, kept far away from the shores of Italy.
> Is this the reward for duty? Is this the way you restore us to royal
>   power?" (*Aeneid* 1.250–53)

Aeneas's ultimate fate is very different both from the one Achilleus faces and from the one that awaits the Aineias of the *Iliad* (*Iliad* 1.416; 20.332–36). They must both face the finality of death, but Aeneas has been promised a place with the gods. Nevertheless, he and his followers have almost drowned in the storm that Juno sent with the help of Aeolus, king of the winds. Moreover, the bulk of Aeneas's fleet is now missing (*Aeneid* 1.81–123, 170–71). Here the paradox of the undeserved suffering, inflicted on the dutiful figure of Aeneas by Juno, recalls the dilemma brought to the Muse's attention by the narrator at the start of the Aeneid (*Aeneid* 1.8–11). But now Jupiter's reply to Aeneas's divine mother makes clear that, in the long term, Venus's anxieties are unfounded. The future fate of her people remains unaltered, and Aeneas's ultimate deification is assured. Jupiter tells her that "you will bring on high to the stars of the sky / great-hearted Aeneas. No, I have not altered my purpose" (*Aeneid* 1.259–60).[8]

After surviving the near-death experience at sea that first introduces Aeneas to the reader, he sets out the next morning with his companion Achates to discover what he can about the land onto which his surviving ships have been blown, and he is met by his mother in disguise:

---

8. Lyne (1987, 71–99) and Feeney (1991, 137–55) explore the link between fate and Jupiter's will.

His mother placed herself in his path in the middle of the forest.
She had a maiden's face and appearance and the weapons of a
    maiden
of Sparta, or was like Thracian Harpalyce,[9] when she tires the
    horses
and outruns the fast flowing Hebrus in flight. (*Aeneid* 1.314–17)

In the previous scene, Venus speaks to Jupiter as he looks down from "the highest point in the sky" (*Aeneid* 1.223–29). Now, as she appears to her son on the ground in human disguise, the sense that she belongs in another world becomes more complex. The meeting is unexpected, and the cloaking of her identity from her son is thoroughgoing. She has taken care to make herself look like a huntress, and after first boldly attracting the men's attention (*Aeneid* 1.318–24), she opens the encounter by inquiring about her sister huntresses, who are out on a boar hunt. Her appearance and opening words point within the divine world not to her own identity but to that of her antithesis, the maiden-goddess and huntress Diana.[10]

The hiding of Venus's true identity from her son through this elaborate piece of play acting is shared with the reader: "So spoke Venus and so began Venus's son in reply" (*Aeneid* 1.325). Aeneas replies that he has neither seen nor heard any of her sisters. He is uncertain how he should address her and asks her in turn for information:

"O how should I refer to you, maiden? For yours is no mortal
face, nor does your voice sound human. O goddess for certain,
(either the sister of Phoebus or one of the race of Nymphs?),
be gracious, whoever you are, and lighten our labors
and tell us, please, what sky we are under, onto the shores of what
    land
we have been tossed." (*Aeneid* 1.327–32)

In many ways, the scene that now develops between Aeneas and his disguised mother suggests comparison with the meeting between Odysseus and Nausicaa after Odysseus, having nearly drowned, has been washed ashore,

---

9. There is no surviving reference to Harpalyce before Virgil. For a similar but more detailed picture, cf. the description of the maiden warrior Camilla at *Aeneid* 7.806–11.

10. Cf. *Aeneid* 1.498–503; 11.652. In the human world, a boar hunt is shown as a high-risk, male activity; cf. *Iliad* 9.543–46; *Odyssey* 19.392–94, 444–54; and *Aeneid* 4.156–59.

although in the *Odyssey* these details appear in a different order.[11] Recall of the sexual comedy in this scene in the *Odyssey*, which I discuss in chapter 6.3, adds to the complex irony in the manner of Venus's concealment of her identity from her son. The scene has produced a wide range of critical response. R. G. Austin writes, "The following scene shows Virgil's touch at its lightest and most charming" (1971, 118). Oliensis (1997, 306–7) offers a darker reading of the scene, making much of its "incestuous undertones."[12] A comparison with a later scene, in which Athene in disguise helps Odysseus be on his way (*Odyssey* 7.18–79), produces a similarly complex result. In both this and the present passage in *Aeneid* 1 a goddess disguises herself as a young girl, and in both, the goddess makes the traveler(s) invisible for protection against a potentially hostile reception (*Odyssey* 7.14–17, 39–42; *Aeneid* 1.411–14). However, the setting for these two encounters is different. In the *Odyssey*, Odysseus is already approaching the city when he meets a young girl carrying a pitcher. In the *Aeneid* the encounter is set out in the wilds, in the middle of the forest, and both sexes are armed for hunting. Here, by contrast, is a potentially more dangerous context for an encounter between man and goddess.[13]

Venus preserves her disguise with the ironic claim that she is not worthy of divine honor, such as Aeneas has just promised. She speaks briefly of the local Tyrian girls and their traditional dress as huntresses before answering Aeneas's question and explaining to him where he is (*Aeneid* 1.335–39). The bulk of her speech, however, gives an account of those events in Dido's earlier life that have led to her holding power in this region of North Africa. In that it focuses attention on the importance of the local queen, this account can be compared with that of the disguised Athene in the *Odyssey*. But unlike Arete, Dido has no husband or child. In this context, with its intimate details of Dido's personal life, the fiction that Venus is no more than a local girl, temporarily parted from her sister huntresses, is allowed to recede. Here, as Aeneas himself takes for granted (*Aeneid* 1.328, 372), is a goddess speaking.

11. Cf. *Odyssey* 6.149, 122–24, 119, 175–77; 8.467–68; 6.102–4, 150–52.

12. For further discussion, see Oliensis (2009, 61–63).

13. For the relatively safe setting of the first of these meetings, cf. the double fountain under the walls of Troy, used in peacetime by the women of the city for washing clothes, at *Iliad* 22.147–56. For the potentially more dangerous setting of the second of these meetings, cf. Circe's home in the middle of a forest at *Odyssey* 10.150.

At the end of her speech the fiction returns, and with its return, the irony in the scene becomes more somber. The disguised Venus now starts questioning Aeneas and Achates, and at this Aeneas sighs and reflects sadly that the whole day would be too short for him to give a full account of their troubles (*Aeneid* 1.369–74). First he explains that they have come from "ancient Troy," if by any chance she has heard "the name of Troy," and then he introduces himself and his mission:

> "I am dutiful Aeneas, and in my fleet I carry with me the house-
>   hold gods,
> snatched from enemy hands, my fame is known above the sky.
> It is Italy that I seek, my homeland, and my origin is from
>   almighty Jupiter." (*Aeneid* 1.378–80)

He explains how he started with twenty ships on the journey allotted to him by fate, "with my mother showing me the way." Now barely seven storm-tossed ships remain, while he himself is "unknown" and in need. As he continues his account of his sufferings, Venus interrupts him: "Whoever you are, you are not, I believe, hated by the immortals, / as you draw the life-giving air, you who have reached the Tyrian city" (*Aeneid* 1.387–88). Her advice to him is "to carry on" along the path until he reaches the queen's threshold. As for the missing ships and their crew, she gives him an authoritative interpretation of an omen, which now appears in the sky: either they have already landed or they are safely sailing into port (*Aeneid* 1.389–401).

Here and in the following lines, which draw the encounter to a close (*Aeneid* 1.402–17), the ironic gap widens between the two worlds of human son and divine mother. Venus makes no response to the words of Aeneas, which suggest with increasing irony cues to which she might respond. Before this encounter between son and disguised mother, first the narrator in dialogue with his Muse and then Venus herself in earnest conversation with her father Jupiter raise the issue of Aeneas's undeserved suffering. But when her son himself speaks despondently about his own situation, his divine mother withholds her identity from him and does not allow him even to finish his account of his sufferings. For Aeneas this is an important moment, a chance to articulate, after a near-death experience, his own identity, his sense of purpose and his pain. This moment makes an ironic contrast with the comparable moment in Odysseus's experience. In the *Odyssey*, it is Odysseus himself who has for long remained incognito and who finally reveals his identity in the warm, public context of a banquet held in his honor:

"I am Odysseus, son of Laertes, and all men know of me
for my tricks, and my fame reaches the heavens.
I live in bright Ithaca." (*Odyssey* 9.19–21)

Aeneas has no home, only the search for an elusive, distant "homeland" for himself and his people. Odysseus, the master trickster, can speak confidently of his fame reaching the heavens, but Aeneas, the man of duty, speaks one moment of his fame being known above the sky and the next moment of being "unknown." For the reader this word carries the further, ironic sense that his identity is not acknowledged by his own divine mother.

Attention now focuses on the moment of parting:

She spoke and, as she turned away, the light shone back from her
    rosy neck,
her heavenly head of hair breathed forth a divine
scent; her dress flowed down to her feet,
and as she walked, she revealed herself a true goddess. When he
    recognized
his mother, he followed after her fleeing figure with these words:
"Why do you so often cheat your son—you too are cruel—with
    false
appearances? Why is it not granted to join
hand in hand and to hear and utter our true voices?" (*Aeneid*
    1.402–9)

Venus makes no reply but flies away. She is last seen arriving happily in Paphos, to be welcomed by the fragrance rising from her altars (*Aeneid* 1.415–17).[14]

The complex irony surrounding this encounter and coming in large measure from its interaction with the earlier, Homeric passages makes a contrast with the more straightforward intervention by divine mothers to help their human sons in the *Iliad*. Thetis makes reassuring physical contact with her son (*Iliad* 1.361–63; 19.6–7; 24.126–27), and Aphrodite, intent on saving Aineias from death in battle, folds her son in her arms and brings part of her dress over him to conceal him from flying weapons (*Iliad* 5.311–18). Aeneas's sudden encounter with his disguised mother brings him some much-needed information and guidance, but her efforts to ease his despondency with assur-

14. For Venus's departure to Paphos with its sweet-smelling altars, cf. the final description of Aphrodite in Demodokos's song of her affair with Ares at *Odyssey* 8.362–63.

ances that the gods take an interest in him are coupled with a thorough-going denial of a mother's emotional support for a hard-pressed son. In this sense there is no bridging of the gap between the divine world and the human world, no longed-for physical contact to reassure the son, and no openness on his mother's side in their communication. Also it is far from being the first time Aeneas has felt himself cheated in this way by a cruel mother.

From the start of the encounter, Aeneas is put at a disadvantage by his mother's careful disguise. Venus here takes on a new persona, one in which she appears, not in a proto-Roman context with her father, but in a potentially hostile and dangerous Carthaginian context and in Carthaginian dress. In this context, Aeneas can be allowed to identify himself and his sense of purpose, but his heartfelt complaints about his wretched fortune fall on deaf ears. The divine transformation brought about at Venus's parting brings Aeneas a moment of sharp pain, as sudden recognition is coupled with a sense of emotional rejection. Gone now is the disguise, and in its place stands a figure turning away from him. Aeneas realizes that it is his mother and that she is leaving him. The meeting ends with agitated, unanswered questions from Aeneas and the parting of their ways.

Later, in the course of his account of the fall of Troy, Aeneas recalls how his divine mother appeared to him (*Aeneid* 2.589–623). The preceding lines, which I discuss in chapter 5.2, describe his fury at catching sight of the half-hidden figure of Helen and his desire to kill her (*Aeneid* 2.567–88). They lead without a break into his mother's appearance:

> when she presented herself for me to see her, my kindly mother,
> never before so clear to my eyes, and in pure light she shone
> through the night, manifesting herself as a goddess, in nature
> and in size as she appears to the gods of heaven. She seized my
>   hand,
> restrained me and, in addition, she spoke these words from her
>   rosy lips. (*Aeneid* 2.589–93)

The two appearances are in sharp contrast. Now Venus appears, not as a young, foreign girl, but in the full majesty of her divinity. Now, as he looks back to this experience, Aeneas's mother is not "cruel" but "kindly." Now there is urgent, restraining physical contact[15] as well as direct communication from her (*Aeneid* 2.594–620).

---

15. Cf. Athene's intervention to restrain Achilleus from killing Agamemnon at *Iliad* 1.193–222.

Venus's opening words are colored by criticism of her son's behavior:

"Son, what great pain arouses this uncontrollable anger?
Why are you so furious? What has become of your care for me?
Will you not first see where you have left your weary old father,
Anchises, whether your wife, Creusa, is still alive
and little Ascanius?" (*Aeneid* 2.594–98)

Venus sets a duty of care toward herself in place of the murderous frenzy that her son feels toward Helen. Such care should make him think, rather, of the safety of his family, particularly in view of the care that Venus herself has shown to protect them (*Aeneid* 2.598–600). The tie between human son and divine mother, as well as the future of Aeneas's own young son, make up a central strand in the *Aeneid*'s grand narrative and direct the reader's thoughts, not toward Aeneas's past life,[16] but toward the glorious future that is waiting to unfold. On the present occasion, however, Venus opens her son's eyes to a different big picture, to "the pitilessness of the gods," as the Olympians wreak destruction on Troy (*Aeneid* 2.601–18). She gives him clear orders to escape, echoing the earnest instructions of the dream figure Hector (*Aeneid* 2.289–92). She ends with a reassuring promise before disappearing into the night: "I shall not leave you, but will set you safe on your family threshold" (*Aeneid* 2.620).

Once Aeneas meets Dido, the dual role of Venus—as goddess of sexual attraction and as mother of the man of duty destined to play a central part in the foundation of the Roman nation—adds further ironic complications to the relationship between son and mother. Despite the sympathetic picture she has given, while in disguise, of Dido's past life, and despite giving her son a godlike appearance in readiness for his first meeting with Dido (*Aeneid* 1.588–91),[17] Venus views the queen and her hospitality to the Trojans as a threat and fears that her enemy, Juno, will benefit from the delay. Her response is to make a preemptive strike on Dido; she will disguise Cupid, her divine son and Aeneas's brother (*Aeneid* 1.667–69), as Aeneas's own young son. By a trick, she will use him to ensure that Dido is consumed by a burning passion for Aeneas such that no power will be able to change her: "but that with me she will be held in a great love of Aeneas" (*Aeneid* 1.675). Here the distinction

16. For details in the *Iliad* of the past life of Aineias, cf. *Iliad* 2.820–21; 5.247–48 (his birth) and 13.465–66 (his early upbringing).

17. Cf. Athene's intervention to enhance the physical appearance of Odysseus, both in his meeting with Nausicaa and later in his meeting with Penelope (*Odyssey* 6.227–38; 23.156–63).

between a mother's love for her son and the arousal of desire for her son in a woman is blurred, and the latter is shown as a means used by the mother to entrap a potential enemy. Aeneas himself is compromised by the means chosen by his mother to neutralize the threat to the Trojans from Dido and her Carthaginians. When rumor of his affair with Dido is brought to Jupiter's ears (*Aeneid* 4.173–221), part of the damning charges against Aeneas, which he tells Mercury to deliver, is that "This is not the man whom his most beautiful mother / promised us, nor was this why she twice rescued him from Greek weapons" (*Aeneid* 4.227–28). At this stage, the *Aeneid*'s big picture, already unfolded to Venus by Jupiter (*Aeneid* 1.257–96), faces a new threat from "lovers forgetful of a better fame" (*Aeneid* 4.221). Gone now is the Venus recently seen artfully contriving to hold Dido in her son's power and playfully acquiescing in Juno's wedding trick to draw the two together. In her place, as reported by Jupiter, stands the beautiful mother, betrayed by her son's lapse into the role of lover and his temporary forgetfulness of his destiny.

The relationship between divine mother and mortal son becomes more straightforward once Aeneas has left Dido and has resumed his travels. Concern for her son's troubles prompts Venus to ask Neptune for help (*Aeneid* 5.779–98). Later, as Aeneas follows the Sibyl's instructions to search for the Golden Bough that will enable him to journey through the Underworld to meet the spirit of his dead father, twin doves appear and guide him to the spot. Aeneas recognizes "his mother's birds" and is "happy" as he prays for their help and for the support of "his divine mother" (*Aeneid* 6.185–97). Later still, when a great new war threatens Aeneas in Italy, Venus approaches her husband Vulcan and begs him for arms, "a mother asking on behalf of her son," though not her husband's son. This is a request to which Vulcan, sexually aroused by his wife's advances, readily agrees (*Aeneid* 8.370–406).

Before she brings the divinely created arms to her son, Venus gives a spectacular sign in the sky (*Aeneid* 8.520–29). Aeneas's companions are bewildered, but he recognizes the meaning of the portent:

"I am being demanded by Olympus.
My divine mother sang in prophecy that she would send this sign,
if war were to fall upon us, and that she would bring arms from
    Vulcan
through the air, to assist me." (*Aeneid* 8.533–36)

Soon after this, Venus herself appears in the sky, bringing the arms. From a distance, she sees Aeneas standing apart. Of her own accord, she goes to meet him and addresses him with these words:

> "See, the gifts are all completed by my husband's promised
> skill. Soon you need not hesitate to demand battle
> either with the proud Laurentines or with violent Turnus."
> The goddess of Cythera had spoken and came to embrace her son,
> and the gleaming arms she placed before him, beneath an oak
>   tree. (*Aeneid* 8.612–16)

The reassuring immediacy of physical contact comes with his mother's gift and her clear instructions for the forthcoming war, and Aeneas is left with a glowing sense of pride and wonder as he takes hold of these gifts from his divine mother and starts to examine them.[18]

In the *Iliad*, "laughter-loving Aphrodite" is among the gods ranged on the Trojan side when the gods themselves enter the fighting (*Iliad* 20.40), but her experience when she comes up against both a human and a divine adversary (Diomedes and Athene) shows beyond doubt that she does not belong on the battlefield (*Iliad* 5.330–80; 21.418–34). Venus, by contrast, plays an active part in the war in Italy as it gathers momentum and moves towards its climax. Her commitment to the Trojan cause, first seen in *Aeneid* 1, comes into prominence once again in the council of the gods summoned by Jupiter (*Aeneid* 10.16–62). On the battlefield, "kindly" Venus defends her son from danger, brings support to the Trojan forces, and she and Juno watch from opposite sides as the fighting rages (*Aeneid* 10.331–32, 608–9, 760). When Aeneas is wounded by an arrow and the doctor is unable to treat the wound, Venus shows a mother's concern for her son's "undeserved pain" and secretly brings the crucial medicinal aid to help the doctor extract the arrow and allow her son to return to the fighting (*Aeneid* 12.398–431).

Finally, Venus intervenes in her son's direction of the war:

> Here his mother, in all her beauty, put it in Aeneas's mind
> to go to the walls, to turn his forces more swiftly against the city
> and throw the Latins into confusion by this sudden disaster.
>   (*Aeneid* 12.554–56)

---

18. Cf. *Iliad* 19.6–18 for the moment when Thetis brings the new armor to Achilleus.

With this comes a new stage in the sequence of support Venus gives to the completion of her son's military mission: first a favorable omen in the sky, then the delivery of the divine arms, and now the divine directive to conduct a war of terror on the hitherto unscathed civilian population of the enemy. A final, fleeting moment in the relationship between son and mother comes in the course of Aeneas's duel with Turnus: Aeneas's spear becomes stuck in a tree root and Venus pulls it out for him (*Aeneid* 12.786–87). Tarrant writes, "This is Venus's last appearance in the poem—hardly a glorious ending for her" (2012, 289).

4.3 🐔 Problems with Mother

Telemachos does not have an easy relationship with his mother.[19] Murnaghan gives a sensitive analysis of the difficulty facing Penelope. She still considers herself married to her missing husband and longs for his return. Her social position, however, is unsustainable since she is a husbandless woman in a male-dominated world imbued both with the belief that "wives in general are not to be trusted" and "by the inclination to blame women for the circumstances by which they are constrained" (2009, 236, 242). Penelope's prolonged indecision over what response to give to her numerous, self-seeking suitors and the inroads they are making into the family wealth contribute much to Telemachos's state of depression at the start of the *Odyssey*. He even tells his guest, Mentes (Athene in disguise), that he has only his mother's word for it that Odysseus is his father (*Odyssey* 1.215–16). He does not know his father. Instead the peculiar circumstances of his home life force him to see the sons of the local ruling class, members like him of the younger generation, treating his home as their own and raucously expressing their desire to go bed with his mother (*Odyssey* 1.365–66). Telemachos's relations with his enigmatic mother are not made any easier by what he hears of family life outside his own experience: the story of Agamemnon murdered on his homecoming by his unfaithful wife and her lover (*Odyssey* 1.298–302; 3.254–75, 303–10). Rather than creating solidarity against a common enemy, his home situation has driven a wedge between Telemachos and his mother. At her first, brief

---

19. De Jong (2001, 20–21, 363, and 36–38) gives a useful summary of the main features in the characters of Telemachos and Penelope and of the relationship between son and mother. For further discussion of the complex characterization of Penelope, see Foley (1995) and Felson-Rubin (1996). Rutherford (2013, 93–97) gives a concise survey of the issues raised by her characterization.

appearance in the presence of himself and her suitors (*Odyssey* 1.328–61), he makes a show of taking a stand against her. He systematically counters her attempt to alter the singer's choice of subject, which she finds too upsetting, tells her to bear with fortitude the loss of her husband, and with a new-found sense of his own authority orders her to leave:

> "But go to your room and see to your own work,
> the loom and the spindle, and give orders to your maids
> to attend to their work. Talk will be a matter for the men,
> all of us, but especially me, for the power in the house belongs
> to me." (*Odyssey* 1.356–59)

Telemachos's words are similar to those used by Hektor to Andromache at *Iliad* 6.490–93, which are discussed in chapter 6.1. There, however, it is war that is specified as being men's work. Later, at *Odyssey* 21.350–53, Telemachos uses similar words again to his mother, but now it is the bow on which his attention is fixed. These expressions of male authority impose on the female sex a fixed role, "your own work," while allowing the characteristic task of the male to be adapted to suit the occasion.

The following day at the public assembly that Telemachos has called to force his mother's suitors to leave the house, he finds himself challenged by Antinöos, who blames the situation on the mixed signals and delaying tactics that Penelope employs toward her suitors (*Odyssey* 2.85–112). Murnaghan (1995) notes that the association of women with weaving in a literal sense and with the metaphorical idea of "weaving a plot" overlap in the case of Penelope's plot to trick her suitors (*Odyssey* 2.93–110; 19.137–58; 24.128–48).[20] Antinöos and Eurymachos,[21] Penelope's two leading suitors, put forward a counterproposal that Telemachos should tell his mother to leave the house and return to her own father so that he can decide on a new husband for her. But this is out of the question as far as Telemachos is concerned:

> "Antinöos, I could not possibly drive out of the house, against her wishes,
> the mother who gave birth to me and brought me up, while some-where in the world,
> my father is either alive or dead." (*Odyssey* 2.130–32)

---

20. For "weaving" in this latter sense, cf. *Odyssey*. 13.303, 386.
21. Stanford (1959, lii–lv) has a useful collection of the characteristics of these two leading suitors.

Telemachos may feel confident enough to tell his mother to go to her room, but he explains that with his father's fate still unknown, it would be quite unacceptable for him to force her to leave the house (*Odyssey* 2.132–37). And so the problem remains unsolved. Meanwhile Telemachos tells the assembly his plan to sail off in search of news of his missing father, but he keeps this plan hidden from his mother. He makes Eurycleia, the old family nurse, swear to keep the secret, at least for the time being, for fear of upsetting his mother before it is absolutely necessary: "so that she does not damage her lovely face with crying" (*Odyssey* 2.376).

Penelope's worries over her son, however, soon go beyond anything that Telemachos can imagine. The first she hears of his departure is when the herald brings her news of the suitors' plot to ambush and kill him on his return. Coming on top of the years of pining for her husband, this new blow overwhelms her and is coupled with the sense that she could have stopped her son from leaving if only she had been told of his intention (*Odyssey* 4.732–34). When Penelope, still worrying about her son, finally falls asleep, Athene sends her a comforting dream. In her sleep Penelope pours out her fresh troubles to the dream figure of her distant sister:

> "Now, what is more, my beloved son has gone on his hollow ship,
> and he no more than a child, with no knowledge of hardship or of
>   speaking in public.
> I grieve for him even more than for my husband." (*Odyssey*
>   4.817–19)

The dream figure calms her fears, at least as regards her son's safety, and when Penelope wakes, she feels comforted by her dream (*Odyssey* 4.840–41).

As the first four books of the *Odyssey* unfold, the tensions in the relationship between son and mother develop. Here is a situation very different from those in the *Iliad* and the *Aeneid,* where a divine mother periodically visits her adult human son to intervene in his life. Telemachos's relationship with his mother is beset by anxieties on both sides and is an arena for potential conflict. On one side is a son, brought up by a single parent and now, on the verge of adult life, with much to feel angry and insecure about. On the other side is a lonely mother, exhausted and on the verge of submitting to intense pressure both to accept that her missing husband will not return and to choose against her wishes a second husband among a horde of arrogant, self-seeking, and unscrupulous suitors who display increasingly abusive behavior.

In the early scenes in the palace and after the public assembly, the disguised Athene seeks to strengthen Telemachos's sense of confidence in himself as the child of Penelope and Odysseus (*Odyssey* 1.222–23; 2.270–80). But the prophecy she gives him of Odysseus's imminent return and his subsequent realization of her divinity (*Odyssey* 1.200–5, 323) create an ironic gap from now on between what Telemachos and the reader have been told and what the suitors and Penelope herself know. Thus when Telemachos first demonstrates his authority over his mother in the presence of her suitors, there is an element of play acting. However, it soon becomes clear that, beyond the role play, there is an emotional bond between son and mother. Telemachos does not like to think of tears staining his mother's lovely face, even though this is not going to stop him from leaving home and carrying out the mission given him by Athene to find news of his father. In her waking state, Penelope instantly obeys her son's orders and respects the wisdom with which he speaks to her in adult, male company (*Odyssey* 1.360–61). But to her sleeping mind Telemachos is still her child, unready for all the dangers and challenges that a hostile adult world is now thrusting on him. Thus as son and mother are parted from one another in physical terms, their relationship has been shown to be both complex and fraught with problems.

When the time comes at the start of *Odyssey* 15 for Telemachos to return home, Athene arrives, finding him unable to sleep and worrying about his father. She stands close by and speaks to him, warning him of the continuing threat to the family property and reviving his fears about his mother's intentions:

> "But quickly now urge Menelaos of the great war cry
> to send you off, so that you may still find your excellent mother at
>   home.
> For already her father and brothers are telling her
> to marry Eurymachos. For he surpasses all
> the suitors with his presents and keeps increasing his bridal gifts.
> You do not want her taking anything out of the house, without
>   your consent.
> For you know what a woman's heart is like:
> she wants to enrich the house of whoever is marrying her,
> and as for her former children and her dear husband,

once he is dead, she does not remember them or think of them."
(*Odyssey* 15.14–23) [22]

Much of the uncertainty surrounding Penelope's actions, intentions, and future life comes from the fact that she is talked about in her absence in different ways. Here Athene is preparing the way for Telemachos to disentangle himself politely from the pressing hospitality of Menelaos in faraway Sparta and to return home safely. To do this, she steers Telemachos's thoughts back to his altercation with Eurymachos over his mother in the course of the public assembly (*Odyssey* 2.182–211), and she now pictures Penelope being egged on by her close male relatives to succumb to Eurymachos's advances. Athene also revives Telemachos's anxiety about the fate of the family property in his absence (a concern expressed to him earlier in his travels by Nestor at *Odyssey* 3.313–16). Telemachos uses these concerns about the family property to explain to Menelaos why he must leave now, although he discreetly modifies the picture presented by Athene and edits his mother out of it (*Odyssey* 15.86–91).

In the course of his return journey, Telemachos speaks of his mother to a stranger, the exiled prophet Theoclymenos, and now he presents a different picture of her. Theoclymenos begs for help, and on their arrival in Ithaca, he asks if he should go straight to the home of Telemachos and his mother. Telemachos explains that in the present circumstances, this would not be a good idea since he himself will not be there and his mother will not see his guest: "For she does not often appear in front of her suitors, / but works at her loom, away from them, in her upper room" (*Odyssey* 15.516–17). Here Telemachos's description of his mother conforms to the pattern of secluded, domestic activity that he laid down for her in the presence of her suitors (*Odyssey* 1.356–61). Telemachos proposes instead that Theoclymenos should approach Eurymachos, explaining that he is looked on as the leading man in the community and is the keenest of the suitors to marry Telemachos's mother and replace Odysseus as the local ruler (*Odyssey* 15.519–22). As Telemachos speaks now, gone is the painful association of ideas that accompanied this thought as he lay awake at night. Instead Eurymachos's courting of Penelope is presented as something to be expected in view of his standing in the community.

When Telemachos arrives at the hut of Eumaios, the loyal swineherd, at the start of *Odyssey* 16, he finds that Eumaios already has a guest. Conversation

---

22. For this hostile generalization about women, cf. *Odyssey* 11.456, discussed in chapter 7.1 of this volume, and *Aeneid* 4.569–70, discussed in chapter 6.3 of this volume.

soon turns to the subject of Telemachos's mother. Telemachos is keen to learn from Eumaios whether his mother is still living at home or whether she has remarried. In his reply, Eumaios speaks movingly of Penelope's faithfulness and of the emotional cost to her of her long separation from her husband (*Odyssey* 16.37–39). A little later, Telemachos's thoughts turn to the identity of Eumaios's guest, who, as the reader already knows, is Odysseus in disguise. Telemachos is upset that he cannot offer the stranger the appropriate hospitality in his own home, and despite Eumaios's reassuring words, this idea leads his thoughts back to his deep-seated anxiety over his mother:

> "My mother's mind is split and keeps wavering between two
>   courses:
> either to remain there with me and look after the house,
> and to respect her husband's marriage bed and public opinion,
> or to go off with the best of the Achaean suitors,
> who court her in the palace, the one whose gifts are the greatest."
>   (*Odyssey* 16.73–77)

When the stranger, still maintaining his disguise, joins in the conversation, Telemachos reverts to the painful description of events at home that he originally gave to Athene-Mentes (*Odyssey* 16.122–28, repeating the description at *Odyssey* 1.245–51). In these scenes in *Odyssey* 15–16, in which attention returns to Telemachos before he sees his mother again, his picturing of his mother both to himself and to others is shown to be affected by both mood and context. Here, in the safe haven of Eumaios's hut, that picturing takes place in the presence of his disguised father. It follows a glowing account of Penelope's fidelity from the family's faithful slave, and now, as Telemachos spells out the first course of action over which he pictures Penelope wavering, he uses prescriptive terms to color it with approval.

After an emotional reunion, father and son get down to plotting their revenge on the suitors. Odysseus insists that his return must be kept a secret from the rest of the household, even from Penelope herself (*Odyssey* 16.303).[23] Now that the tie between son and long-lost father has been established, the emotional distance between son and mother established in *Odyssey* 1 is extended. At this point, Eumaios has not yet been taken into the confidence of father and son, and as Telemachos, instructed by his father, prepares to rejoin the suitors, he is keen to establish a convincing motive in Eumaios's

---

23. The significance of this part of Odysseus's revenge plan is analyzed by Murnaghan (2009, 234–40).

mind for his imminent departure. Now is no time for Telemachos to think regretfully of tears spoiling his mother's lovely face:

> "For I do not think that she is going to stop
> her hateful wailing and all that crying and groaning,
> until she sees me in person." (*Odyssey* 17.7–9)

Telemachos enters the palace, his mind occupied with thoughts of revenge, and is welcomed home by the womenfolk with tears and kisses. "Thoughtful" Penelope comes out of her room, "looking like Artemis or golden Aphrodite" (*Odyssey* 17.37). Penelope enters the hall where her son is, and later reenters that same hall, which now contains her husband in disguise (*Odyssey* 19.54). As she does so, the narrator adds his own voice to those voices within his narrative that draw attention to the different, and at times ambiguous, aspects of Penelope's appearance in the eyes of the male figures around her, voices that invite her to be seen either as a model of chastity or as a model of self-conscious sexual attraction.

Penelope's response to seeing her beloved son again is highly emotional: she cries, flings her arms around him and kisses him on his head and on his eyes, and speaks to him "with winged words" (*Odyssey* 17.40–44). Telemachos's response is curt and unemotional. The reader knows that his father's plans must remain a secret from her, but Telemachos can safely allow himself to tell his mother to offer a vow to the gods if Zeus grants them revenge. Meanwhile, he will go out again to collect a guest he has met on his travels (*Odyssey* 17.45–56): "So he spoke and speech remained wingless in her" (*Odyssey* 17.57). Relief, affection, residual anger, and burning curiosity find vent in "winged words" from Penelope to her son. His reply abruptly puts an end to this flight of communication, and Penelope is left speechless.[24]

On Theoclymenos's arrival, the household busies itself with providing the due hospitality. Penelope, fresh from her bath and change of outfit, is present at the meal to welcome her son's guest and now appears as a model of domesticity: "His mother sat opposite, by a pillar of the hall, / resting on a

---

24. The interpretation of the words translated here as "speech remained wingless in her" has long been disputed. Two points are at issue here: whether the word translated as "wingless" should be taken instead as a variation on the term "winged," and whether the word translated here as "speech" should be taken to refer to the speaker (Telemachos) or the person addressed (Penelope). The view adopted here takes the word "apteros" to mean "wingless" and the word translated as "speech" to refer to Penelope. See Stanford (1958, 282–83). For further discussion, see Russo, Fernandez-Galiano, and Heubeck (1992, 22–24).

reclining chair and turning the fine thread on her distaff" (*Odyssey* 17.96–97).[25]
After the meal, Penelope tells Telemachos that she intends to go upstairs and
lie down on her bed, which is wet with her constant tears. She continues:

> "and you have not had the heart
> to tell me if you have heard any news of your father's return,
> before the proud suitors come to the house." (*Odyssey* 17.104–6)

The business of entertaining a guest makes the occasion more relaxed than
the tense, first moments of reunion between mother and son, and words in
consequence come more easily. Telemachos duly responds now to this cue
from his mother and recalls his time away from home. He passes on the
story told first by the Old Man of the Sea to Menelaos (*Odyssey* 4.554–60) that
Odysseus is alive but marooned on Calypso's island (*Odyssey* 17.138–45). At
this point, Telemachos quickly brings his story to an end, but Penelope has
heard enough to be deeply moved (*Odyssey* 17.150).

In *Odyssey* 18, a further ironic component is added to the already complex
picture of Telemachos's relationship with his mother. Now it is displayed not
just before one composite audience made up of Penelope's wicked suitors
but also simultaneously before a second, secret audience in the form of her
long-lost husband, as yet unrecognized by her. At *Odyssey* 18.158–62, Athene
puts it into Penelope's mind to appear before her suitors. Athene's motive in
doing this is a double one: to make quite clear what is in the hearts of her
suitors and to bring Penelope more honor both in the eyes of her husband
and of her son. Penelope gives a hysterical laugh before broaching the subject
with her maid and giving her own account of her motivation:

> "Eurynome, I have not felt like this before, but now my heart longs
> for me to show myself to the suitors, loathsome though they are
>   to me,
> and I would like to say a word to my son, that would be profitable
>   to him,
> and tell him not to spend all his time with these arrogant suitors,
> who speak fine words but are planning evil in their heart."
>   (*Odyssey* 18.164–68)

Here Penelope, under Athene's influence, is shown to be pulled emotionally
in different directions and hence is presented in a comparatively complex

---

25. Cf. Nausicaa's description of her mother Arete at *Odyssey* 6.305–7.

psychological light. Eurynome approves wholeheartedly of her mistress's idea, but the two of them disagree about how Penelope should look. Eurynome thinks that she should wash her face and use some makeup (*Odyssey* 18.172–76). Although Penelope roundly rejects this idea, Athene intervenes again, sending her into a sudden, deep sleep, in the course of which she makes her look as lovely as Aphrodite when she dances with the Graces (*Odyssey* 18.187–97). Penelope comes downstairs and appears once again in the hall.[26] The effect on her suitors is one of instant arousal (*Odyssey* 18.206–13).

Penelope scolds her son for bringing disgrace on himself by allowing the stranger to suffer shameful treatment from her suitors. This public criticism has a self-conscious ring and, in this sense, mirrors the words spoken by Telemachos to his mother in the presence of the suitors at *Odyssey* 1.345–59. She begins with these words:

> "Telemachos, you have not the brain or the sense that you once
>   had.
> When you were still a boy, you had more sense of how to act
>   profitably.
> Now that you are big and have reached the prime of life,
> an outsider, seeing how big and good-looking you are,
> would certainly say that you were a prosperous man's son.
> Yet you no longer have the brain to see what is proper behavior."
>   (*Odyssey* 18.215–20)

Telemachos's instructions from his father are to mix with the suitors (*Odyssey* 16.270–71). And despite his mother's misgivings about his spending so much time in their company, the reader knows that there is no danger of his being taken in by the hypocritical suitors. Telemachos must now play a delicately calibrated double role, maintaining contact with his disguised father, who is surrounded by his enemies and who must not be recognized before he is ready to act, and responding appropriately to his mother's words spoken publicly in their presence. For so long tormented by loneliness, grief, anxiety, and indecision, Penelope has here, under Athene's direction, a moment to take control of events, a chance both to make clear her loathing of her suitors and their unacceptable behavior and to shift the balance of power between herself

---

26. For Penelope's appearances in the hall, cf. *Odyssey* 1.332–35; 16.413–16; 21.63–66. On the first two occasions, she acts on her own initiative; on the present and subsequent occasion, as the climax approaches, she acts under prompting from Athene.

and her adolescent son. Crucial in this context is the fact that Telemachos is no longer a child but stands on the threshold of adult life. In this sense, Telemachos is unique among Homeric characters in that he is seen to be passing through a stage in the process of growing up. His coming of age has a special significance for his mother. Eurynome has reminded her of this (*Odyssey* 18.175–76), and soon it becomes apparent that this is the time at which Odysseus told Penelope she should leave home and remarry if he had not returned from the war (*Odyssey* 18.269–70). As Murnaghan notes (2009, 233), the narrator does not in general tell the reader what is going on inside Penelope's head in the second half of the *Odyssey*. This leaves a fertile area of ambiguity for the reader to enjoy. With much, it may be imagined, on her mind, and with all eyes on her, Penelope embarrasses her son by telling him how much more she approved of him when he was a little boy. Also her glowing estimation of what people would think of him now stands in marked contrast to his own feelings that he expressed to Athene-Mentes (*Odyssey* 1.217–20).

Telemachos has plenty here to make him feel irritated, but he does not lose control; his response is calm and measured:

> "Mother of mine, I will not get annoyed with you for being angry,
> but I do take things to heart and know all that is happening,
> good things and bad things alike. Before now I was a child.
> But I cannot think sensible thoughts all the time.
> All these people sitting all around me, with their evil thoughts,
> knock the sense out of me, and I have no helpers." (*Odyssey*
>   18.227–32)

Here is a gentle correction of his mother's hostile view of her son's behavior. For a moment, the focus of attention in the son-mother relationship is no longer the vexed issue of whether Penelope will remarry, and angry confrontation can give way to reason and understanding. But the context cannot allow complete transparency on Telemachos's part. He is keen to defend his reputation for thinking sensibly and has no illusions about the suitors, but the need to mix with them forces him now into claiming himself compromised by their company. To Penelope's ear his words "and I have no helpers" may have a heartfelt ring, but the reader, remembering the presence of his disguised father and the agreement of father and son about the powerful support of Athene and Zeus in their endeavors (*Odyssey* 16.259–65), knows them to be disingenuous.

When they are no longer together and engaged in elaborate play acting before an audience, both Penelope and Telemachos have reasons for portraying the other in a comparatively unfavorable light. As she confides more and more in the stranger, who is still unrecognized by her, Penelope is keen to win his sympathy for the predicament she is placed in by her suitors. In this context, the significance in her mind of her son's contribution to this predicament gains strength. Initially she says of him:

> "and my son is annoyed that they are eating up his living.
> He can see it. He is a man now, quite able to take good care
> of the house, someone to whom Zeus grants glory." (*Odyssey*
>   19.159–61)

Later she speaks movingly of her insomnia and explains in more detail how she is racked by indecision. In this context, Telemachos appears in a new light:

> "While my son was still a boy, with childish thoughts in his head,
> he did not allow me to leave my husband's home and marry,
> but now that he is big and has reached the prime of life,
> he begs me to go back and leave the house,
> worrying about the possessions, which the Achaeans are
>   consuming." (*Odyssey* 19.530–34)

Mother and son are now shown to share a similar response to the long period of agonizing uncertainty about the breakup of the family home. After being the prey to insomnia (*Odyssey* 15.7–8; 19.515–17), each pictures the other's part in their shared troubles in a manner that is not supported by the surrounding narrative.

For his part, Telemachos speaks disparagingly of his mother to Eurycleia as he inquires whether their visitor was given the appropriate food and bedding for the night or was left without proper care:

> "For my mother is just like that, for all her discretion.
> It is senseless the way she gives honor to one man,
> if he is bad, and dismisses a good man in dishonor." (*Odyssey*
>   20.131–33)

By contrast, the narrative has recently lingered over Penelope's care to offer her visitor the comfort and honor due to him (*Odyssey* 19.317–34), and Eurycleia herself roundly rejects Telemachos's criticism of his mother (*Odyssey* 20.134–43). In this protracted context of concealment and disguise and against the background of persistently abusive behavior by Penelope's suitors, the relationship between mother and son allows the reader to enjoy a complex irony, centered on the idea of good and bad behavior. Penelope has launched into a verbal attack on her son for his inability, now that he is grown up, "to see what is proper behavior" (*Odyssey* 18.220). As Telemachos asks a servant for information about his mother's treatment of their visitor, he constructs in his mind a comparable failure on her part to act in an appropriate way, and at the same time he applies to her a more thoroughgoing failure to distinguish between good and bad behavior. Much of the ironic humor here lies in the fact that the critical view adopted by each of the other, in the midst of all their problems, is shown by the narrative to be misplaced.

As the time for revenge approaches, the irony in the son-mother relationship ceases to involve Telemachos directly with his mother and focuses instead on the gap between what Telemachos knows is about to happen and what the suitors are expecting. One of the suitors proposes that Telemachos himself should tell his mother to choose a new husband, now that there is no possibility that Odysseus will be coming back, and Telemachos is reminded of his self-interest in this outcome. With his mother safely installed looking after her new husband's home, Telemachos will have every prospect of enjoying his own inheritance (*Odyssey* 20.333–37). Instead of flatly rejecting such an idea, Telemachos now swears that he is ready to go along with it, provided that the decision is left for his mother to make:

> "I am not delaying my mother's marriage. In fact, I tell her
> to choose a husband, and I will give her enormous wedding gifts
> but, in all conscience, I could not force her out of the house,
> against her wishes. May a god never let that happen!" (*Odyssey*
>   20.341–44)

A little later, when Athene prompts Penelope to propose the archery test for the selection of her new husband, and she expresses her resolve, albeit regretfully, to leave her beloved family home (*Odyssey* 21.68–79), this ironic gap widens. Athene has already induced hysterical laughter on the part of the suitors at Telemachos's recent words (*Odyssey* 20.345–46), and now it seems that it is Telemachos's turn to be afflicted with a fit of such laughter:

> "Oh dear, oh dear! Zeus, the son of Kronos, has taken away my
>   senses.
> My dear mother, in her discretion, tells me
> that she will leave this house and go off with someone else,
> but I am laughing and my senseless mind is enjoying itself."
>   (*Odyssey* 21.102–5)

Once again the reader can enjoy the ironic humor, both here and in the following lines, as Telemachos advertises his mother as the unique prize for which the suitors are competing and throws in the additional detail that he would be less sad to see his mother leave home if he himself managed to pass the archery test (*Odyssey* 21.106–17).

The shifting irony in the description of the relationship between Telemachos and Penelope displays one final transformation in *Odyssey* 23. After being a prey to protracted indecision, Penelope cannot quickly shake off this state of mind, and she wavers now between excitement and doubt at Eurycleia's news that her husband has returned and has killed the suitors.[27] In the midst of this agonizing, new uncertainty, Telemachos remains one fixed point in her thoughts. Certainly, if Eurycleia could be believed, she and her son would be overjoyed, and she must go with Eurycleia to see her son and whoever has killed the suitors (*Odyssey* 23.60–61, 83–84). Now a new uncertainty troubles her: how should she react when she first sees her husband? Penelope enters the hall and sits looking at her husband, bewildered. Sometimes, as she gazes at his face, she can see who it is; at other times she cannot recognize him in his filthy rags. Odysseus too remains sitting in silence, waiting for her to speak. This pregnant silence is broken by angry words addressed by Telemachos to his mother:

> "You are a bad mother, mother of mine. You have a hard heart.
> Why do you remain apart like this from my father? Why do you
>   not sit
> beside him and talk to him and ask him things?
> There is no other woman who could be so cold-hearted,
> who would keep away from her husband, when he has suffered so
>   much
> and has taken twenty years to return to his homeland.
> But your heart has always been as hard as stone." (*Odyssey*
>   23.97–103)

In reply Penelope calmly explains to her son that in her bewilderment she can neither speak nor look the man full in the face. But if it really is Odysseus, there will be signs, known only to the two of them, which will give a better

---

27. Emlyn-Jones (2009) explores the complexities of their reunion. The significance of their marriage bed is the center of a wide-ranging discussion by F. I. Zeitlin (1995).

indication of how well they know each other. At this Odysseus smiles and tells Telemachos to leave his mother to test him, now that he is home. This will soon make her think better of him. It is because he is dirty and dressed in rags that she dishonors him and says that she does not recognize him (*Odyssey* 23.104–16).

Now that the climax of violence has passed, the silence of wife and long-lost husband, reunited in their son's presence, creates a hiatus that Telemachos cannot endure. He rounds angrily on his mother for causing it. A mixture of feelings toward his mother, which the reader may imagine has long been festering in Telemachos's mind, now comes to the surface: anger, incomprehension, and the suspicion that she has a cold, unfeeling heart. There is no longer any risk of derailing the revenge plan and thus no need to be circumspect in what he says about good and bad behavior. Now, in the presence of his father, is the time for some straight talk from son to mother. Penelope, for her part, no longer needs to fear the anger of her son since the death of the suitors has removed the cause of her anxious indecision. She can speak to him openly as a mother—"my son" (*Odyssey* 23.105)—while at the same time treating him as a young adult who has claimed the ability to "know all that is happening" (*Odyssey* 18.228). Thus she gently corrects his false impression of her. The spell of silence is broken. Odysseus smiles at her hint of the intimacy of their life together and explains in "winged words" the situation to his son, complementing the words already spoken by his wife and deferring the moment when her lingering doubts about his identity can be overcome. Thus the problems of the son-mother relationship finally play a part in the complex reunion of his mother and his father. Unlike the earlier reunion between father and son at *Odyssey* 16.155–212, this one has no divine intervention by Athene to facilitate matters. Meanwhile father and son can turn their attention to dealing with the aftermath of the killings.

5

Helen and the Men in Her Life

5.1 ✒ Helen of Troy

In the *Iliad* Helen's name is first spoken by Hera and Athene. Hera is shocked when she sees the Achaeans' single-minded rush for their ships, produced by Agamemnon's ill-conceived attempt to test his men's loyalty to their mission, and she shares her concern with Athene:

> "For shame! This way, child of aegis-bearing Zeus,
> Atrytone,[1] the Argives will run away home
> to their beloved country, across the broad-backed sea,
> and they will leave Argive Helen for Priam and the Trojans
> to boast of as their prize. Yet it was for her sake that many of
>   the Achaeans
> lost their lives in Troy, far from their beloved homeland."
>   (*Iliad* 2.157–62)

Hera sends Athene to hold back the army, and when Athene meets Odysseus, she enlists his help (*Iliad* 2.163–81). As Agamemnon's war on Troy looks set to collapse, Hera's words, and the challenging manner in which Athene relays them to the firm-hearted Odysseus, bring into sharp focus the unacceptable consequences of such an outcome. The Argive army may return home safely, but they will be running away, and their colleagues who lost their lives fighting

---

1. The probable meaning of this name, applied to Athene, is "she who is unwearied."

for Helen's sake will not be so lucky: their fate will be to have died in vain for her sake, far from the home they loved.[2] Later, when the truce for the duel between Menelaos and Paris is broken and Menelaos is suddenly wounded by an enemy arrow, Agamemnon makes a similar connection between Helen and the need to continue the war. Agamemnon, however, is preoccupied, not with the men who will have died in vain, but with the dishonor he personally will suffer should his brother be killed and the men start thinking of going home without achieving their mission (*Iliad* 4.169–75).

Helen's name is also linked to the war on two other occasions in the early stages of the *Iliad*: first by Nestor and again by the manner in which Menelaos' entry is given in the list of Achaean forces. Once the mood of the men has been brought around in favor of continuing hostilities against the Trojans, Nestor gives a hard-line speech, adding his weight to the call for unswerving commitment to the Achaean war effort. Their first thoughts, he tells the men, should not be of returning home but rather of sleeping with the wives of the Trojans. A little later Menelaos states his aim of gaining revenge, as he is shown inciting his men to war (*Iliad* 2.356, 589–90). In both these contexts a phrase occurs that links Helen closely with the words "struggles and groans." This phrase has given rise to a long-standing controversy since the words can be understood in two different ways: either as meaning "in revenge for Helen's struggles and groans" or "in revenge for the struggles and groans caused by Helen." If this ambiguity is accepted, it leaves the reader free to decide whether it suits the purposes of the two leaders—the aggrieved husband and his older, hawkish companion—to portray Helen as an innocent victim or as a willing accomplice in marital infidelity. N. Austin characterizes "doubleness" as Helen's defining characteristic and writes, "In the *Iliad* Helen's status depends on the viewer" (1994, 83).

Whatever the connection made among the Achaean fighting forces between Helen and the war, when she herself first appears in the privacy of her own room, her activity subtly shows her awareness of herself as the cause of conflict in the world of men:

> She was weaving a great web,
> a double-sided, purple cloak, and was making a pattern on it of the
>   many sufferings

2. J. Griffin (1980, 106–10) explores the motif "far from home" and in particular its application in the recurring idea of "dying far from home" in the *Iliad*.

of the Trojans, tamers of horses, and the bronze-clad Achaeans,
which they were enduring for her sake, at the hands of Ares.
    (*Iliad* 3.125–28)

Elsewhere Odysseus listens to Demodokos singing about the part he himself
played in the Trojan War and cries at the memories the experience evokes,
while Aeneas sees his part in these events represented in sculpture on a
temple under construction, and he too cries at the sight. Helen, by contrast,
creates through her weaving her own representation of the war and her part
in it, and now the narrative gives no emotional response from her to this
artistic representation of the sufferings of the two warring sides. In one
sense, the pattern she chooses confers fame on Helen: she commemorates
in her weaving her own central role as the ultimate prize of war, a prize for
which both sides were willing to endure "many sufferings." In another sense,
it confers notoriety on her since she also commemorates the inextricable,
causal link between herself and those sufferings that, as she weaves, the two
sides are still enduring. Helen's choice of pattern makes a contrast with that
of Andromache at *Iliad* 22.440–41. Rather than suggesting her place at the
center of a world of male conflict, Andromache creates a floral design, and
this design is part of a description of domestic activity, into which the tragic
news of her husband's death in battle is about to burst.

Led by the goddess Iris disguised as Laodike, Helen's Trojan sister-in-law,
Helen now leaves her room to see something amazing: the Trojans, tamers of
horses, and the bronze-clad Achaeans, the very subject of her weaving, are no
longer fighting each other but are sitting in silence, waiting for Alexandros
(Paris) and warlike Menelaos to fight a duel.[3] Iris tells Helen that she will
be called "the dear wife of the winner" (*Iliad* 3.129–38). The uncertainty of
the outcome on the battlefield is suddenly made a matter of immediate and
intimate concern to her. Iris's words have a strong effect on Helen:

> So saying, the goddess cast a sweet yearning into her heart
> for her former husband, her city and her parents.
> At once, hiding her face behind a white linen veil,
> she set out from her room, shedding a tender tear,
> not alone, but her two maids also followed her. (*Iliad* 3.139–43)

---

3. As Taplin (1992, 98–99) notes, the duel of Paris and Menelaos and its aftermath provide an opportunity to explore the question of the responsibility for the Trojan War. However, it is not until near the end
of the *Iliad* that mention is made of the starting point for the whole sequence of events: the Judgment of
Paris (*Iliad* 24.28–30).

Helen brings a past life, with all its former emotional associations, to her present experience in Troy, and the goddess's sudden, unexpected words evoke in her a "sweet yearning" for the way things used to be. A moment ago, Helen controlled the miniature figures whom she was creating in static form in her weaving and who represented the real-life figures fighting and suffering "for her sake" on the battlefield. Now any sense of control has gone and been replaced by a longing for the past and uncertainty about the immediate future. As she steps out into the world of men, Helen keeps her face veiled.[4]

She makes her way toward the tower by the Scaean gate of the city, while Priam and the Trojan elders sit there watching her. N. Austin (1994, 31) notes that in this scene Helen does not only gaze out, she is also the focus of the male gaze. The old men of the community are beyond the age for fighting but are great talkers and quietly pass comment on her to each other:

> "No cause for anger that the Trojans and the Achaeans with their
> fine greaves[5]
> have for a long time endured suffering for such a woman.
> She looks uncannily like the immortal goddesses.
> But even so, such as she is, let her get on the ships and go away,
> and not stay here to bring misery on us and our children after us."
>   (*Iliad* 3.156–60)

The ambivalence of Helen's place within the world of male conflict is now spelled out as the old men of Troy watch her and talk to one another about her. Priam himself, by contrast, speaks directly to Helen:

> "Come over here, dear child, and sit before me,
> so that you may see your former husband, relatives, and friends.
> I do not hold you responsible; it is the gods I hold responsible,
> who brought on me this war with the Achaeans and all its
>   tears—." (*Iliad* 3.162–65)

Here too, expressed in a subtler form, there is an ambivalence. Priam is affectionate and refuses to blame Helen, but he also draws her attention insistently to the consequences of her past actions, inviting her to see among the enemy forces below the city walls her "former husband, relatives, and friends." He does more and asks her to pick out and name for him key individuals among

---

4. Cf. Penelope's entries into male company, discussed in chapter 4.3 of this volume.
5. Armor worn to protect the shins.

the enemy commanders, beginning with a mighty figure, who has the air
of being a king (*Iliad* 3.166–70). As noted in chapter 1.2, the second, third,
and fourth books of the *Iliad* have the effect of taking the reader back to
the early stages of the war. It would be implausible, as Kirk (1985, 286–87)
remarks, that after nearly ten years of war, Priam did not know the identity
of the enemy leaders laying siege to his city. The way he phrases his inquiry
to his "dear child," with its elaborate and complimentary description of the
man who has caught his eye, carries a hint of irony as the reader waits for
Helen to name for her Trojan father-in-law the kinglike figure visible below
among the enemy forces.

In her reply to Priam's question, Helen speaks first of Priam and herself
before answering him:

> "I revere you, dear father-in-law, and am in awe of you.
> How I wish that cruel death had been my pleasure, when I
>   followed
> your son, leaving behind my marriage-bed, my relatives,
> my daughter, my only child, and all my sweet companions!
> But that did not happen, and so I dissolve in tears.
> I will answer the question, which you ask me.
> This man is Agamemnon, the wide-ruling son of Atreus,
> both a good king and a mighty warrior,
> and I, with my bitch's face, once called him brother-in-law, if ever
>   that time was." (*Iliad* 3.172–80)[6]

Helen has, she makes clear, a model relationship with her Trojan father-in-law,
combining deep respect with love for him. Her self-portrait invites sympathy,
corroborating her father-in-law's view that she is in no way to blame and
thereby subtly undercutting the mutterings of his elders. It would be churlish
for the old men to resent a beautiful woman, who now says that she wishes
that she had died instead of leaving home and loved ones at the instigation of
the king's son. She is a daughter-in-law who has the affection and support of
her father-in-law, the king, and who still apparently feels bad about herself.
A contrast can be drawn again here between Helen and Andromache. Helen
looks back and briefly wishes that she had died, before dismissing the idea and
moving on. Faced with the prospect of losing her husband on the battlefield,

---

6. For other instances of the rueful idea "if ever that time was," cf. *Iliad* 11.762; 24.426; *Odyssey*
15.268; 19.315; 24.289.

a prospect soon to be realized, Andromache says that it would be better for her to die and gives a detailed account of the sufferings that lead her to make this wish (*Iliad* 6.410–32).

At the same time, Helen's words hint at a steely control of past events and their consequences for the present, and Helen cannot avoid being part of her own naming process. She may hide behind preemptive self-denigration and a hazy sense that the past is little more than a dream to her now, but for all that, Agamemnon used to be her brother-in-law. Here the power of naming takes on a new form. As seen from the current viewpoint of Priam and Helen, Agamemnon is redefined for the reader. No longer is he a selfish and divisive figure, woefully out of touch with the hearts and minds of his men. Now he appears as an honored king and mighty warrior, at the head of a staggering array of armed forces. Priam's response to Helen's answer is to express, in glowing terms, his admiration for Agamemnon and the unparalleled scale of the armed forces under his command (*Iliad* 3.181–90). His reply to her subtly draws attention once again to the ambiguity in Helen's position. As sister-in-law of a man so blessed by fortune and with such vast forces under his command, Helen will have enjoyed some of his reflected glory, but now that she has given all that up, her status as his ex-sister-in-law brings a reminder of how close her link is with the presence of the overwhelmingly large enemy forces, which now pose such a threat to Priam and his city.

Reminders of Helen's past life continue in the rest of the conversation and retain for the reader a hint of irony in the communication between the elderly men and the beautiful woman who has joined them. When Priam's attention is caught by a second figure, Odysseus, whom he describes in detail and asks her to identify, her characterization of him as "knowing all kinds of tricks and cunning plans" (*Iliad* 3.202) prompts one of Priam's companions, Antenor, to tell Helen that he can vouch for the truth of what she says, and he proceeds to give a pithy anecdote about the time when Odysseus and Menelaos came to Troy and stayed with him:

> "For once upon a time godlike Odysseus came here.
> It was about a message concerning you, and warlike Menelaos
>   came with him.
> They enjoyed my hospitality and a warm welcome in my house,
> and I learned to recognize their looks and their cunning plans."
>   (*Iliad* 3.205–8)

Antenor's reminiscence draws attention to the talk about Helen that went on between the two sides before the start of hostilities,[7] and it brings the name "Menelaos" to the ears of Helen and those around her three times (lines 206, 210, and 213). After a careful comparison of the two men in the Achaean delegation, Antenor concludes that it was Odysseus who was the more commanding, and certainly the more eloquent, of the two men (*Iliad* 3.209–24).

Helen makes no reply to this assessment of her ex-husband, but when Priam sees the mighty figure of Aias and asks her to make a third identification for him, she quickly responds and volunteers information about the man standing next to him. He is Idomeneus, the godlike leader of the Cretan contingent, and she continues: "Many is the time he enjoyed the hospitality of warlike Menelaos / in our home, whenever he came from Crete" (*Iliad* 3.232–33). Helen makes clear that she has no problem naming Menelaos or even talking about "our home" and the "hospitality" that her ex-husband used to extend if a friend came to stay from overseas. Now, however, she signals that the question time is over (*Iliad* 3.234–35), but the narrator brings the passage to a close with an irony of a more somber nature. Helen is surprised not to see her brothers Kastor and Polydeukes among all the figures visible below her. She wonders if they never left Sparta, or if they perhaps came with their ships to Troy but were unwilling to take part in the fighting for fear of "the shame and the many insults that surround" her (*Iliad* 3.242). The narrator continues: "So she spoke, but the life-giving earth already covered them, / there in Lakedaimon, in their beloved native land" (*Iliad* 3.243–44). Time has passed and things are not as they were. In exchanging her life in Sparta for her new life in Troy, Helen has, in the case of her two brothers, cut herself off from her former relatives in the most profound sense. Kastor and Polydeukes have died without her knowing it, without her being there to mourn them. Helen's anxiety over the absence of her brothers' familiar faces is well founded, though her attempts to manage that anxiety are shown to be misplaced.[8]

Once started, the duel quickly comes to an end, but the outcome is inconclusive since Aphrodite saves Paris from being killed by Menelaos, snatching him away and covering him in a thick mist. She then sets him down in his

---

7. Later Agamemnon refers to a proposal put before the Trojan assembly that Menelaos, who had come on an embassy with Odysseus, should be put to death (*Iliad* 11.138–42).

8. For a different account of the fate of Kastor and Polydeukes, cf. *Odyssey* 11.298–304. There they are accorded a special privilege by Zeus and alternate daily between life and death.

sweet-smelling bedroom and goes to fetch Helen, who is still on the watchtower but now with a group of Trojan women (*Iliad* 3.373–84). Aphrodite is disguised as an old serving woman who helped Helen in her former life and was much loved by her. She now gives Helen's dress a tug and speaks to her:

> "Come along now. Alexandros is calling you to come home.
> There he is, in the bedroom, lying on the lovely bed,
> radiantly handsome in his fine clothes. You would never say
> that he had come from fighting a man, but rather that he was
>   going
> dancing or was just sitting down at the end of a dance." (*Iliad*
>   3.390–94)

These words make Helen's heart pound, but she is not taken in by the disguise:

> And so when she had recognized the goddess, with her exquisite
>   neck,
> her beautiful breasts and her flashing eyes,
> she stood in amazement and spoke out and addressed her. (*Iliad*
>   3.396–98)

News of the duel has caused sudden, great uncertainty for Helen, and its inconclusive outcome prolongs her state of emotional conflict. Although the duel has not produced a fatality and hence an outright winner, as envisaged by Menelaos and Agamemnon (*Iliad* 3.101–2, 281–91), nevertheless, on the formula proposed by Paris himself and subsequently relayed to both sides (*Iliad* 3.71–72, 92–93, 255), it has shown one of the two contestants to be the winner insofar as he was the stronger. On these terms, the winner is Menelaos. Under Aphrodite's control, however, events have been moving fast to annul this result, indeed too fast for Helen. Images of her past life have occupied her heart and her mind since news of the duel came, and the female figure who now speaks to her and touches her appears to maintain a comforting, emotional link with the past. But the words Helen hears her speaking direct Helen back to her present home and straight to bed with her present husband. Helen can recognize Aphrodite beneath the disguise, the divine counterpart of her own sexuality. Taplin writes, "It is part of the subtlety of the scene that it is impossible to pin down definitively the degree to which Aphrodite is an outside compulsion and the degree to which she is an externalization of Helen's own mixed feelings" (1992, 101). But it is unacceptable for Paris to claim her back as his prize and for Aphrodite to speak to her in such terms.

Paris may embody for her the ideal of physical appeal in a man, but the moment is not right for Helen to entertain such thoughts.[9] Both in his first, high-profile encounter with Menelaos (*Iliad* 3.15–37) and in his subsequent quick defeat after proposing the duel for Helen, Paris has lost face, however much Aphrodite may shield her favorite. The sudden switch from the image of a warrior returning from battle to the image of Paris as hero of the dance floor cannot conceal this; if anything, it strengthens the inappropriateness of such thoughts.[10] Then there are Helen's present companions for her to consider. She may have had little difficulty in managing Priam and his elders, but now she needs the emotional support of her own sex, which she might lose were she to do what Aphrodite says and hurry back to bed with her beaten partner.

Such pent-up feelings now burst out in a temper tantrum directed at Aphrodite, which is a mixture of wild accusations, defensiveness, dismissive arrogance, and self-pity (*Iliad* 3.399–412). In her mind's eye, Helen already imagines herself taken home, not by Paris but by Menelaos. In such a vision, she sees herself as she imagines Menelaos will see her, as "hateful," and it is for this reason, so it seems to her, that Aphrodite is now standing beside her, scheming to prevent this by taking her once again to some distant place. This time Helen will not cooperate. Aphrodite can go and humiliate herself with her favorite, but Helen herself will certainly not go. Aphrodite responds to this outburst with imperious anger and the threat of terrible retribution (*Iliad* 3.413–17). Helen is being "a wicked woman." In provoking Aphrodite's anger, she is in danger of turning the goddess's very special love for Helen into an equally strong hatred, and Aphrodite has the power to make the Trojans and the Danaans hate Helen equally[11] and so destroy her. Helen is at once terrified into submission. She goes in silence, wrapped in her bright robe and unobserved by her Trojan companions, and the goddess leads the way (*Iliad* 3.418–20). Aphrodite has the power to silence opposition and to render her favorites invisible to those around them, enemies and friends alike, but she must not be rejected or insulted. Paris himself acknowledges the power of her gifts (*Iliad* 3.64–66), and Aphrodite rescues him from the consequence of his actions, the potentially lethal blow from his cuckolded

9. Griffin (1980, 5–9) analyses the characterization of Paris and writes, "since Paris is the archetypal Trojan, the sin of Paris is one in which Troy is inextricably implicated."

10. Cf. the picture given of Paris's behavior by Hektor in his attack on his brother, at *Iliad* 3.38–57, and the angry words of Priam to Paris and his surviving brothers, at *Iliad* 24.248–62.

11. For this reaction cf. *Aeneid* 2.571–74, discussed in chapter 5.2 of this volume.

rival. Under Aphrodite's power, all thought of battle has gone in an instant, and Paris awaits his partner in his sweet-scented bedroom. But Helen must cooperate with this: she must play the part that is expected of her and come when her husband calls.

Once Helen reaches Paris's beautiful house, Aphrodite can forget Helen's insults and even take a little part in their foreplay, bringing with a smile a chair for Helen to sit on in front of Paris (*Iliad* 3.423–24). But the communication between wife and second husband, which takes place in the privacy of their own bedroom, need not reflect the Helen and Paris of the public world, and the narrative now explores this ironic discrepancy. Helen, "daughter of Zeus, who holds the aegis," sits down, keeps her eyes averted, and launches into a bitter attack on her husband: "You came back then, from the war. You should have died there, / brought down by a strong man, who was my former husband" (*Iliad* 3.428–29). Helen lashes out against Paris, and now it is her turn to speak Menelaos's name three times (lines 430, 432, and 434) in order to bring home to Paris his inferiority to her former husband.

Paris's response is relaxed and conciliatory. Helen should stop scolding him. Menelaos has with divine help won this time, but another time it will be Paris's turn. Any thought of the terms on which the past duel was fought, a thought that has been worrying Helen, is out of his mind. All that Paris can think about now is the unrivalled strength of his present desire for Helen, of "the sweet yearning" that he feels for her (*Iliad* 3.441–46). The expression of his overwhelming desire for her and his physical closeness to her in their bedroom are sufficient for the time being to dispel Helen's conflicting emotions: her own "sweet yearning" for her life with her former husband (*Iliad* 3.139–40), her vicious anger at her second husband's inadequacy in combat, and her initial repression of the arousal of her own desire for Paris. She follows her husband to bed and the two make love (*Iliad* 3.447–48). Thus in N. Austin's words, "the libido is declared victorious over honour" (1994, 37).[12]

Meanwhile the angry, frustrated Menelaos storms over the battlefield, trying to see where Paris has gone. None of the Trojans or their allies can tell him, not that they keep his whereabouts concealed out of love for him: "For he was hated by every one of them like black death" (*Iliad* 3.454). Helen and Paris are for the time being cocooned from the outside world by Aphrodite,

---

12. Griffin (1980, 5–6) takes a different view. He believes that Helen's hatred of Paris remains constant, but she "still finds herself forced to go on sleeping with him." Rutherford (2013, 103–7) agrees with this. He writes, "Paris is the comical, lustful figure, in contrast with Helen, a tragic victim."

while Menelaos frets and searches in vain. Thus the situation reached by the end of the abortive duel in *Iliad* 3 recalls the circumstances of Helen's first disappearance, the starting point for the war. Now, however, the consequences brought about by this are clear. A vast Achaean army supports the aggrieved husband and threatens Troy itself with destruction, while among the Trojans and their allies, there is universal loathing for the man who won the beautiful wife of another and has thereby brought war on their community, a man who has now mysteriously disappeared after losing the duel for her with her former husband.

After the duel, Helen is once more the subject of conversation among the Olympian gods. Now it is the turn of her father, Zeus, to speak of her. His motive in speaking is to rile Hera over the outcome of the duel, but there is also a serious question to be addressed. Victory in the duel belongs to Menelaos, and now the gods must decide whether there is to be war or peace between the two sides. If the latter is acceptable to them all, then people may go on living in Priam's city and Menelaos may take "Argive Helen" back (*Iliad* 4.5–19). Such an outcome is angrily opposed by Hera. In that case, all her energy and sweat expended on the Achaean war effort against Priam and his children would go for nothing. Here is the complementary argument to the one she used in *Iliad* 2 for the continuation of hostilities. Thus, to Hera's mind, the thought of Helen's staying at Troy and the thought of her returning to Menelaos lead to the same conclusion: the war must go on. After this point, Helen is not mentioned again by the gods, but her name appears a number of times on the lips of individual warriors on both sides. The most memorable of these is when Achilleus, in his grief for Patroklos, speaks bitterly of fighting in a foreign land "for the sake of loathsome Helen" (*Iliad* 19.324–25).[13]

The focus of attention from now on is the relationship between Helen and her Trojan brother-in-law. When the heavily armed figure of Hektor arrives in order to summon his troublesome brother back to the fighting (*Iliad* 6.280–85), he finds husband and wife together but engaged once more in their own, separate worlds: Paris has his hands on his armor and his bow,[14] while Helen sits among her maids and gives them instructions for their craftwork (*Iliad* 6.321–24). In this setting, half domestic, half preparatory for war, Paris

---

13. The other occasions are *Iliad* 7.354–56; 9.135–40, 277–82; 11.122–25.

14. Edwards writes, "Paris is by preference an archer, shooting at his enemy from a safe distance, rather than a hand-to-hand fighter in heavy armor" (1987, 194). For Paris in action with his bow on the battlefield, cf. *Iliad* 11.369–400, 504–7, 581–84; 13.660–72.

is safe from the violence of Hektor's earlier tirades. Now Hektor's approach is to shame his brother back into action, while Paris's response to criticism once again is relaxed and conciliatory (*Iliad* 6.325–41). In the course of his reply, he cites Helen's part in making him see the need to do as his brother says:

> "But now my wife, persuading me with her gentle words,
> has urged me to return to war, and I too think that would be
> the better thing to do." (*Iliad* 6.337–39)

Helen has last been heard telling her husband in private that she wishes that he had been killed by her former husband and that he had better not risk another encounter with Menelaos (*Iliad* 3.428–36). And when she speaks of Paris in Hektor's presence, it is in terms highly critical and dismissive. Paris's reference to her "gentle words of persuasion," coming as it does between these two outbursts, gives an ironic hint once again of the discrepancy between the image projected to the outside world and the relationship as seen in private.

Paris's words receive no reply from Hektor. Instead, it is Helen who now speaks to her brother-in-law "with soothing words" (*Iliad* 6.343). This speech and her earlier response to the sight of her former brother-in-law, Agamemnon, display a similar combination of ideas. Now, however, there is more detail and a stronger, emotional coloring. Now her denigration of herself as "the cold, scheming bitch" (*Iliad* 6.344) frames her fifteen-line speech:

> "But do come in now and sit on this chair,
> brother-in-law, since it is you, above all, who have the worry
> on my account, bitch that I am, and on account of Alexandros's
>   [Paris's] mad folly." (*Iliad* 6.354–56)

Helen imagines her mother with herself as a newly born baby, and she pictures the destructive storm wind carrying the baby off to die on the mountainside or to drown in the roaring sea (*Iliad* 6.345–48). Her words court the listener's sympathy.[15] This heart-rending picture of herself as a victim of infant mortality is, however, only the first half of a carefully balanced pair of wishes. Since the gods have decreed the present troubles (as Hektor's own father has freely conceded at *Iliad* 3.164), her second wish is that she now had a better man for her husband. Here she shrewdly takes up Paris's claim that he is

---

15. Cf. the words spoken by Penelope at *Odyssey* 20.63–65. Penelope, however, goes on to speak of the heightened sense of grief for her missing husband, which comes to her at night, together with bad dreams (*Odyssey* 20.83–87).

not particularly bothered by the thought of the Trojans' anger toward him (*Iliad* 6.335–36), and she aligns herself with Hektor in criticizing Paris for his failure to take note of the adverse public response to his behavior, anticipating the worst for her husband from the continuation of such empty-headedness (*Iliad* 6.350–53). Referring to her husband in the third person as "this one" and "him" (*Iliad* 6.352–53) also brings a hint of ironic humor into Helen's efforts to distance herself from Paris, and Hektor speaks in similar terms in his reply (*Iliad* 6.363).

Nevertheless, Helen cannot, in the presence of the two men, dissociate herself from all responsibility for the situation, as she effectively managed to do in speaking to Priam. This point is made with subtle irony when she refers to herself and Paris in the last words of her speech: "on whom Zeus has set an evil fate, that in the future / we should be a subject of song for generations to come" (*Iliad* 6.357–58). When she first appears in the privacy of her room, Helen, through her weaving, takes control of the artistic representation of her central place in the world of male conflict, though the narrator subtly endows that place with a sense of ironic ambiguity. Now she appears again in a domestic setting and speaks for the last time until the closing scenes of *Iliad* 24. This time she is in the presence both of her second husband and of his brother, who are in varying degrees of readiness to fight on her behalf. In a moment Hektor leaves, never to see her again (*Iliad* 6.359–69). As this moment of parting approaches, once again Helen is associated with an artistic representation of her life, this time "as a subject of song."[16] However, as she speaks of herself together with Alexandros, her control over this representation has gone. Once again there is a balance to be struck between fame and notoriety, but with her talk of "an evil fate" shared by her, "bitch" that she is (*Iliad* 6.356), and by Alexandros, with his "mad folly," the tilt suggested by her words is towards the latter, although as before an element of ironic ambiguity remains.

At *Iliad* 24.761–75, Helen follows Andromache and Hekabe in leading the ritual lament over the body of Hektor. The only other words spoken by a character after this are the four lines spoken by Priam, ordering preparation for the funeral and relaying the time limit allowed by Achilleus (*Iliad* 24.778–81). Each of the three women defines in her own way what Hektor's death means to her and, in doing this, defines herself in relation to the dead Hektor. This

16. Similarly in the *Odyssey* Alkinöos speaks of the gods causing the fall of Troy and all the destruction associated with it "so that there might be song for men to come" (*Odyssey* 8.577–80).

point is discussed in chapter 8.1. Helen's address to the dead man begins as follows:

> "Hektor, in my heart the dearest of all my brothers-in-law,
> my husband is godlike Alexandros,
> who brought me to Troy, and how I wish that I had died first."
>   (*Iliad* 24.762–64)

During the twenty years since she left her native land (*Iliad* 24.765–66),[17] she has never heard an unkind word from Hektor, and if ever her Trojan relatives criticized her, including her mother-in-law:

> "You with your words used to take my side and make them stop,
> with your gentle kindness and your gentle words.
> So I weep for you, and my heart grieves for my own unhappy fate,
> for there is no-one else throughout broad Troy
> to be kind or loving toward me, but they all shudder at me." (*Iliad*
>   24.771–75)

The desire to undo the past is now expressed with great simplicity and may be felt to be all the stronger for that. In identifying herself in this way as she addresses the dead Hektor as the *Iliad* draws to a close, Helen reminds the reader of her central part in the events narrated. It is for her sake and for the sake of her "godlike" husband that Hektor has died. While Andromache and Hekabe have both recalled Hektor on the battlefield, where he was anything but gentle (*Iliad* 24.739) and where his ultimate fate was to meet a violent death and repeated attempts to inflict posthumous mutilation on him, it is left to Helen finally to commemorate an important, nonheroic feature of Hektor's life: his gentleness and gallantry, characteristics that aroused a special affection in the heart of his beautiful sister-in-law.

A number of commentators express unqualified sympathy for the Helen of the *Iliad*. Bespaloff writes, "She is the prisoner of the passions her beauty excited" (1962, 100). Kirk describes her as "a creature both gentle and unhappy" (1985, 286). Edwards writes of "not only the self-reproach but also the utter loneliness and isolation of this unhappy woman" (1987, 193). However, there is also another side to Helen, and this can be seen in this farewell speech. In this

---

17. The events of the *Iliad* are set in the tenth year of the Trojan War (*Iliad* 2.134), so that it may be imagined that more than ten years have passed since Helen left home. Richardson (1993, 358) notes that Homer commonly uses "twenty" as the next standard figure for a number greater than "ten."

context of formalized lamentation, her words are at their most self-revelatory. Now she has no veil to hide behind, no elderly sparring partners to play games with, no attentive male listener either to please or to shock. Unlike the two speeches that precede hers, Helen's speech is almost exclusively self-centered. Her brother-in-law, whom she loved and with whom she felt safe, has met a violent death. The city is now doomed to fall. His widow, in common with the women of Troy, will become a slave and his infant son will be the victim of a brutal revenge killing, but Helen must not be hurt by unkind words from her relatives. This includes her mother-in-law, who has just expressed her grief for her dead son. Here, finally, is a complex and ambivalent figure: a woman who in her beauty resembles a goddess and is the prize for whom the two warring sides kill and are killed in turn, a woman who has had two husbands and who can still think with longing of her former life, a woman whose sudden change to a new life with a new partner brings no inner peace and contentment. Here is a figure who courts sympathy for her fate and whose fate is a high-profile blend of fame and notoriety, a figure who displays a strong sense of self-preservation, and who, excepting her kindly Trojan father-in-law (*Iliad* 24.770), finally expresses the view that she has no one left in her new homeland to be kind to her or show her affection or challenge the sense of universal loathing for her.[18]

5.2 🖌 Helen and the Fall of Troy Remembered

In the *Aeneid,* Helen is situated at a point between the end of the *Iliad* and the start of the *Odyssey,* in the second crisis of her life, the fall of Troy and the victory of the Achaean forces. As Aeneas journeys through the Underworld, he meets the ghost of Deiphobus, Helen's third husband, who tells Aeneas how his death and horrific mutilation were brought about through Helen's betrayal of him (*Aeneid* 6.494–530). Beyond this, Helen's place in the *Aeneid* is the subject of a long-standing controversy. Earlier, in the course of Aeneas's eye-witness account of his experiences on the night Troy fell, a twenty-two-line passage describes how Aeneas catches sight of Helen trying to conceal herself. The sight of her prompts in him a surge of rage and the desire to kill her in revenge for all the misery she has caused (*Aeneid* 2.567–88). The authenticity of this passage, the so-called "Helen Episode," is very much in

---

18. For the complex and enduring appeal of Helen, see Hughes (2005).

doubt.[19] The lines are included in the Oxford Classical Text edition, although they are enclosed in square brackets. As such, they form part of the present reading. If the vexed question of their authorship is put to one side, three things can be said before the lines are discussed. First, the removal of lines 567–88 does not leave a coherent sequence of ideas. Something is needed to mark the transition. Second, the lines are both highly effective in themselves and also provide the necessary transition. Third, an unresolved problem remains involving the unity between the portrayal of Helen in *Aeneid* 2 and the portrayal of her in the later scene in *Aeneid* 6.

Gone is any ambivalence in Helen's place within the world of male conflict. Instead, each of the two male figures from the defeated Trojan army—one living, one dead—recalls Helen with violent loathing.[20] Aeneas records the time he spent on the roof of the palace (*Aeneid* 2.458–632), where he had a view over the city. At the end of this time, when he is alone, his eyes travel over the scene below him, lit up by the fires of burning buildings, and he sees Helen silently hiding in the doorway of the temple of Vesta. The impulse this arouses in him to kill her comes as a sudden, violent interruption to his growing realization that his first duty is to protect his own family (*Aeneid* 2.559–63, 596–600). He describes Helen in these words:

> "She was dreading the Trojans' hostility to her for destroying their
>   city,
> and punishment from the Danaans and the anger of her aban-
>   doned
> husband, a destroying Fury alike to Troy and to her own land.
> She had hidden herself away and was sitting, a hateful figure,
>   beside the altar." (*Aeneid* 2.571–74)

There she sits, skulking amid the flames of destruction, "a destroying Fury,"[21] seeking sanctuary in a holy place that is the embodiment of the pure flame, the symbol of hearth and home, honored by the Vestal Virgins who are the antithesis of Helen.

---

19. Goold (1990, 60–126) makes a strong case against its authenticity.

20. This does not, however, stop Aeneas from offering as a present to Dido the clothes Helen took with her from Mycenae for her "unlawful marriage" in Troy, which were rescued from the destruction of the city; cf. *Aeneid* 1.647–52.

21. Earlier, at *Aeneid* 2.337–38, the word "*Erinys*," translated here as "a destroying Fury," is used by Aeneas as a personification of the Fury of war. For the description of the Fury Allecto and her cave home, cf. *Aeneid* 7.323–29, 335–38, 447–51, 561–71.

As Aeneas's own fury burns within him, he gives vent to it in a soliloquy (*Aeneid* 2.577–87). How he imagines Helen now changes: the cowering figure is transformed into the proud queen, safe at home once again in her familiar Greek world. She revels in the triumph won over Troy and is attended by the Trojan women, who have become her slaves. Meanwhile Priam is slaughtered, Troy is torched, and the shore is soaked with Trojan blood. These unbearable pictures are presented in a series of agonized rhetorical questions. The conclusion they lead to is a paradoxical one:

> "No! For even if there is no name to be remembered
> in punishing a woman, this is a victory and brings its own glory;
> I shall be praised, all the same, for having extinguished evil, for
>   having exacted
> from her the punishment she deserves." (*Aeneid* 2.583–86)

Here once again is the *Aeneid*'s morally problematic world. The sufferings of Aeneas, as he sees the horrors of destruction all around him, clamor for revenge. But can it be called "a victory" that "brings its own glory" to kill a defenseless woman? She may be an "evil" in Aeneas's mind, but she too, like Priam, whose death has caused such revulsion, seeks sanctuary at an altar. Will Aeneas, the man of duty, be "praised" as the man who killed Helen of Troy in this way? Will there be agreement that this is "the punishment she deserves"?

Such problems are resolved by an epiphany. Venus at once calms her son's rage, redirects his immediate thoughts, and enables him to see what is happening all around him from a divine perspective rather than from his own limited, human viewpoint:

> "I tell you, it is not the hated beauty of the woman of Sparta, Tyn-
>   dareus' daughter,
> nor Paris, the one they blamed:[22] it is the gods, the merciless gods,
> who have overthrown the wealth of Troy and laid low her towers."
>   (*Aeneid* 2.601–3)

In Homer, Helen is the daughter of Zeus (*Iliad* 3.418; *Odyssey* 4.184). A different tradition gives her a human father, Tyndareus, and it suits the present context (*Aeneid* 2.569, 601) to follow this tradition and dissociate Helen from a

---

22. For other references to Paris, cf. *Aeneid* 1.26–27; 5.370; 6.56–58; 10.702–6. Both Dido's rejected suitor Iarbas and Juno herself speak contemptuously of Aeneas as "another Paris"; cf. *Aeneid* 4.215–17; 7. 319–22.

background of divinity. In the *Iliad*, Helen enjoys the special favor of Aphrodite but is warned by her not to turn the goddess's unbounded love for her into unbounded hatred (*Iliad* 3.413–17). In her Roman manifestation as Venus, the goddess now protects Helen from mortal danger (much as Aphrodite protects Paris in his duel with Menelaos) but speaks to her son of Helen's "hated beauty." In the *Iliad*, Priam holds not Helen but the gods responsible for all the suffering brought by war (*Iliad* 3.164–65). In the *Aeneid*, as Venus seeks to calm her son's homicidal blend of pain and anger, she joins Helen and Paris together and absolves them from blame for the war, showing her son instead how the fall of Troy results from "the gods, the merciless gods." Thus the electric moment passes when Aeneas, without Helen knowing it, enters her life and almost takes it from her, and Aeneas moves on.

Nevertheless, Helen is reinstated as an evil force from Aeneas's past life in Troy when he meets the ghost of Deiphobus in the Underworld.[23] The Trojan warriors are now ghosts, keeping company with warriors of an earlier epic past. They flock eagerly around Aeneas, making him linger as they ask him about his journey (*Aeneid* 6.477–88). But one is singled out for attention. It is the trembling figure of Priam's son, Deiphobus, mutilated almost beyond recognition. When Aeneas asks him who could have wanted to inflict such cruel punishment on him, Deiphobus replies: "It was my fate and the deadly crime of the woman of Sparta / that overwhelmed me with these sufferings. This is the monument she has left" (*Aeneid* 6.511–12). He then explains what happened, taking Aeneas back to the horrors of that terrible night when Troy fell, but now a central part in the plot to destroy Troy is given to Helen:

> "She was mimicking a religious dance and was leading the Trojan women round,
> as they made the ritual call to Bacchus, and in their midst she held
> a huge flame and was calling the Danaans from the top of the citadel." (*Aeneid* 6.517–19)

Meanwhile, as Deiphobus lies sound asleep in his ill-fated bedroom:

> "This outstanding wife removes all my weapons from the room,
> my trusty sword she had taken out from under my head,

---

23. Deiphobos plays a significant part in the fighting in *Iliad* 13, and Athene disguises herself as him in the duel between Achilleus and Hektor (*Iliad* 22.226–47, 294–99). He is also mentioned in the *Odyssey* at 4.276 and 8.517–18. After Paris's death, he becomes Helen's third husband.

and she calls Menelaus into the room and throws open the door,
no doubt hoping that this would be a great gift for a lover
and that the reputation of her earlier wickedness could thus be
    blotted out." (*Aeneid* 6.523–27)

This is Aeneas's final revisiting of the horrors of the Trojan War, and
as this defining experience receives its closure, Helen is reinstated at the
center of events. But she is no longer merely the woman for whose sake the
two sides fought. Now she appears as a wicked, hypocritical, and merciless
schemer. Aeneas has seen her polluting the sanctity of the temple of Vesta.
In Deiphobus' memory of her, she goes further and uses religious ritual
to mask her real, devious purpose. In this she is a worthy counterpart of
Sinon, both of them deceiving the Trojans, while all the time being in secret
communication with the approaching enemy. Through Helen, destruction
is brought on Troy and death and mutilation on her unsuspecting husband.
This husband is no longer the ambivalent figure of Paris but the war hero,
Deiphobus, of all Hector's brothers the one closest to him in emotional terms.
Helen's motive in being an accomplice in this atrocity is, "no doubt," to gratify
her former husband by presenting him with an easy opportunity to exact a
bloody revenge on a hated successor to his wife's bed. This, she thinks, will
wipe out her notoriety for running off with another man. Such is the record she
leaves behind her. Once again, as in the earlier scene, Aeneas's thoughts are
deflected from Helen and her wickedness by the voice of feminine authority.
Now the Sibyl moves him on: it is time for the next stage of his supernatural
journey. After learning of "the deadly crime of the woman of Sparta," it is
time for Aeneas to glimpse the eternal punishment of the wicked in Tartarus
(*Aeneid* 6.535–627).

5.3 🌿 Helen of Sparta Again

At *Odyssey* 1.284–88, Athene in her disguise as Mentes advises Telemachos to
visit Nestor in Pylos and to go on from there to see Menelaos in Sparta in the
hope of hearing news of his missing father.[24] For the second stage of his trip
his traveling companion is Nestor's son Peisistratos, who is the same age as
Telemachos and, like him, still unmarried and living at home (*Odyssey* 3.49,
401, 412–16). When the two young men arrive at Menelaos's palace, they find

---

24. De Jong (2001, 91–92, 97–98) gives a brief summary of the characterization of Menelaos and Helen.

a party under way for a forthcoming double wedding. Hermione, the only child of Menelaos and Helen, is about to leave home to join her bridegroom, Achilleus's son. Her half-brother, Megapenthes, Menelaos's son by a slave girl, is marrying a local girl, the daughter of Alektor. Here (*Odyssey* 4.1–19) is a scene of lavish, family celebration, which creates a sharp contrast with the persistent travesty of such celebration back in Telemachos's own home in Ithaca. But for all the glitter of the occasion, it quickly fades from view as attention focuses on the reception of the two new visitors.

Before Menelaos considers asking them who they are, Telemachos and his companion are treated with the courtesy accorded to honored guests. When Telemachos draws his friend's attention in a whisper to the almost Olympian luxury of their surroundings, Menelaos overhears him and speaks at length to them of his wealth and his travels. There has been plenty of trouble in his life too: the unforeseen murder of his brother with the connivance of his brother's accursed wife, and the loss of an earlier well-endowed house of his own. He says that he would gladly give up two-thirds of his wealth if he could bring back all those friends who died far away in Troy. But the one friend above all for whom he grieves is Odysseus, whose efforts in the war were unsurpassed and who is now lost without trace, to the great sadness of Odysseus's father, his wife, and his son, Telemachos, whom he left as a baby (*Odyssey* 4.69–112). These words make Telemachos cry, and although he cloaks his tears, Menelaos realizes who he is. After his fluent and impressive account of himself, his successes and his troubles, and the graceful, gently probing conclusion to his speech, Menelaos is unsure whether to wait for the young man to mention his father or to test his idea by asking him questions (*Odyssey* 4.113–19). This is the moment at which Helen makes her entry: "Helen came out of the sweet-smelling bedroom / with its high roof, looking like Artemis with her golden distaff" (*Odyssey* 4.121–22). Three named maids come with her, bringing Helen's things: a beautiful chair; a soft, woolen rug; and a silver work basket running on wheels with golden rims, part of a lavish set of presents given to the couple by friends in Egypt. The work basket contains her yarn and her golden distaff with its dark wool, and when it has been set beside her, Helen sits down on her chair with a stool for her feet and asks her husband about the guests (*Odyssey* 4.123–37).

In the *Iliad*, Helen's name is on the lips of both mortals and immortals before she makes her first appearance, but in the *Odyssey*, beyond the fact given by the narrator that she has had no further children after Hermione (*Odyssey* 4.12–14), there is no mention of her before her entry. Nestor, in his reminiscences given in answer to Telemachos's questions, has much to say about Menelaos in *Odyssey* 3. But he does not speak of Helen, nor does Menelaos himself mention her when he gives his newly arrived young guests an account of his life and its troubles. Time has passed since the Trojan War, and Menelaos, it is now clear, is living once again with his beautiful former wife. Now, however, it is Helen's lovely daughter, Hermione, who invites comparison with "golden Aphrodite" as she sets out to embark on her married life. Helen herself still looks divine as she makes her entry, but in her case the resemblance now is to "Artemis with her golden distaff." At the moment when the initial meeting between host and his young guests is poised to move forward with the revelation of their identity, the lady of the house makes her entry into male company. She is surrounded by her own intimate and individualized circle of female companions, who bring for her all her paraphernalia, showing both her role as the model housewife[25] and her wealth and status in the eyes of a world stretching all the way to the fabulously rich land of Egypt.

Helen's opening words gracefully resolve her husband's dilemma: "Menelaos, cherished by Zeus, do we know who these people / say that they are, who have come to our house?" (*Odyssey* 4.138–39). Helen must say at once that she has no doubt about the identity of one of them since he looks exactly like the son of great-hearted Odysseus:

> "Telemachos, whom he left at home as a newborn baby,
> when for the sake of me, with my bitch's face, the Achaeans
> went to Troy, devising bold war." (*Odyssey* 4.144–46)

Menelaos agrees with his wife. He has already noticed a striking physical resemblance to Odysseus in the young man, and he tells her that when he mentioned all Odysseus's sufferings and efforts on his behalf, it brought floods of tears to his visitor's eyes, even though the young man tried to conceal it (*Odyssey* 4.147–54). Peisistratos now joins in the conversation (*Odyssey* 4.155–67). Menelaos is right: Peisistratos's companion is Odysseus's son, but he is discreet and hates the idea of coming into the company of such a godlike speaker and engaging at once in "flinging words around" before him. Peisistratos explains that he himself has been sent by Nestor to act as an escort to his friend, who is anxious to see Menelaos and ask him for advice and help with all the troubles he faces at home: "So it is with Telemachos: his father has

---

25. Cf. the picture Nausicaa conjures up of her mother Arete at *Odyssey* 6.305–7.

gone and there are no others / at home who could protect him from wicked people" (*Odyssey* 4.166–67). Here is another example of the power of naming. When he first appears in the Odyssey, Telemachos is full of uncertainty. He cannot be sure that Odysseus is his father, and the prospect of meeting Nestor and having to speak to someone so much his senior fills him initially with misgiving (*Odyssey* 1.215–16; 3.21–24). Now when he has to face both the magnificence of Menelaos and the elaborate splendor of Helen's entrance, he finds the way already paved for him since first Menelaos, then Helen, and finally Peisistratos utter his name in a sympathetic, reassuring, and in the last instance explanatory context before Telemachos himself speaks a word.

Menelaos now exclaims at the thought of this visit from the son of such a close and supportive friend. He now explains that he had planned to empty one of the cities in his power for Odysseus and his people to live in so that the two friends could meet regularly. This idea, however, must have been resented by some divine power, and instead the wretched Odysseus alone has been denied his homecoming (*Odyssey* 4.155–82). Menelaos's words move them all to tears:

> Argive Helen, offspring of Zeus cried,
> and Telemachos and Atreus's son, Menelaos, cried
> nor indeed did Nestor's son remain without tears in his eyes.
>   (*Odyssey* 4.184–86)

Menelaos and Helen now live together again in great luxury, but neither can escape from the past, from their involvement in all the sufferings that came upon the Achaeans as a result of the war at Troy. The face of the new generation only reinforces this link with the past, and an echo from that past can be heard when Helen briefly characterizes herself as "me, with my bitch's face." Telemachos had already been moved when Menelaos first spoke sympathetically of his missing father, and the tears are quick to flow again when Menelaos speaks of his grandiose but fruitless plans for supporting his old friend's family (*Odyssey* 4.104–14, 171–82). Peisistratos cries at the memory of his older brother, Antilochos, killed in the fighting at Troy, as he explains a moment later (*Odyssey* 4.187–89, 199–202). Both young men, though not directly involved in the fighting themselves, have been emotionally scarred by it. Menelaos's words bring tears to his own eyes too. A few moments earlier he had spoken of his recurring tears at the memory of all those who died far from home at Troy, and of his vain wish that he could pay somehow to bring them back to life (*Odyssey* 4.97–103). Now the contrast between the regular companionship with Odysseus that he had eagerly looked forward to and Odysseus's own disappearance brings a special poignancy in the presence of Odysseus's grieving son. So the men, young and old, are joined by their tears, tears of suffering and tears of regret. In Telemachos's case, this unspoken form of communication precedes speech. The narrator does not, however, attempt to penetrate the mind of "Argive Helen, offspring of Zeus" to seek the cause of her tears, as attention is drawn first to her.[26]

Peisistratos and Menelaos now make polite efforts to turn attention from tears back to food, and Menelaos promises to have a talk with Telemachos in the morning (Odyssey 4.190–218). Helen goes further than this in her efforts to make them all feel better:

> At that point, Helen, offspring of Zeus, had another idea:
> at once she dropped a drug into the wine they were drinking,
> to remove all grief and anger and to bring forgetfulness of all
>   troubles. (Odyssey 4.219–21)

Now Helen appears as the healer rather than the cause of all the sufferings of the Trojan War. A highly theoretical approach to this scene is adopted by Bergren (2009). She analyses the underlying patterns of thought and traces a correlation between the ideas associated with the word "drug" and the ideas associated with "speech/story/poetry." This form of detailed analysis illustrates the contribution made to Homeric studies by structuralist and poststructuralist criticism.[27] The temporary effects of Helen's "happy" drug are guaranteed by the narrator: after taking it mixed in wine, no one could feel like crying even if forced to witness the violent death of close family members (Odyssey 4.222–26). This drug, like her magnificent work basket on wheels, comes from Egypt. Helen and her husband have seen a wider world than their two young visitors, and they have brought their experience of foreign travel back into their home life. Sitting comfortably with food in front of them and yielding to the soothing influence of their drinks, which have been given an extra boost by their hostess, the menfolk are encouraged to forget their troubles while Helen reminds them of an important lesson: "But to different men at different times / Zeus gives now something good and now something bad, for He can do it all" (Odyssey 4.236–37). As they enjoy their meal, Helen herself will tell them something to fit the occasion, but first

---

26. For tears expressing a sense of shared grief, cf. Iliad 19.300–302, 338–39; 24.507–21, 773.
27. For this contribution, see Doherty (2009, 13–17).

she makes clear the limits of what she can tell them: "But as for everything, every single ordeal, which the stout-hearted Odysseus / underwent, I could not speak of them or name them" (*Odyssey* 4.240–41).[28]

The anecdote Helen is about to recount must serve as no more than an example of what Odysseus was willing to go through and what success he achieved. It happened at Troy when, as she reminds her listeners without specifying her connection with events, "you Achaeans endured sufferings." It tells of Odysseus's undercover activities behind enemy lines, after he had gone to great efforts to disguise himself as a beggar. She herself, she tells them, was the only one who penetrated his disguise, and when she started asking him questions, he skillfully evaded answering them. She continues:

> "But when I gave him a bath and anointed him with olive oil
> and dressed him, and swore a mighty oath
> not to reveal the presence of Odysseus among the Trojans,
> until he reached the swift ships and the tents,
> then he went through with me all the details of the Achaeans'
>   plan." (*Odyssey* 4.252–56)

Odysseus then kills many Trojans before returning to the army with much inside information. The other Trojan women are loud in their cries of grief:

>   "But my heart
> was glad, for already I had had a change of heart and was set
> on coming back home, and I was sorry for the blind folly that
>   Aphrodite
> gave when she led me there from my beloved home country,[29]
> leaving my little girl, my marriage, and a husband,
> who lacks nothing when it comes to intelligence or good looks."
>   (*Odyssey* 4.259–64)

Menelaos at once answers her. His wife is quite right about Odysseus. In all his travels he has never seen the like of his dear friend, the "stout-hearted Odysseus." He too has an anecdote to show what Odysseus went through and

---

28. For the impossibility of giving a complete account of a subject, cf. the words of Nestor at *Odyssey* 3.113–17, of Odysseus at *Odyssey* 11.328–30, 517–20; 14.195–98, and of Aeneas at *Aeneid* 1.372–74. For similar thoughts expressed by the *Iliad*'s narrator, cf. *Iliad* 2.488–92; 12.176; 17.260–61, which I discuss in chapter 1.3 of this volume.

29. The use in Homer of the word translated here as "blind folly," induced by a divine power, is analyzed by Dodds (1951, 2–8). Paris (Alexandros) is nowhere named in the *Odyssey*.

what he achieved. The starting point for Menelaos's anecdote is a little later than that of his wife. It concerns the wooden horse and the time when he, along with all the best men in the army, was sitting inside it intent on bringing destruction on the Trojans. Addressing his wife, he continues:

> "Then you came along. It must have been some divine power,
> keen to bring glory on the Trojans, who told you to do it,
> and, as you came, godlike Deiphobos followed you over.
> Three times you walked round our hollow hiding-place, putting
>   your hands around it,
> and you called out the names of all the best of the Danaans,
> imitating the voice of each of their wives." (*Odyssey* 4.274–79)

He himself, he continues, was sitting in the middle with Diomedes and Odysseus and could hear her shouting, and it was only Odysseus who restrained the two of them from jumping up and getting out of the horse or answering her back from inside it. After that, all but one of them remained silent:

> "Antiklos was the only one who wanted to reply to you,
> but Odysseus put his strong hands over Antiklos's mouth
> and kept it shut, and saved all the Achaeans,
> and kept hold of him, until Pallas Athene led you away." (*Odyssey*
>   4.286–89)

Telemachos has come on a long journey at a difficult time, intent on finding news of his missing father and so putting an end to the gnawing uncertainty that plays a large part in his present troubles. Nestor has given him a glowing account of his father's war record and has shown Odysseus setting sail from Troy. But he has not been able to take Telemachos any further in his search for his father (*Odyssey* 3.120–29, 162–64, 218–22). Nevertheless, Nestor raises Telemachos's hopes that Menelaos, safely home at last after his extensive travels, may be able to help him, and when Peisistratos explains the purpose of their visit, Menelaos promises a good, long "talk" with Telemachos in the morning (*Odyssey* 4.214–15). In the meantime, the courteous reception of the two visitors by the host and his wife and the need for the whole company to forget their tears and begin to enjoy themselves lead to dinner-table "talk" of a different kind (*Odyssey* 4.234, 238–39). In this context, the purpose of Telemachos's visit recedes temporarily from view, and a number of other agendas come into play, bringing plenty of ironic humor for the reader to enjoy.

Helen is the first to offer a reminiscence of the wartime Odysseus, and in it she herself occupies center stage, perhaps even hinting at a romantic interest between herself and Odysseus. She can see straight through Odysseus's lifelike disguise, and this puts her in control of the situation. Now her uncovering process moves across into the outer, physical world as she sees to the "beggar's" needs on arrival and personally gives him a bath.[30] Having shown her control by laying Odysseus bare in this double way, she can begin a comparable re-covering process: first she clothes the physically naked Odysseus, and then she swears a great oath to keep his identity a secret until he is out of danger. Once again she demonstrates control, since Odysseus must trust, on the strength of her oath, that his secret is safe with her. So great indeed is Odysseus's confidence in her that he now volunteers all the information concerning the Achaean war plans, and his confidence is well placed since he is able to take back plenty of inside information. This image that Helen presents of herself as a mole, intimately involved in the crucial espionage leading to an Achaean victory, she now corroborates by recording her response to the multiple killings inflicted on the Trojans by the disguised Odysseus. In the *Iliad*, Helen in the company of Trojan women is keen to ensure their approval of her and shares in their grief at the loss of their city's war leader (*Iliad* 3.411–12; 24.761–76). In this new context and in retrospect, she distances herself emotionally from them. It appears that already, even before the Achaean victory, she has had a change of heart and is "sorry for the blind folly that Aphrodite gave." But her tale has a happy ending: she is back where she belongs, in her own beloved country, near her daughter on her daughter's special day, and married (once again) to the perfect husband.

The irony takes on a sharper edge when Menelaos in turn produces an anecdote for the benefit of his fellow diners. Ostensibly he is in complete agreement with his wife, as he tells her (*Odyssey* 4.266). He too can illustrate Odysseus's prodigious power of endurance and ability to achieve success (*Odyssey* 4.271, which repeats 4.242), but his anecdote systematically dismantles the image his wife has given of herself and replaces it with a very different one. Helen claims a special relationship with Odysseus, which places her firmly in support of the Achaean side in the closing stages of the Trojan War. Menelaos appropriates Odysseus instead, and Odysseus is shown as part of the cream

---

30. For the most part elsewhere in the *Odyssey* it is a maid or maids who give the men their baths. However, Calypso and Circe (both of whom have maids of their own) personally give Odysseus a bath, and Circe gives a bath to members of Odysseus's crew (*Odyssey* 5.263–64; 10.360–65, 449–51).

of the Achaean forces, sharing with Menelaos himself the dangerous, secret mission inside the wooden horse. This is a secret mission that very nearly turns disastrous when Helen arrives on the scene, followed by Deiphobos, and calls out the names of the men inside the horse, mimicking in turn the voice of each of their wives. Once again Helen shows how clever she is, but now it seems she is being driven by some supernatural power keen to give success to the Trojans since it is clear that she is aware of the wooden horse's secret. She now seems to be playing wilfully with that secret knowledge, perhaps to demonstrate how alluring she can make herself sound, or perhaps to align herself with the Trojan side, or perhaps both. Only Odysseus saves the day, keeping his comrades quiet until Athene leads Helen away.

In immediately following Helen's own account of herself and Odysseus, the image now presented of her appears as a revision. Menelaos speaks directly to his wife—"Then you came along"[31]—and suggests the possibility of corroboration by those other male figures, both named and unnamed, who were present on the occasion inside the horse. As the events are recounted, male control almost slips away into female hands at a crucial moment and in such a way as to be both deadly serious and amusing. Helen's own anecdote strongly suggests a sense of safety and cooperation. Menelaos's anecdote strongly suggests the opposite: a sense of mischief and danger. He and the men with him sit in the dark belly of the wooden horse, all keyed up to play their crucial part in the plan to destroy Troy. The secret of their presence inside enemy territory must at all costs be preserved, but Helen seems intent on destroying that secret and with it the lives of the men inside the horse. Now Helen and Odysseus are no longer partners but adversaries in a lethal game of her making, and had it not been for Odysseus, control would once again have been in her hands. Here once again is Helen's "doubleness." With a potential allegiance to both sides, she moves effortlessly in these anecdotes between the categories of friend and enemy.

Beyond this war of reminiscences, the narrator adds another level of irony for the reader to enjoy, since talk of concealed identity and the threat of premature disclosure in enemy territory offers an ironic overlap with subsequent developments, and so helps tie together different strands in the *Odyssey*'s wide-ranging narrative. Telemachos hears from Helen of his father, disguised as a beggar, intent on concealing his identity from the eyes of the

---

31. For the comparatively rare form of a narrative of events addressed to the listener in the second person, cf. the words of Zeus to Hera at *Iliad* 15.18–30, of Achilleus to Aineias at *Iliad* 20.188–94, and of Poseidon to Apollo at *Iliad* 21.441–57. For a more extended example, cf. *Odyssey* 24.36–94, which I discuss in chapter 7.1 of this volume.

enemy, and these are the conditions in which he will first meet his father and will subsequently work with him to gain revenge on their enemies. Helen, as she bathes Odysseus, knows who he is, and this puts his safety potentially at risk. She may swear to keep the secret, but her ability to keep her mouth shut is fatally compromised by the anecdote that Menelaos tells against her. Later, even Penelope herself must be kept in ignorance of her husband's identity until the enemy have been destroyed, and when the loyal old nurse, Eurykleia, washes Odysseus's leg and recognizes him from the tell-tale hunting scar, she must be forcibly silenced for fear of raising the alarm (*Odyssey* 19.209–12, 386–96, 467–504).[32] Reminiscences of the war, set in the faraway magnificence of a Spartan palace, and events that are later to unfold back home in the embattled palace in Ithaca are thus shown to be part of an overlapping world.

When Menelaos finishes talking, "wise" Telemachos replies to him: "Atreus's son, Menelaos cherished by Zeus, leader of the people, / that makes it worse" (*Odyssey* 4.291–92). He at once explains this laconic comment: granted that Odysseus had such an iron will, the fact that this did not save him from bitter destruction makes it worse. Helen's drug, for all the claims made for it, has not worked for Telemachos, whose thoughts cannot be distracted from their anxiety. Telemachos does not let himself get drawn into the hostilities that have now appeared below the unruffled surface of Menelaos's marriage. Instead he proposes that they should all retire and get a good night's rest. This gives the cue to Helen to take control of the sleeping arrangements. Soon the two young men are led off to the guests' quarters, and Menelaos goes to bed: "and next to him lay the illustrious Helen, in her flowing nightdress" (*Odyssey* 4.305).

When the time comes for Telemachos to end his visit and start on the journey home, husband and wife are united in their desire to send their visitor off with valuable presents as keepsakes. Helen goes to her clothes chests and selects for him the most stunning and most intricate of the robes, which she herself has woven. It is now down at the bottom of the chest (*Odyssey* 15.104–8). When her husband has made a little speech over his parting gift, it is Helen's turn:

> Helen with her beautiful cheeks stood beside them,
> holding the robe in her hands, and spoke out and addressed
> Telemachos:
> "I too am giving you a present, dear child. Here it is,
> a reminder of Helen's handiwork, something for your wife to wear,

32. For a discussion of the lying stories that Odysseus tells to Penelope and others in the second half of the Odyssey, see P. Walcot (2009).

when the time comes for love and marriage. In the meantime, let
    your dear mother
keep it in the house. I wish you a happy arrival
at your fine house in your own homeland." (*Odyssey* 15.123–29)

This exquisite robe has none of the complex associations that connect Helen
with the Trojan War in the *Iliad* and hint at a guilty liaison in the *Aeneid*.
However, its place at the bottom of the clothes chest perhaps hints at the
passing of time since Helen was in her heyday. Telemachos receives the gift
with pleasure, and Peisistratos, looking with wonder at all the presents, stows
them away, ready for departure. As they part, Menelaos and Telemachos
exchange graceful farewells, and at this moment an eagle appears in the sky,
carrying off a white goose. The omen is received with general excitement and
pleasure, and Peisistratos asks Menelaos for whose benefit he thinks it has
been sent. While Menelaos pauses to reflect on a fitting way to respond to
this, Helen once again takes the initiative and interprets it as showing either
that Odysseus will come home and get his revenge or that he is already home
and planning it (*Odyssey* 15.160–68). Telemachos prays that her words come
true and adds: "Then, when I am back, I would say prayers to you, as to a god"
(*Odyssey* 15.181),[33] and with that they leave.

    Here then, presented early in the *Odyssey*, are Helen and Menelaos. There
is much that is godlike about their existence in faraway Sparta. Indeed, as the
"offspring of Zeus," Helen makes Menelaos the son-in-law of Zeus and thereby
confers future immortality on him. He will not die in his native Argos but
will be taken by the gods to a life of ease in Elysion at the ends of the world
(*Odyssey* 4.561–69). In the meantime, here is a fabulously rich and famous
middle-aged couple for the impressionable young Telemachos and his friend
to meet. Menelaos is a grand figure, charming and self-satisfied, eager to talk
about himself but sensitive also toward his young guests and their lives. He
is even at times a little unsure of himself in their company. Beyond thoughts
focused on the war, there is also another sadness in his life: he and Helen have
not had a son, and he has had to be content with a son, Megapenthes (Great
Grief), given to him by a slave girl. This absence in his life is reinforced by the
arrival of the two noble young men: earnest Telemachos, who is the image
of his father, and Peisistratos, who talks with a wisdom beyond his years and

---

33. The same words form part of Odysseus's farewell to Nausicaa; cf. *Odyssey* 8.467.

who, despite losing a brother in the war, still has five elder brothers to look after his father, Nestor, in old age.

In physical terms, Helen lives a life of ease and luxury. She is still beautiful in midlife and is attentive to her young guests, but her control is in some ways less secure. Now it requires the assistance of a drug to deaden emotional pain. On the arrival and again on the departure of their young guests, husband and wife present a picture of harmony, but the talk at the dinner table reveals tensions below the surface. No one mentions Paris, but even when he has been edited out of the couple's past life and thoughts are focused on Odysseus, Helen's place in the events marking the second crisis of her life—the imminent fall of Troy and return into her life of Menelaos—remains a matter of contention between husband and wife. Helen's flattering presentation of herself at that time is at once countered by her husband's presentation of her. There are elements of family comedy here, but it is comedy of a bittersweet nature, with so much continued suffering lurking so close to the surface. Telemachos and his friend arrive in the middle of a wedding party, and as he leaves, Telemachos's thoughts are steered by Helen toward the time when it will be his turn for "love and marriage." Ironically, coming from Helen's lips, these words have a comforting ring. As the visit comes to an end, Helen can make all appear well. Telemachos is both a "dear child," happy to be given his special, parting present, and also a young man who one day will have a wife of his own. Helen can also mention Telemachos's "dear mother" without causing pain and with no more than a hint of sounding patronizing. With queenly blandness, Helen brings her little speech to an end: "I wish you a happy arrival / at your fine house in your own homeland" (Odyssey 15.128–29), despite the enormous problems that have caused his visit. A few moments later, the parting view of Helen is of a revered prophetess, inspired by the immortal gods to utter words whose truth is not yet known to Telemachos, but which is already shown to the reader to be unfolding.

Nevertheless, from the middle of the Odyssey up to its climax in Odyssey 22, with Helen herself no longer present, she is widely recalled by the male world with bitterness as the woman for whose sake so many men died at Troy. This is how Odysseus speaks of her to Agamemnon's ghost (Odyssey 11.436–39). Eumaios, the faithful servant, wishes that instead of Odysseus, Helen and her whole tribe had died, since it was she who sent so many men to their death (Odyssey 14.68–69). Despite the parting gift with its charming little speech, this is how Telemachos thinks of Helen when he tells his mother how he met her: "There I saw Argive Helen, for whose sake Argives and Trojans / suffered much, at the whim of the gods" (*Odyssey* 17.118–19), and in the thick of the fighting with the suitors, Athene goads Odysseus into showing the same valor as when he fought at Troy for Helen's sake (*Odyssey* 22.226–30).

The last word on Helen in the *Odyssey*, however, comes from a female viewpoint. When Penelope can doubt her husband's identity no longer, she begs him not to be cross with her for being unsure of him at first and for failing to respond with sufficient emotion (*Odyssey* 23.85–95). She speaks then of the danger of a woman being deceived and led astray by a man. At this her thoughts turn to Helen:

> "Argive Helen, daughter of Zeus,
> would never have gone to bed and made love to another man,
> if she had known that the warlike sons of the Achaeans
> were going to take her back to her beloved country.
> It was a god who made her do that shameful act.
> Never before had such blind folly entered her mind,
> bringing so much bitterness, and that was the start of all our
>   sufferings." (*Odyssey* 23.218–24)

In her present circumstances, Penelope can take a lenient view of Helen and confidently say that, with hindsight, Helen would never have acted as she did. It was a god who stirred her to act shamefully, and this visitation of "blind folly" was quite out of character.

With these words Penelope retrospectively corroborates Helen's account of herself at *Odyssey* 4.261–62, and thoughts of Helen remind Penelope of the starting point of the sufferings that she and Odysseus have endured.[34]

---

34. Schein sees an element of revisionism here in this final, sympathetic verdict on Helen. He turns this into a general point, suggesting that "the *Odyssey* implies that its own main values and most frequently expressed viewpoints are neither unproblematic nor the only ones possible" (1995, 25–26).

6

Parting

6.1 ✍ Returning to Battle

At the start of the *Iliad*, the reader is plunged straight into events in the Achaean camp. Nearly ten years have passed since the Achaean forces left their families and went off to fight in Troy (*Iliad* 2.134, 295–96, 326–30).[1] The narrator takes pains to show the tensions that this war imposes on the relationship between the young leader of the beleaguered city's forces and his wife, Andromache, and their baby son. As Edwards writes, their brief meeting after Hektor leaves the battlefield and reenters Troy (*Iliad* 6.390–502) "draws into clear focus some of the strongest and most universal of human emotions" (1987, 209). Tragically, the death in battle that Hektor confronts as a possibility is soon to be his fate, so that when he parts from them it is for the last time. Setting this family parting not at the start but in the midst of hostilities enhances its emotional complexity. Time is short. Hektor's first thoughts are for the hard-pressed men under his command, and only after he has completed his assigned task of rousing the old women to seek the support of Athene for their city and has secured the return to the battlefield of his problematic brother, Paris, does he allow his thoughts to turn to his own immediate family. By now an atmosphere of impending disaster has been established (*Iliad* 6.311, 367–69), and this atmosphere colors both the meeting and its aftermath, when Andromache returns home.[2]

---

1. For Penelope's recall of the moment when Odysseus went off to the war cf. *Odyssey* 18.257–71.

2. After *Iliad* 6, there are only two, glancing references to Andromache (*Iliad* 8.185–90; 17.206–8) before *Iliad* 22.

Just as Hektor crosses from the world of the battlefield to "the lovely dwelling that was his home" (*Iliad* 6.370, 497), so Andromache moves in the opposite direction. Hearing news of the collapse of the Trojan forces and in great distress, she has left the scene of her domestic life with her husband and rushed to the vantage point of the great tower on the city walls. As a result, the two initially miss each other, and Hektor has to retrace his footsteps. When they meet, they are both running, and their meeting takes place midway between the two worlds, close to the city gate through which Hektor will leave to return to the battlefield (*Iliad* 6.371–73, 386–95). Andromache is accompanied by a nurse, who carries the baby close to her breast. The narrator lingers over the description of the baby:

> an innocent child, just a baby,
> Hektor's own dear son, like a beautiful star,
> whom Hektor called Skamandrios but the others called
> Astyanax, for Hektor alone protected Troy. (*Iliad* 6.400–403)

Here too is a suggestion of the bringing together of two worlds. Hektor has his own intimate name for his beautiful, darling baby son. The name "Skamandrios" recalls the name given by men to the main river of Troy (*Iliad* 20.73–74). However, the child is already known by another name in the outside world—"Astyanax," or "Lord of the City"—and this name places him firmly at the center of a public world and carries with it the strong association of his father's role as sole protector of that world.[3] As husband and wife meet, Hektor first looks at the child and smiles in silence (*Iliad* 6.404). This is the only time Hektor smiles in the course of the *Iliad*. Graziosi and Haubold write that here is "a moment of loving silence in a poem full of noise and speeches" (2010, 193).

Andromache cries as she stands beside her husband and takes hold of his hand. Her speech to him (*Iliad* 6.407–39) is dominated by one idea, an appeal to him to pity his wife and baby son and not to court death amid the massed ranks of the enemy. She begins with a simple and stark warning—"your valor will destroy you" (*Iliad* 6.407)—and tells him that she would rather die than lose him. Since her father and her seven brothers have all been killed by Achilleus and her mother is dead, she has no one else to comfort her: "'But you, Hektor, are father to me and honored mother, / and brother, and you are my strong husband'" (*Iliad* 6.429–30). She urges him to adopt the different strategy of staying on the battlement rather than making his son an orphan

---

3. It is by this second name, "Astyanax," with its by now painful associations, that Andromache refers to their child when she sees that her husband has been killed; cf. *Iliad* 22.499–507.

and his wife a widow. From there he could marshal his forces to defend the city at its weakest point, where Andromache says that three enemy assaults have already been attempted (*Iliad* 6.431–39).

Hektor responds sympathetically to his wife's concerns, but he sees things differently. His speech (*Iliad* 6.441–65) is a little shorter than Andromache's. In it he makes three distinct points, which are expressed with increasing emotional intensity. First he tells her that he would be deeply ashamed to act like a coward and avoid the dangers of war, and in this way lose the respect of the men and women of Troy (*Iliad* 6.442, repeated at 22.105). This combination of a sense of shame and the need to maintain public respect is a central part of the heroic code discussed in chapter 4.1. Schein analyzes it in the following way: "Aidōs ("shame" or "respect") is both an individual and a social concept; it is an internal, emotional impulse towards correct behaviour in conformity with what is expected of one by others" (1984, 177). Hektor does what his heart tells him to do:

> "since I have learned to be brave
> always and to fight in the forefront of the Trojan army,
> winning great fame both for my father and for myself." (*Iliad*
> 6.445–46)

Thus it is neither in his own nature to act as Andromache has suggested, nor does it fit his self-image to do so.

After such an emphasis on bravery, fame, and the avoidance of public disgrace, Hektor's second point comes as a surprise:

> "For I know this well in my heart and in my mind:
> the day will come when sacred Ilios will be destroyed
> and Priam and the people of Priam with the fine ash wood spear."
> (*Iliad* 6.447–49)

These words, spoken in a tone of melancholy foreboding, echo those spoken in a tone of vindictiveness earlier by Agamemnon (*Iliad* 4.163–65). Hektor's mood is colored by the pervasive sense of impending catastrophe, and in particular by the anguished vision of his wife, who stands beside him holding his hand. It contrasts both with the more hopeful mood that he displays when Paris joins him (*Iliad* 6.526–29) and with the confidence in victory that he subsequently displays when things are going well for him on the battlefield.[4]

---

4. Cf. for example *Iliad* 8.175–76, 526–28; 12.231–36.

It also gives the reader an ironic glance forward to the coming fate of Hektor himself and the ultimate outcome of the fighting.

Hektor is now led on to the thought that occupies the remainder of his speech (*Iliad* 6.450–65). As he looks ahead, the pain he feels is not so much for the sufferings of his people as for the misery Andromache will endure in being enslaved by the victorious enemy. The obligations Hektor feels as defender of a public world and as defender of his own private world are, as Schein notes, "mutually contradictory" (1984, 179). Here the all-embracing nature of his feelings for Andromache mirrors what she has expressed toward him. In an agonizing image of her life as a slave, he imagines what will be said to her face, and in so doing, places his fame as the great warrior in a tragic context:

> And then someone will say, as he sees the tears pouring down
>   your face:
> "This is the wife of Hektor, who was the greatest warrior
> of the horse-taming Trojans, when they were fighting around Ilios."
> That is what they will say, and fresh pain will come to you,
> at losing such a man to keep from you the day of slavery. (*Iliad*
>   6.459–63)

Just as Andromache would rather die than lose her husband, so he now prays for death rather than the knowledge that such a fate has befallen her (*Iliad* 6.464–65). This final outpouring of emotion, however, contains a bitter paradox. Hektor prays that he does not live to see his wife dragged off into slavery, and tragically his prayer will be answered. But the death he prays for is also the death his wife earnestly begs him to avoid out of pity for her subsequent fate.

Hektor has not spoken of their son in his reply to Andromache, but now once again the baby becomes the focus of attention. As Hektor finishes speaking, he reaches out toward his son, but the baby screams and turns back to his nurse's breast. The narrator describes closely the baby's feelings:

> alarmed by the sight of his dear father,
> terrified by the bronze and the horse-hair crest,
> seeing the terrible way it nodded from the very top of the helmet.
>   (*Iliad* 6.468–70)

His father and mother laugh at this, and at once Hektor takes off his helmet, lays the gleaming object on the ground, gives his darling son a kiss, and jogs him up and down. Then he utters a solemn prayer:

"O Zeus and you other gods, grant that this son of mine
may become as I am, outstanding among the Trojans,
just as brave and mighty, and may rule in strength over Ilios,
and may they say of him: 'This man is much better than his
    father,'
as he comes back from war. May he kill the enemy, bring back
the bloody spoils, and may his mother rejoice in her heart." (*Iliad*
    6.476–81)

With these words, Hektor puts his son in his wife's hands, and she takes him to her breast, with tears showing through her laughter (*Iliad* 6.482–84). Edwards notes, "The usual indication of the gods' response to the prayer is omitted" (1987, 211).

A sudden, unexpected response to his father by the baby dispels the sadness that has been weighing so heavily on the minds of his parents. Hektor's "glancing helmet" is a defining characteristic of the great warrior,[5] but when this object, charged with associations from the world of war, obtrudes into the intimate, domestic world of a baby clinging to a woman's breast, it looks terrifying to the baby's eye. Thus the very child whom the father is risking his life to defend from the enemy cries out in alarm at "the sight of his dear father." Here is a different kind of paradox from the one that has immediately preceded it, one that can relieve the tension and provoke both parents to laughter. Hektor at once takes off his helmet before paying further attention to his beloved baby son. Now, for a moment, he is Hektor, the dedicated father, rather than Hektor, the mighty warrior. But his thoughts turn at once to the code of behavior engraved on his heart. Just as Hektor sees his own task as winning fame for his father and for himself in battle, so now he earnestly prays that his own son may far outshine him on the field of battle. This aspiration has the power to transform Hektor's outlook on the future. With a powerful mood swing, he envisages a Troy and its people, not destroyed, but ruled over in strength by the son, who lives up to his public name, "Lord of the City." Now he hears an imaginary observer speaking words that fill him not with grief but pride, and now he imagines his wife, not crying and screaming as she is dragged off into slavery, but rejoicing at the proof of the overthrow of the enemy by her brave warrior-son.

---

5. It has been prominent in the preceding scene, where Hektor meets Paris and Helen. It appears in the line introducing Hektor's reply to Andromache and reappears a little later as Hektor is about to return to the fighting; cf. *Iliad* 6.342, 359, 369, 440, 520. It was given to Hektor by Apollo; cf. *Iliad* 11.353.

With such a vision conjured up in prayer, Hektor entrusts his baby son to the protection of his wife, and as she hears it she blends her tears with laughter. In her speech, Andromache entreated her husband to show pity, and this he now does, up to a point, as he sees the signs of mixed emotion on her face: "As he saw this, her husband felt pity for her, / he stroked her with his hand and spoke out loud to her" (*Iliad* 6.484–85). He tells her not to let her heart be too troubled: no one will kill him before his appointed time, and no one can escape his fate. His last four lines bring closure to the meeting and to the subject of their conversation:

> "But go to the house and attend to your own tasks,
> the loom and the shuttle, and give orders to your maids
> to go about their tasks. War will be a matter for the men,
> all those who were born in Ilios, and particularly for me."
>   (*Iliad* 6.490–93)

Hektor shows tenderness toward his wife, as he has done toward their baby son, and tries to calm her fears. He feels pity for her, but this will not make him agree to her request. The division of roles according to gender goes too deep for that. Andromache should keep herself profitably employed in her own domestic world and not try to interfere in the male world of war and power.[6]

So saying, Hektor puts on his helmet again and Andromache makes her way home. Graziosi and Haubold write, "There is no resolution, no common perspective. At the end of this most loving encounter, there is simply a parting" (2010, 47). Now Andromache does not run but keeps turning around, and the tears are once more pouring down her face. On returning to the lovely home of "Hektor the man-killer," she finds herself in the midst of her maids, but the task she sets them is not what her husband might have expected:

> "and she aroused them all to lamentation.
> They lamented for Hektor in his house, alive as he still was.
> For they said that he would not come back from the war,
> or escape being overwhelmed at the hands of the Achaeans."
>   (*Iliad* 6.499–502)

Here the passage leaves the reader with a final, complex paradox. The masculine mind sets the division of labor for the two sexes: for the man, the world of

---

6. The role of women in the Trojan community is discussed by Schein (1984, 172–77), who notes how in this scene between Hektor and Andromache "each is made to participate in the other's sphere of activity."

war, with its opportunity to show outstanding courage and to win honor and a fame that crosses over the generations; for the woman, domestic life and the rearing from birth of the new generation of warriors. But at a moment of crisis, it is the feminine mind that questions the values invested in the world constructed by the masculine mind and points to their cost in terms of life expectancy and the legacy of human suffering. It looks at the problem and suggests a different approach: in this case, a strategic withdrawal. More than that, when this suggestion is summarily dismissed, it sidesteps the domestic task expected of it and, in the company of its own sex, intuitively sees into the future in a way both prophetic and disturbing in that it anticipates the worst and acts as if it has already happened.

6.2 🖋 Abandoning Home to the Enemy

Aeneas recounts a family parting that has taken place in the midst of war. This forms the climax of his eyewitness account of the fall of Troy (*Aeneid* 2.634–795). It is discussed by Lyne (1987, 146–51, 167–71, 183–86, 188–89). Here the atmosphere is one of disaster that has already struck the city and that threatens any moment to engulf the whole family. Aeneas plans to remove his father, Anchises, to the safety of the mountains, but his plan meets an insuperable difficulty: Anchises will not leave *(Aeneid* 2.637–46). Aeneas now reproduces for his internal audience three speeches: his father's, his own slightly longer speech, and his wife's short speech, which brings the protracted crisis to its climax (*Aeneid* 2.638–49, 657–70, 675–78). Anchises urges the others to escape and to leave him to die. He remains adamant despite the tears and entreaties of his family and of the whole household, and now the crisis intensifies. In desperation at this impasse, Aeneas rushes back for his weapons, intent on dying in battle. As Aeneas arms himself for battle and hurries to leave the house, on the threshold his wife clings tightly to his feet and holds little Iulus out toward his father as she addresses him in passionate words:

> "If you are leaving to die, then take us with you to face what comes;
> but if you know that you can place some hope in taking up arms,
> first protect this house. To whom is little Iulus being abandoned,
> and your father and I who was once called your wife?" (*Aeneid*
> 2.675–78)

As she speaks, Creusa fills the whole house with her cries of anguish.

The conflict in Aeneas's family at this crucial moment differs from and is more complex than that shown in *Iliad* 6. Now the conflict is set in the emotionally charged context of the family home, which is soon to be overrun by the enemy. The initial point of conflict is between father and son rather than between husband and wife, and now the conflict spills over so that three rather than two adult figures are involved. All three, together with Aeneas's little son, are threatened with immediate, violent death as a result of it. The conflict begins not so much as a clash of worlds as a clash of wills. Anchises says a firm "No" to the idea of life after Troy. His perception of the will of the gods, the feeling of déjà-vu at the repetition of a past trauma, and the sense of being old, cursed, and worthless create an impregnable emotional barrier.[7] This produces an impossible dilemma for Aeneas. His guiding principle is the performance of his duty toward the gods and toward his fellow men, and he owes a special duty toward his father as the head of the household. His divine mother tells him to protect his father and the rest of his family and to escape. His human father tells Aeneas to escape with them but to leave him behind to die. The problem cannot be solved, and soon it will be too late to agonize over it.

Aeneas graphically recalls his sense of frustration and despair. He responds by reverting to his initial fight-or-flight reaction and opting to share death in battle with his defeated comrades. But for the man of duty, abandoning his family to their fate is not an option either, as Aeneas's wife at once makes clear, both by her two dramatic gestures and by her succinct and powerful reformulation of his dilemma. Now the clash of wills extends to include a clash of worlds. Here the pressure Creusa puts on her husband is stronger than the pressure on Hektor from Andromache. Andromache begs her husband to modify his activity on the battlefield out of concern for his family. Creusa instead presents Aeneas with a stark choice: either to take his family with him to share his fate on the battlefield or to give up his urge to return to the fighting and instead to protect first the family home. A few moments earlier, Aeneas attributes the responsibility for the family plight jointly to the gods and to his father's intransigence (*Aeneid* 2.659–61), but Creusa's impassioned words now strongly suggest that by his response Aeneas is transferring that responsibility onto his own shoulders.

---

7. For Anchises' allusion to an earlier capture of Troy, cf. the words of Herakles' son, Tlepolemos, at *Iliad* 5.638–42. In lines 648–49, Anchises speaks of a time when he was scorched by Jupiter's thunderbolt after boasting of his affair with Venus. Here, very briefly, a moment from the past life of Aeneas's family is allowed to appear. For another, similar moment, cf. Dido's awareness of the circumstances of Aeneas's birth (*Aeneid* 1.617–18).

As in *Iliad* 6 it is the child within the family who brings a sudden relaxation to adult tension. Now, however, this is brought about not through a
baby's natural response to the adult world but rather through a supernatural
intervention that centers on the passive figure of the little child. E. L. Harrison
writes of "the instantaneous efficacy of that most striking feature of Roman
religion, the prodigy" (1990, 57). A tongue of fire appears at the top of the
child's head, shedding its light and playing harmlessly around his hair and
forehead. The family's response to this portent is mixed, but for the moment
all thought of their crisis is laid aside. Aeneas and Creusa are frightened and
try to extinguish the sacred fire, but "father Anchises" is transformed. Now
he is "happy" and reestablishes positive contact with the divine world. Once
again, Aeneas reproduces three speeches: two short speeches from his father,
one a prayer, the other the expression of his readiness to leave Troy, enclosing
a further prayer; and finally Aeneas's own somewhat longer speech (*Aeneid*
2.689–91, 701–4, 707–20). Anchises asks that Jupiter may be moved by their
prayers to help them as a just reward for their "dutifulness," and that he may
give them confirmation of this omen. When this duly comes and a shooting
star reveals their path to safety in the mountains, any lingering doubts in the
old man's mind are overcome. Now Anchises is eager to be going and ready
to let his son take the lead: "For my part, I yield and do not refuse, my son, to
go as your / companion" (*Aeneid* 2.704).

Aeneas's own speech in reply begins and ends with his father:

> "Come then, dear father, put your arms round my neck,
> and I will lower my shoulders for you. That labor will not weigh
>   heavy on me.
> Whatever may befall us, both will share one danger,
> one escape to safety. Let little Iulus
> be my companion, and let my wife keep track of us at a distance."
>   (*Aeneid* 2.707–11)

He gives instructions about a meeting place to the family slaves and ends
by telling his father to hold the sacred images of the household gods (*Aeneid*
2.717–20). Then he takes his father on his shoulders, little Iulus holds onto
his hand and runs to keep up with his father, and his wife follows behind as
they make their way through the darkness (*Aeneid* 2.721–25).

In the nick of time, divine intervention has resolved the human impasse,
and the family has begun its escape. But disaster now strikes. When they have
almost reached the city gate unharmed, there is a sudden sound of enemy

footsteps. Anchises peers ahead through the shadows and exclaims, "Get away, son, get away!" He can see the enemy approaching. In this terrible split second of panic and confusion, Aeneas veers off the familiar path and contact with Creusa is lost. Aeneas's otherwise authoritative account of events wavers for a moment as he comes to this point:

> "Alas for my suffering, my wife, Creusa, did she stop, snatched
>   away
> by fate, did she stray from the path or did she slip
> and remain there? It is not known. I never saw her after that."
>   (*Aeneid* 2.738–40)

Aeneas explains that he became aware of his wife's absence only when he and the others reached the meeting place. He recalls, in words that combine great emotional power and brevity, the bitterness of his anguish at the discovery (*Aeneid* 2.745–46). Making sure that his son, his father, and the household gods are safe, he retraces his steps into the dangers and horrors of the burning city, looking endlessly for Creusa among the buildings and constantly calling out her name (*Aeneid* 2.747–71). Lyne draws an ironic contrast here, writing that "when Creusa is dead, Aeneas displays in abundance . . . the love and emotion which, for one reason or another, he did not display when she was alive" (1987, 170). His nightmarish search for her ends when Creusa's ghost appears to him and, with soothing words, directs his thoughts away from the pain of the present and toward his own future. As night draws to a close, Aeneas returns to the meeting place to find it thronged with refugees from the city, keen to entrust themselves to his leadership. He yields to the situation, lifts up his father, and makes for the mountains, and in this way *Aeneid* 2 comes to an end.

The contrast between these two scenes of family parting in the *Iliad* and the *Aeneid* can now be explored in more detail. The narrator tells the events of *Iliad* 6 as they happen, and this gives them a sense of immediacy colored by a growing sense of foreboding. When the voices of Andromache and Hektor are heard, they each speak at length (*Iliad* 6.407–39, 441–65, 476–81, 486–93). This helps create a sense of balance between the two voices, before the male voice takes control of the situation. Aeneas, by contrast, reproduces the terrible events that took place in his own life seven years earlier (*Aeneid* 1.755–56), and he does this in the public context of an after-dinner speech. Thus the narrative of his experiences is under his own control and is produced for an internal audience, and in this sense his narrative is like Odysseus's much longer account of his experiences given to the Phaeacians (*Odyssey* 9–12).

Aeneas spends much of his time reproducing the speeches of the characters involved in this family parting, himself included, and this gives the narrative a sense of drama. Rhetoric plays a part, both in the construction of Aeneas's entire speech to his present audience and in the construction of the speeches embedded within it. Attention is focused on the interplay of highly charged and rapidly changing emotions, and such highly charged emotion is not confined to the dramatic events Aeneas unfolds. Within his audience, Dido listens avidly and, as the surrounding narrative makes clear, is already the subject of a passionate and hopeless infatuation with the speaker (*Aeneid* 1.748–56; 4.1–5). Here then is the setting for an account of a highly emotional family parting in time of war, which in place of the comparative directness of the *Iliad* narrative offers the reader both something more self-conscious and the possibility of emotional engagement at a number of different levels.

Both scenes also enable the reader to look beyond the events being narrated, but this sense that the family parting opens out to reveal a big picture behind it is much more developed in the *Aeneid*. In *Iliad* 6 Hektor knows that Troy will be destroyed, and Andromache and her maids say that Hektor will not come back alive. Here the prophetic ability of the human mind, both male and female, to glimpse into the future adds greatly to the pathos of the scene of parting, but it does not overlay it with a sense of divine providence. The family parting in the *Aeneid*, by contrast, is charged with a sense of divinely ordained change. This is a central part of the *Aeneid*'s big picture: the turning point from the old world of Troy to the start of a new world, in which the survivors from the devastation of Troy are led by Aeneas to find their divinely fated new home, with all its promise of future greatness. Here then, underlying the clash of wills, there is also a clash of worlds in another sense, a clash between the old and the new, the past and the future. The trauma of this clash and its unforeseen, divine resolution are conveyed within the context of this family parting.

Dominant throughout all this is the bond between Aeneas and his father. Anchises' stubborn refusal to leave Troy places the lives of Aeneas, Creusa, Iulus, and the whole household in jeopardy since Aeneas cannot leave without his father. More than this, his father's death wish at once communicates itself to his son and thus intensifies the pressure on the rest of the family. The turning point comes when Anchises, with the intuition of the old, at once grasps the divine significance of the flame playing around Iulus's head. Here is a miraculous moment (*Aeneid* 2.680) in which the divine world and the human world are in communication, and at the same time, communication within the human world leaps over a generation, ironically the generation of the *Aeneid*'s central character.

Grandfather and grandson are united by this wordless communication at the very moment when Iulus is "midway between the hands and the faces of his sad parents" (*Aeneid* 2.681). Its effect is to dispel Anchises' depression and to evoke in him not only a sense of the "dutifulness" of the whole family but also their right humbly to ask for divine help and duly to be rewarded by it. Thus just as Anchises' negative emotion has an immediate, destructive effect on the other members of the family, so his sudden, miraculous change of heart reunites them and brings them divine recognition of the all-important sense of duty as the guiding principle in their lives.

As the scene in the *Aeneid* develops, the symbolism becomes more pronounced. In the *Iliad*, Hektor strives to bring fame on his father by his superiority in battle, and he prays that his own son may outshine him in war. Here the three, male generations are tied together in a vision of ever-increasing military glory.[8] In the context of flight from defeat, the image of Aeneas bending down to carry his father on his shoulders and holding on tightly to his little son's hand as the child runs to keep up with his father creates a more complex association of ideas. The grandfather's emotional state has been transformed, and with this transformation the whole family can move on, away from the brink of death. Anchises understands the omen. From now on he acts as spiritual guide and carries the images of the household gods, a potent reminder of the religious continuity with the past. But in physical terms he remains a frail old man with not long to live.[9] He must be willing to sit, like a child, on his son's shoulders and to entrust himself to his son's physical strength and strength of purpose to save him. Aeneas, upright now and with his father on his shoulders, is at the center of the image and strides forward. Conflict with his father has given way to cooperation, expressed in glowing terms (*Aeneid* 2.709–10). Now is the opportunity for the new head of the household to show leadership in a crisis, together with the responsibility for the protection of his father and his young son (*Aeneid* 2.728–29). Little Iulus[10] does not shrink from his father but runs to keep up with him. Rather than shrieking at the sight of a "glancing helmet," Iulus himself has a divine

---

8. For a practical demonstration of a grandfather's delight to see his son and his grandson competing in military valor, cf. Laertes, Odysseus, and Telemachos at *Odyssey* 24.505–15.

9. For Aeneas's expression of grief as he subsequently recalls his father's death, cf. *Aeneid* 3.708–13.

10. Aeneas's son is like Hektor's son in having two names, Ascanius and Iulus. In the *Aeneid*, however, the public significance of the second of these names is made clear in the context of the poem's grand narrative (*Aeneid* 1.267–71, 286–88).

light playing around his own head, a light that, when coupled with the guiding light of the shooting star in the sky, gives Anchises the confidence to entrust himself, his family, and even the future of Troy itself to the hands of the gods (*Aeneid* 2.689–91, 701–3). The three male figures, representing past, present, and future, can now move forward as one, confident in the strength of the present to hold them together as they move away from the lost world of Troy with all its heartache and toward the bright future that awaits them with the foundation of Rome.

All this gives Creusa a very different role from that of Andromache in *Iliad* 6. As Aeneas and his divine mother express their concerns about the safety of his family, Creusa appears alongside Aeneas's father and their little son in their thoughts (*Aeneid* 2.560–63, 596–97, 664–67). She plays a brief but important part in the rapidly developing family crisis, but no indication is given of Aeneas's feelings for her, nor is she involved in its resolution. As Aeneas takes control of the family parting, she recedes into the background. Her presence does not complicate the image of the male members of the family bonding across the generations as they set off. Whereas Hektor displays tenderness and a degree of pity toward Andromache before they part for the last time, Aeneas speaks of his wife only in the third person and makes clear that the onus is on her not to lose track of them as she follows behind. As the family embarks on its hazardous, nighttime escape, his anxious thoughts are given over to the safety of his father and his son. The loss of Creusa produces a variety of responses. R. G. Austin speculates that "perhaps . . . she at least was more able to look after herself than the old man and the little boy" (1964, 267). Lyne is more persuasive here when he writes that Aeneas's arrangement for the departure from Troy "contributes to, if not causes, Creusa's loss" (1987, 169), and Perkell goes further. In her view, "To Creusa Aeneas is fatally inattentive" (1981, 370), and she reminds the reader of the male-dominated nature of Aeneas's sense of duty and of the political-military drive to found the Roman Empire. The discussion returns to this point toward the end of the next section of this chapter.

The account Aeneas gives of the loss of his wife is a complex one and plays a central part in the closing stages of his account of the fall of Troy. His words evoke the pain of loss. However, any suggestion that there might be a causal link between the sudden swerve to avoid the enemy and the loss of Creusa, who is following along behind in the dark as ordered, is no more than a hint, a hint subsequently surrounded in ambiguity by the unanswered question "did she stray from the path?" Divine providence has enabled the family to escape just in time, but it is not an all-encompassing divine providence. There is still room for a malign power outside human control to intervene, and its victim is the woman in the family, out of reach of the three male generations and the tutelary protection of the household gods. Having drawn attention to the fatal moment, and having aroused the sympathy of his internal audience and of the reader for his loss, Aeneas retrospectively asks three questions about Creusa's disappearance and leaves the matter unresolved, though beyond doubt ("I never saw her after that"), before acknowledging that he did not look back for her as he changed direction or notice that she was missing until he had reached the meeting place.[11]

The subsequent realization of his wife's absence brings an extension to the family crisis, but at least now it is a managed crisis. Aeneas ensures that his father, his son, and the household gods of Troy are as safe as circumstances will permit before retracing his steps to look for Creusa. Now it is Aeneas's turn to experience a terrible sense of déjà-vu as he makes his way back into the horror of the sacked city, back to his home, which is now being torched by the enemy, and back to Priam's palace. His search and his agonized cries of his wife's name are set against the images of his home city in enemy hands: fires raging, holy treasures being looted, and long lines of panic-stricken mothers with their sons.[12] The relationship between the fallen city and the members of Aeneas's family has changed since the start of the crisis. Initially the old man could not bear to part with his home and preferred to die there, but a miracle changed all that. Initially Creusa joined with the others in trying to make Anchises change his mind and choose the possibility of life rather than the certainty of violent death, but it is not part of the *Aeneid*'s big picture that she should continue her life after the sack of Troy. Her life is lost, the cause of death never established. As Aeneas reaches the end of his account of the fall of Troy, he focuses once again on the bond with his father. Just as Anchises "yields" (*Aeneid* 2.704), so Aeneas recalls his acceptance of the new situation, and father and son are once more shown moving as one: "I yielded and, lifting my father up, I made for the hills" (*Aeneid* 2.804).

11. As Creusa, intent on escaping from death, follows behind Aeneas, she is in some ways like Eurydice following behind Orpheus; cf. *Georgics* 4.485–93. Eurydice, however, is lost when Orpheus looks back for her, whereas Aeneas does not look back until it is too late.

12. And then—nothing. The gap where the remainder of line 767 remains incomplete leaves an eloquent silence.

6.3 ✹ Separating

Among Odysseus's experiences in the course of the long journey home from Troy are two extended periods spent living first with one and then with a second goddess, and a short encounter with a beautiful and intelligent girl who is the daughter of a friendly, local king. Great subtlety interlaces the accounts of these three experiences of feminine company and the way in which each is brought to an end. Each is set far away from Ithaca, and together they explore many different aspects of the relationship between the sexes before Odysseus finally returns home to resume, after the long physical and emotional separation, his own married life with Penelope.[13]

Calypso ("The Concealer"), her cave home, and her desire to make Odysseus her husband are introduced at the start of the *Odyssey*, and by the time Odysseus is first seen by the reader in *Odyssey* 5, the sense that he is desperate to leave her and to return home has been well established (*Odyssey* 1.13–15, 48–59; 4.556–60; 5.82–84). Odysseus spends his nights with the goddess, but she no longer brings him any pleasure: "At night-time he slept with her, by necessity, / in her hollow cave. She wanted him but he did not want her" (*Odyssey* 5.154–55). He spends the days in tears, gazing out at "the barren sea."[14] When Hermes delivers Zeus's command to Calypso that she must let Odysseus go, she responds with a shudder and with words that convey a mixture of emotions: bitterness, grudging acceptance tinged with a moment's petulance ("let him get lost!"), and finally generosity as she promises that she will do what she can to send him safely on his way (*Odyssey* 5.116–44). The breaking of the tie between Odysseus and Calypso, with whom he later tells the Phaeacians that he spent seven years (*Odyssey* 7.259), is described in detail (*Odyssey* 5.149–227). First Calypso goes over to Odysseus, and this physical proximity brings with it a new willingness to see the situation from Odysseus's point of view: "'Poor man, please do not grieve here any more, do not let your life / waste away, for now I will send you on your way, with a good will'" (*Odyssey* 5.160–61).

Calypso conceals her visit from Hermes. Her words come as a shock to Odysseus, who is lost in sad thoughts, and he too reacts with a shudder.

---

13. For an introduction to the complex portrayal of Odysseus in the *Odyssey*, see De Jong (2001, 133–34, 221–27). For a survey of his portrayal both inside and beyond the *Odyssey*, see Stanford (1963).

14. Achilleus also looks out in tears at the sea, but for him the presence of the sea brings relief; cf. *Iliad* 1.348–50 and 23.59–62.

Initially he is wary of doing as she says and entrusting himself to the perils of the sea on a raft, and he insists that the goddess swear a great oath that she is not planning him any harm (*Odyssey* 5.171–79). This human mistrust of the word of a goddess has the paradoxical effect of bringing the two of them together at this highly charged moment: "So he spoke and Calypso, the divine goddess, smiled / and stroked him with her hand and spoke out to him" (*Odyssey* 5.180–81).[15] There is no sense of anger or resentment here but rather a smile on Calypso's face and a playful reprimand from her before she duly swears the oath. She then goes even further, assuring Odysseus that she can imagine herself in his plight and is not so hard-hearted that she cannot feel pity for him (*Odyssey* 5.182–91).

Calypso quickly leads the way back to her cave. After their meal Calypso reopens the subject of Odysseus's departure:

> "Offspring of Zeus, son of Laertes, Odysseus of many devices,
> so now you want to go home, right this moment,
> to your native land, do you? Well, all the same, I bid you farewell."
>   (*Odyssey* 5.203–5)

They sit on opposite sides of the table, enjoying their meal together but already separated by the nature of their food: mortal food on one side of the table and immortal on the other. Odysseus's departure is now offered to him in the form of an open question, so that the decision is his to make. Calypso breaks her tie with Odysseus without rancor, but not without a note of pique, telling him that if he knew what troubles were in store for him before reaching his native land, he would stay and look after "this home" and accept her offer of immortality, however much he might pine to see his own wife again. Calypso's concealment of Zeus's order to release Odysseus now borders on an invitation to transgress that order. The irony, with its hint of hidden danger, continues as Calypso ends her speech by dwelling on her mortal rival for Odysseus's affections.

Odysseus's reply (*Odyssey* 5.214–24) is courteous but firm: Calypso should not be angry with him, for she herself knows that his own "thoughtful Penelope" is no match for her in looks since she is mortal, while Calypso is immortal and ageless. Odysseus's longing to be reunited with his own, mortal wife can now be recognized without any snub to her immortal rival, and any

---

15. This light-hearted gesture contrasts with the serious mood in which Thetis strokes her son's hand at *Iliad* 1.360–61 and Hektor strokes his wife at *Iliad* 6.485. Later the disguised Athene also strokes Odysseus playfully, at *Odyssey* 13.287–89.

lingering fear of the horrors of the sea, which Calypso might try to use to make him stay, is dismissed by his proven ability to endure such suffering. Assuming some measure of control of the situation, Odysseus goes now with Calypso to a corner of the cave as the sun sets, and, before they part, they return to the earlier, shared pleasure of making love:

> So he spoke, and the sun set and darkness fell,
> and the two of them came to a corner of the hollow cave,
> and enjoyed making love and staying in each other's arms.
>   (*Odyssey* 5.225–27)

Dawn brings the start of four days of feverish activity as Odysseus builds the raft. Calypso provides him with all the equipment and information at her disposal. She duly bathes him, dresses him, gives him provisions, and as promised sends him off on the fifth day. So Odysseus sets off with a happy heart on the next leg of his journey home (*Odyssey* 5.228–77).

Two near-death experiences enclose the time that Odysseus spends with Calypso and help set it apart as something approaching a living death.[16] Exhausted after his fresh struggle to avoid drowning, Odysseus clambers ashore and makes a bed of leaves for himself among the bushes before falling into a profound sleep. As *Odyssey* 6 opens, Nausicaa, the daughter of the local king, is also asleep, safe in bed in her father's palace and dreaming of her wedding day. Sleep instantly soothes the pain of Odysseus's sufferings, and he wakes to find himself in a new world where girls are playing with a ball while the washing dries in the sun, a world where they all shriek when one of them misses a catch and lets the ball fall into the river. Working behind the scenes throughout this transitional sequence of events is the goddess Athene, intent on Odysseus's safe homecoming (*Odyssey* 6.13–14, 112–14). Odysseus's brief encounter with Nausicaa radiates a sense of amusement and optimism, of attraction and cooperation between the sexes after the initial shock caused by the circumstances of their meeting and despite the gulf separating their two worlds. Here too, however, there is a serious undertone, which appears in Odysseus's praise for the unequalled blessings of a harmonious married life:

> "For nothing can surpass this:
> when two people, man and woman, share each other's
> thoughts and home" (*Odyssey* 6.182–84)

16. For the first of these experiences, cf. *Odyssey* 7.248–54; 12.420–53; 23.330–32, and for the second, cf. *Odyssey* 5.291–463; 7.267–84.

Still the incongruity of the situation—an all-but naked, middle-aged war veteran who has been sleeping rough, extolling the harmony of an ideal marriage to a beautiful, dreamy young girl whom he has never seen before and whose maids he has just sent flying for their lives—remains for the reader to enjoy. Odysseus's civilized behavior and eloquence and Nausicaa's recognition of her obligation to respond to the ritual of supplication quickly turn the threat of the wild into a natural backdrop for communication between a man, albeit without his clothes on, and a young woman.[17] From this point on, his reintegration into human society, with its controlled interaction between the sexes, proceeds quickly, and it soon becomes clear in Odysseus's conversation with Nausicaa's parents that he is once again well in control of the situation.

The following evening, after a day of entertainment given in honor of their guest and after preparations for his forthcoming departure, Odysseus goes to join the men with their drinks, and Nausicaa stands by a column in all her divine beauty. As she speaks, the gaze she directs on him is full of admiration: "'I say farewell, stranger, so that when you are in your own homeland, / you may remember me, since you owe me first the reward for saving your life'" (*Odyssey* 8.461–62). In his reply, Odysseus prays for his safe return home and expresses his gratitude to Nausicaa in the form of a final, graceful compliment before taking his place beside the king:

> "Nausicaa, daughter of great-hearted Alkinöos,
> just so may Zeus, the loud-thundering husband of Hera,
> now grant that I may come home and see the day of my return.
> Then I would pray to you there, for ever more,
> as to a god, for you, maiden, gave me life." (*Odyssey* 8.464–68)

The circumstances of their meeting, when Nausicaa saw the naked Odysseus and for a moment held his life in her hands, remain a private bond between them, a narrative excluded from Odysseus's married life with Penelope.[18] Odysseus's bath and dressing have now taken place in the customary, domestic setting, rather than out in the country as on the occasion of his first meeting Nausicaa, and she looks at him once again in admiration. Now, however,

17. J. F. Johnson (2016, 25–47) discusses ritual acts of supplication in Homer. He notes the religious nature of supplication and writes of an "aggregate of religious, social and personal feeling" that prompts the person supplicated to assist the suppliant (27).

18. After Odysseus and Penelope have made love, he gives her an account of his adventures, which the narrator summarizes. But when the narration comes to Odysseus's time with the Phaeacians, no mention is made of Nausicaa (*Odyssey* 23.338–41).

she has no maids with her to whom she can confide her fleeting dreams of marriage as she did before (*Odyssey* 6.239–45). Odysseus remains for her no more than a "stranger," an honored guest whose identity and personal history will not be disclosed until after she has left. To Odysseus, on the other hand, she has openly declared her identity as "daughter of great-hearted Alkinöos" (*Odyssey* 6.196–97) and discreetly revealed her own name, "Nausicaa" (*Odyssey* 6.275–77). Just as Odysseus's first words upon meeting her were a graceful compliment, blurring the distinction between goddess and young girl (*Odyssey* 6.149), so his parting words take on a similar form. Now, however, earnest talk of an ideal marriage is replaced by a closing hint of humor in the paradoxical idea that a "maiden" could have given life to him.

In their different ways, both Calypso and Nausicaa save Odysseus's life, and his experience with these two figures and the manner of his parting from them are described by the narrator.[19] Odysseus's encounter with Circe is both the last of the three to be presented to the reader and the first to have occurred. The encounter combines folk-tale elements with subtle and often ironic characterization.[20] It belongs in Odysseus's own account to the Phaeacians of his adventures since leaving Troy.[21] It differs from the other two experiences in three ways. Since Odysseus, as he looks back, is now in control of the narrative, Circe is presented from his own viewpoint.[22] In place of an external account of events, therefore, there comes a sense of Odysseus presenting his narrative as a performance, given before an appreciative, internal audience. Here is a narrative in which the threat of female control over the male sex is at its most terrifying. This is in sharp contrast to the narrator's own account of life in the Phaeacian royal family, where the queen is accorded great respect and influence by the male population and where an aura of discretion and politeness is shown to exist between the sexes.[23] At the same time, the hero of that narrative appears in the reassuring role of narrator of events, which, however terrifying they may be, he at least has survived and can skillfully articulate as past history.

19. The narrator also deftly incorporates a reminder of both Circe and Calypso immediately before Nausicaa's farewell; cf. *Odyssey* 8.446–53.

20. For further discussion, see Heubeck and Hoekstra (1989, 50–52).

21. De Jong (2001, 221–227) analyses Odysseus's own narrative of his earlier adventures on the way home from Troy (*Odyssey* 9–12, the so-called Apologue).

22. Odysseus gives two further sources for his information about Circe: his conversations with Eurylochos and with Hermes; cf. *Odyssey* 10.251–73, 281–301.

23. For a different but comparable gap between Phaeacian social behavior and the world as presented in entertainment, cf. Demodokos's song of Ares and Aphrodite (*Odyssey* 8.266–367).

Second, at this stage in his adventures Odysseus is still in command of the crew of his ship. They too are players in the drama he is bringing to life. This drama is set not only in a different time but also in a different world, a world of terrifying, supernatural forces. Odysseus's experience with Circe marks a turning point in his account of these adventures. Up to the moment of his impending encounter with her, Odysseus records dangers of which he has had no divine foreknowledge. Now he is told, first by a god (Hermes) and then, more comprehensively, by a goddess (*Odyssey* 10.490–540; 12.25–27, 37–141), what further, terrifying experiences lie ahead and how best to react to them. This difference gives Circe a special role in the construction of the *Odyssey*'s narrative. From now on the reader can make use of this foreknowledge, waiting in suspense to see how Odysseus will meet the challenges that lie ahead and reminded of the warning given by the narrator at the outset (*Odyssey* 1.6–9) that his crew are doomed to die before Odysseus reaches the end of his narrative. Finally, Odysseus and his men meet, stay with, and subsequently part from Circe not once but twice, since they return to her briefly after the journey she has ordered them to make to "the house of Hades and of august Persephone" (*Odyssey* 10.491). This gives Odysseus's parting from Circe an added complexity.

As he recalls the events leading to their two partings they become the focus of an elaborate irony. On first meeting Odysseus's companions, Circe uses her magic to make his men forget all about their homeland and to turn them bodily into pigs. However, with Hermes' help, Odysseus has the power to reverse her magic, and he is enabled to accept without danger her demand that he should go to bed with her. After this, Circe turns into a sympathetic hostess and gives Odysseus and his men the opportunity to take time to recover both physically and emotionally from all their sufferings, and so they enjoy a year of constant feasting. Now it is Odysseus who has to be reminded of their homeland by his own men (*Odyssey* 10.467–75). Once reminded by his companions, Odysseus begins by displaying a measure of control over the situation. He waits for another day of feasting to pass and for his companions to settle down for the night. Then, climbing onto "Circe's exquisitely beautiful bed" where Circe herself has said that they can trust each other (*Odyssey* 10.333–35), he begs her to honor her promise to send him home. Circe makes no problem over releasing her guests, although there is perhaps a hint of archness in her voice: "'Offspring of Zeus, son of Laertes, Odysseus of many devices, / now I would never want you all to stay in my house, against your wishes'" (*Odyssey* 10.488–89).

When he hears that he must go to the house of Hades before he can return home, Odysseus collapses into a state of misery and, ironically, does not want to go on living. Circe shows that she can still reduce men to tears, but she has long ceased to use this power as an enemy, and now she spends the night giving Odysseus instructions (*Odyssey* 10.503–41). In the morning, she dresses first Odysseus and then herself,[24] and Odysseus wakes his men up with the good news of their imminent departure, while keeping the bad news of their immediate destination for a later moment (*Odyssey* 10.541–50, 561–68). When they hear the news, they are all in tears as they prepare to leave.

In this twofold parting from Circe, the gulf between mortal and immortal is suddenly reestablished, and in its starkest form. The presence of Circe, daughter of the Sun, on her island, home of the Dawn (*Odyssey* 10.135–39; 12.3–4), encloses the human journey to the world of the dead, and this point of embarkation and return throws the journey to the darkness of the underworld into sharp contrast. The death of one of the crew, as the journey is about to begin, adds an immediacy to the experience of death. After his crew have spent a year living like gods and feasting constantly, one of their number, the luckless Elpenor, loses his life in the scramble to leave as a result of a drunken accident. Circe herself slips past the men without being seen. Now that her mortal visitors have their thoughts set on death, their immortal hostess is not to be seen. Similarly, on their return to her island, she does not appear until after Elpenor's body has been collected from her house and the funeral rites have been completed. Then, as she welcomes them back, she draws attention to their unique and paradoxical place in the human world: "'You unflinching wretches, you have gone down to the house of Hades alive. / You die twice, while other mortals die only once'" (*Odyssey* 12.21–22). The men enjoy one final day of feasting before they set sail on a voyage that will lead to the deaths of all but Odysseus, who himself has a near-death experience. When night falls, Circe leads Odysseus by the hand away from his companions. She lies beside him, and they spend their last night together deep in conversation. When dawn comes, Circe leaves and goes inland while Odysseus returns to his ship and calls his crew together, ready for departure. They row the ship out to sea. Circe is described for the last time as she sends them a favoring wind: "Circe with her beautiful hair, dread goddess with the power of speech" (*Odyssey* 12.150).

24. The morning after making love to Calypso, Odysseus dresses himself (*Odyssey* 5.228–29); here at *Odyssey* 10.542, after a night of talking, Circe dresses him.

In a number of ways the sequence of events that first brings Aeneas into Dido's life and subsequently leads to their parting resembles the experiences of Odysseus and Calypso. Aeneas almost drowns in a terrible storm brought upon him by divine anger. He comes ashore in an unknown land and is helped by a powerful but husbandless figure who lives close by. She is at once attracted to him and wants to make him her husband. For a time they become lovers, but Mercury intervenes with orders from Jupiter to Aeneas to ensure that he returns to the path he is destined to follow. However, the situation that leads to the parting in *Aeneid* 4 also differs profoundly from the circumstances in which Hermes passes on to Calypso Zeus's orders to release Odysseus. First, the relationship between Dido and Aeneas is shown from the start as an arena in which two divine forces are locked in a complex and far-reaching conflict. Venus fears that the Carthaginians cannot be trusted, and Juno's savage hostility makes her sleepless with worry. In Venus's eyes, Dido is a threat to the completion of her son's mission, and Juno and her plans stand behind the hospitality Dido offers. In this way, the queen becomes an enemy who must be overpowered (*Aeneid* 1.658–75). Lyne (1987, 18–20, 26) examines Venus's involvement in the sequence of events that lead to Dido's suicide and concludes, "Venus does not come well out of the Dido story" (26).

A second set of differences now comes into prominence. Calypso is a goddess, and her efforts to keep the mortal Odysseus with her and to make him her husband are blocked by a higher, divine authority. Thus the human male is allowed to resume his journey home to his wife, and the immortal sea-nymph returns to her own, solitary life. Dido by contrast is a woman, and the narrator goes to great lengths to arouse the reader's interest in her state of mind.[25] When Venus (in disguise) first speaks of Dido, she shows her as an innocent victim, widowed by the impious murder of her husband, Sychaeus, at the hands of her wicked brother, yet strong enough to take her followers overseas to find a new home, "a woman leading events" (*Aeneid* 1.340–68). When the shipwrecked Trojans who have been separated from their leader arrive on the coast of her new home, they are unjustifiably treated as enemies by the Carthaginians (*Aeneid* 1.524–29, 539–41), but in striking contrast to this, Dido herself is generous in her offer of help, holding out not just the offer of assistance for the next leg of the Trojans' journey but even a shared future for the two peoples (*Aeneid* 1.572–74).

---

25. Hardie (2014, 51–76) examines the complex characterization of Dido and her enduring appeal for later writers and artists. Dido, he notes, "is Virgil's most 'intertextual heroine'" (52).

As Dido and her Carthaginians extend their friendship and hospitality to Aeneas and his hard-pressed Trojans, Venus's fears recede for a time into the background, and the narrative explores in detail the queen's feelings. W. R. Johnson (1976, 38–45) gives a sensitive examination of the narrator's description of these feelings, with its carefully "blurred uncertainties." Venus's plan is now beginning to take effect (*Aeneid* 1.709–22), and it becomes clear that Dido is the victim of an ill-fated and destructive passion. Dido feels an equally strong compulsion to remain faithful to the memory of her dead husband, and "barely in her right mind," she confides in her sister, Anna, and explains the effect that this violent conflict is having on her (*Aeneid* 4.9–30). In part the description of Dido is colored by the Roman ideal that a bride's husband should be her only sexual partner and that there should be no question of a second marriage after her husband's death.[26] Her sympathetic sister offers Dido a strong combination of emotional and prudential arguments not to fight the love she feels. These arguments overcome Dido's scruples but still fail to bring her peace of mind (*Aeneid* 4.31–55). The importance in Dido's mental conflict of the idea of remarrying also makes a contrast with the nature of Calypso's relationship with Odysseus. Calypso herself longs to make Odysseus her husband (*Odyssey* 1.15; 5.119–20), but there is no suggestion of a wedding ritual taking place between goddess and man. Both Dido and Aeneas, by contrast, have already lost their first marriage partners, and the possibility that their relationship can in some sense be regarded as a marriage becomes the focus of far-reaching conflict.

Once Dido has become the victim of a frenzied passion (*Aeneid* 1.659–60; 4.65–73, 90–92, 101),[27] Juno and Venus are shown talking to each other (*Aeneid* 4.90–128). Feeney (1991, 129–35) analyzes the complex role of Juno in the *Aeneid*. In part she represents a world element, the upper air; in part her significance is allegorical since she represents the forces threatening the Trojans and their enterprise. Feeney uses the phrase "multivalent frustrating negativity" in this context. In part, she is shown in anthropomorphic form. Despite their natural antagonism, the two goddesses appear for the moment to find common ground in Juno's plan to arrange a wedding between Dido and Aeneas. Juno explains what she has in mind. The next day "Aeneas together

---

26. See Rudd (1990) for a discussion of this ideal. He also notes that in *Aeneid* 3 the three-times married Andromache "is treated with tenderness and respect" (159).

27. For a description of the destructive drive of love in the sense of sexual attraction throughout the whole of the animal kingdom, humans included, cf. *Georgics* 3.242–83.

with poor, wretched Dido" will go out hunting in the forest. A storm will begin
proceedings.[28] While all their companions run for shelter and are concealed
in darkness,

> "Dido and the Trojan leader will arrive at the same
> cave. I will be there and, if your wish is fixed with mine,
> I will join them in a lasting marriage and will name her his own.
> This shall be the wedding." Venus made no objection to her
>   request,
> she nodded and laughed to uncover the trick. (*Aeneid* 4.124–28)

A thunderstorm begins, bringing rain and hail. The hunters run for cover
as streams come rushing down the mountains. For a few, momentous lines
attention focuses now on the cave:

> Dido and the Trojan leader arrive at the same
> cave. First Earth and Juno, the matron of honor,
> give the sign. Fires shone out and the sky above was witness
> to their marriage, and on the mountain top the Nymphs shrieked.
> That was the first day of death, that first day was the cause
> of the troubles. For Dido is not moved by appearance or reputation,
> and she no longer keeps secret the love that occupies her thoughts.
> She calls it marriage and with this name she concealed her fault.
>   (*Aeneid* 4.165–72)

At *Odyssey* 5.194 and 225–27, "goddess and man reached the hollow cave,"
and after a meal and an earnest conversation, Calypso and Odysseus are
discreetly shown making love at night in the corner of the cave. In *Aeneid* 4,
after the emphasized arrival of woman and man at the same cave, neither
is shown to the reader. The love making in the cave, which the reader is left
to imagine, takes place while a storm temporarily turns daylight into the
darkness of night and while the public activity of the hunt, where the two
belong as joint leaders, is temporarily suspended. Calypso's cave home on a
remote island enjoys in its location all the beauties of nature and is warm
and welcoming (*Odyssey* 5.59–74), whereas the cave setting in *Aeneid* 4 is
a trackless, mountain upland where wild animals have their lairs (*Aeneid*
4.151–59). The supernatural marriage ritual recorded here, far from human

---

28. For the association already established between Juno and storms, cf. *Aeneid* 1.82–91, 279–80.

civilization, has a complex and ambiguous quality. In part it is something primitive and elemental in which Earth, Air, Fire, and Water are represented. At the same time, it is marked as ill omened. In place of a wedding hymn, "on the mountain top the Nymphs shrieked."[29] When Odysseus speaks to Nausicaa of marriage, he prays that she may have the unparalleled blessing of a harmonious married home and the good reputation it brings (*Odyssey* 6.180–85), but for Dido the consequences of this marriage ritual are the exact opposite: "That was the first day of death . . . the cause of the troubles." Gone now from her is any concern for how things look and what people will say.

The last line of this passage *(Aeneid* 4.172) subtly prepares the way for Aeneas's subsequent denial of having given any lasting commitment to Dido. When the narrator says, "She calls it marriage," the reader may feel the implication, "even though it was not marriage in the accepted sense of the word." This self-conscious focusing on the word "marriage" continues in the second half of the line, since it is "with this name" that Dido "concealed her fault." Such is the care with which the narrator empathizes with Dido at this point that he leaves it ambiguous whether the word "fault" is to be imagined as being applied to herself internally by Dido, as she has used it of herself earlier in conversation with Anna at line 19, or whether the narrator is taking responsibility for this value term and is setting it as a corrective to the word "marriage" in the first half of the line. Either way, the final image of the marriage ritual is that of guilty concealment on the part of Dido. Calypso (The Concealer) keeps Odysseus hidden away from human society and hides the divine instruction to release him. Dido's concealment takes place within the internal arena of her own mental conflict. Desire has triumphed first over duty and now over caution, and Dido's concealment of the sense that she is at fault takes the form of calling her newly changed relationship the marriage that her sister Anna urged upon her so persuasively, and which Aeneas' enemy, Juno, planned for her out in the wilds with the laughing compliance of Aeneas's mother, Venus.[30]

After this point, communication shifts to the male world. Rumor brings a toxic mix of fiction, distortion, and fact (*Aeneid* 4.188) to the ears of Dido's rejected, North African suitor. Outraged, he demands that Jupiter should see

---

29. For the "shrieking" of women's lamentation, cf. *Aeneid* 2.487–88; 4.667–68.

30. The evaluative word *culpa*, translated here as "fault," carries a wide range of ideas. These are examined by Rudd (1990). Central in the present context is the idea of responsibility for marital infidelity; cf. the description of Paris at *Aeneid* 2.602 as "the one people blamed."

what is going on and act. Jupiter sees the lovers, gives his orders to Mercury, and Mercury takes his message to Aeneas in Carthage (*Aeneid* 4.196–278). Now comes a radical reappraisal of the situation as the focus moves from Dido to Aeneas and his young son. Venus planned that Dido should come under the joint control of Aeneas and herself (*Aeneid* 1.675), but when Mercury sees him, Aeneas appears to be under Dido's control. Wearing Dido's gift of magnificent, Tyrian clothes, Aeneas is taking an active part in her building program. Mercury addresses him dismissively as "wife-server." Venus's plan to control Dido by arousing her desire took Aeneas's young son, Ascanius, as its starting point, but now both Jupiter and Mercury are agreed in viewing Ascanius as the heir-in-waiting for the glory to come in a Roman context, now unreasonably cheated of his hopes by his father's forgetfulness of his mission. Jupiter even speaks of Aeneas's lingering "amid a hostile nation" (*Aeneid* 4.235).

Once he has spoken, Mercury disappears into thin air. Aeneas is horror struck. He longs to run away, despite the pull of "the sweet land," and is in a quandary, as the narrator explains: "Alas! What is he to do? What words dare he now use to get round / the frenzied queen. How can he make a start?" (*Aeneid* 4.283–84). Some quick reviewing of possibilities suggests a twofold response to the changed situation. First, some male bonding and the issuing of orders: "He calls Mnestheus, Sergestus, and brave Serestus" (*Aeneid* 4.288). They are to prepare quietly for the fleet's departure and "disguise" the reason for this change of policy. Meanwhile his own confrontation with "the frenzied queen" can for the moment be postponed. This gives him time to think of her in a different way as "excellent Dido," who is unaware that their great love is being broken apart, and to test out ways of approaching her and so find the best time and manner of speaking to her. All Aeneas's companions are delighted to carry out his orders (*Aeneid* 4.289–95).[31]

Detailed attention is given by the narrator to the breaking of the relationship between Aeneas and Dido (*Aeneid* 4.296–396). When Hektor leaves Andromache and returns to the battlefield in *Iliad* 6, a clash can be felt to take place between two worlds defined in terms of gender. Here in *Aeneid* 4 a comparable clash occurs, but now the division between the genders is internalized into an exploration of different characteristics: the feminine passionate and wide-ranging emotion is set against the masculine suppression of emotion and concentration on the performance and justification of a divinely

---

31. For the mood of Aeneas's companions at this point, cf. *Odyssey* 10.472–74.

given duty. As in *Iliad* 6, the man leaves the woman on his own terms and with tragic consequences, but now it is not the man who dies a hero's death in battle, but the woman who takes her own life, and now their parting focuses on the conflicting views that each takes of the situation.

As the passage opens, the narrator asks "Who can deceive a lover?" (*Aeneid* 4.296). Dido is predisposed to feel fearful, even without good cause, and now she instinctively senses when she is about to be tricked. Rumor brings "to her frenzied mind" the news of the fleet's planned departure. Already Dido has been shown, in the intimacy of her sister's company, as "barely in her right mind" (*Aeneid* 4.8); now she is "out of her mind" and roams "in her inflamed state" all over the city. The simile likening her to a Bacchant, with its suggestion of the world of Greek Tragedy (*Aeneid* 4.300–303),[32] strengthens the image of her as a threat to the world of male order and ultimately a threat to male life and limb. Finally she confronts Aeneas, giving him no time to speak first (*Aeneid* 4.304). Two speeches from Dido frame and throw into sharp contrast one speech of Aeneas (*Aeneid* 4.305–30, 365–87, 333–61). Two-thirds of the passage (sixty-seven of the one hundred and a half lines) take the form of direct speech. Before this point, Aeneas has spoken without interruption about his earlier life. Now once again the reader can respond to the vividness of direct speech and consider the effect of its complex rhetoric, but now the setting is a bitterly adversarial context with the first and last words given to Dido rather than the comparative safety for Aeneas of an autobiographical, after-dinner speech. Feeney makes two general points in his detailed and wide-ranging discussion of these speeches. The first is that "Vergil consistently excludes from his poem the intimacy, companionship and shared suffering which Homer's men and women hold out to each other through speech" (1990, 181). The second is to endorse the view already expressed by Highet, who writes that "Vergil, it seems, held that powerful oratory was incompatible with pure truth, and that every speaker presented his or her case by misrepresenting the facts" (1972, 289).

Dido begins with a series of five, impassioned questions *(Aeneid* 4.305–14). After the increasing complexity of her thoughts shown in the first four of these questions, the last of them is phrased with great simplicity and directness: "'Is it me you flee from?'" (*Aeneid* 4.314). This possibility leads her to make a passionate plea to Aeneas to change his mind:

---

32. Bacchantes were female worshippers of the god Dionysus (Bacchus). They banded together and left the male control of their home life to roam the mountain wilds in a state of orgiastic frenzy. Cf. *Aeneid* 4.469–73 for a further association of Dido with Greek tragedy, this time with male characters.

"By these tears and by your right hand
(since I have nothing else left to me now in my misery),
by our wedding, by the start of our marriage,
if ever I have deserved your gratitude or if anything about me
has seemed sweet to you, have pity on my collapsing house and,
I beg you, if there is still a place for prayers, give up this idea."
     (*Aeneid* 4.314–19)

After making two statements that place full responsibility for her troubles on Aeneas (*Aeneid* 4.320–23), she reverts to agonized questions, a further three this time, as she imagines the future. These include a sad aside in which she notes that the name "guest" is now all that remains of "husband."[33] Finally she expresses a heartfelt longing for the impossible. At least if she had conceived a child before his flight from her, if "a dear little Aeneas"[34] could have played with her in the palace and reminded her, despite everything, of his father's features, she would not seem so utterly "captured and deserted" (*Aeneid* 4.323–29).

Once she has finished speaking, Aeneas's state of mind is succinctly shown to the reader before he speaks. He has been keeping his eyes on Jupiter's commands and has with a great effort been suppressing his emotion. "Finally he says a few things in reply" (*Aeneid* 4.333). He begins by side-stepping the emotional claims Dido makes on him. He acknowledges that the queen has much that she can say on the subject of the gratitude her actions have earned from him, and he assures her that as long as he lives he will not be sorry to remember her (*Aeneid* 4.333–36). The changed circumstances in which he says these words make an ironic contrast with his fulsome expressions of gratitude on the formal occasion of their first meeting (*Aeneid* 1.597–610). In the course of her speech, Dido has used both her own name and Aeneas's name in highly emotional contexts (*Aeneid* 4.308, 329). Aeneas now addresses her first as "queen" and then as "Elissa," a name that helps to distance her from the reader, who has not seen it used before.

Having made a start (*Aeneid* 4.333–36), he continues by echoing the narrator's introductory comment on his speech: "'On the matter let me say

---

33. Cf. *Aeneid* 4.10–11 for the excitement aroused in Dido's mind by her "new guest." To Nausicaa, by contrast, despite dreams of marriage, Odysseus is never more than a "stranger/guest"; cf. *Odyssey* 6.187; 8.461.

34. The Latin word *parvulus*, translated here as "dear little," is the only use of a diminutive in the *Aeneid*. For a moment it introduces a tenderly conversational tone into the speech's complex rhetoric. This is as close as Dido comes to the moment of relaxation in the tension between Hektor and Andromache that is brought to them by their baby son.

a few things'" (*Aeneid* 4.337). In fact, Aeneas's speech is by two lines the longest of the three speeches. In its construction it is the opposite of Dido's speech. Statements expressed in measured language now predominate, and the only question, which occurs in the middle of the speech, is cast in the form of an appeal to reason (*Aeneid* 4.347–50). His first point quickly dismisses the accusation made by Dido in her opening question. He tells her he had no intention of secretly stealing away. No room is given here to the initial element of disguise that Aeneas himself authorized for the Trojan change of plan (*Aeneid* 4.290–91). This rebuttal is immediately linked with a brief but forceful denial of the basis of Dido's emotional claim on him: "'nor did I ever hold out / the wedding torch as your husband or enter into this contract'" (*Aeneid* 4.338–39). This central point of dispute between the two is set out clearly by Feeney. He begins by noting that "Roman marriage was a matter of cohabitation and intent: any accompanying ceremonies had no legal status and were, strictly, irrelevant to the inception of the marriage" (1990, 167–68). On this basis, the indications of their shared life (*Aeneid* 4.260–67, including Mercury's dismissive description of Aeneas as "wife-server") may be felt sufficient to justify Dido "in regarding their liaison as a real marriage," or at least in "imagining that his intention involves marriage." On the other hand, individuals of status and importance, like Dido and Aeneas, "lived a public life in which such connections were formally marked and openly advertised," and no such public recognition of a marriage has taken place. Feeney concludes that the ambiguity does not center on the factual question of whether or not they are married but rather on "the characters' own interpretation" (168).[35]

At this point Aeneas too imagines if things had been different, but in his case this vision of a better but unattainable world widens the emotional distance between the two of them. If fate allowed him to manage his own life and to choose how to resolve his worries, then he would first devote himself to rebuilding the conquered city of Troy. But as it is, "great Italy" is his divinely given objective. "Italy" say the orders of Apollo and his Lycian oracles, and Aeneas is adamant: "'This is my love, this is my country'" (*Aeneid* 4.347). He now makes clear that life with Dido would not have been his first choice, and the appeal she has made to him in the name of "our love" collapses for her devastatingly in the face of the definition he now gives of "my love" (*Aeneid* 4.307–8, 347). After this, he makes two further points: Dido accuses him of

---

35. For the ways Dido subsequently talks about the "marriage," cf. *Aeneid* 4.431, 494–97, 550–52.

wickedness (*Aeneid* 4.306), but on the contrary, the search for a new home, a kingdom overseas, is both something Dido from her own experience should readily be able to sympathize with and something with the full force of a divine mandate (*Aeneid* 4.347–50).

After making these tightly linked points, Aeneas gives the justification for his action (*Aeneid* 4.351–59). In Aeneas's mind, the past and future male generations of his family join in rebuking him for the dereliction of his duty, and it is made absolutely clear to him that he is acting in obedience to the divine will. Now, however, unlike Creusa in the earlier crisis, the woman does not disappear passively into the night. Now she is of a different nationality, and now she puts up strong, emotional resistance. Aeneas's concluding message to her is succinct: "'Stop inflaming both me and yourself with your complaining. / I go after Italy not by my own will'" (*Aeneid* 4.360–61). The second, incomplete line at this point brings one of the *Aeneid*'s most eloquent moments, leaving the brief silence open for the reader's own thoughts to fill.

For a long time now Dido has had her back to Aeneas and has been rolling her eyes. She lets her gaze wander silently over him and addresses him in a blaze of emotion. Initially Aeneas worried about getting around "the frenzied queen," and now in her second speech, as she herself admits halfway through (*Aeneid* 4.376), she is carried away in a blazing frenzy of rage. Her first speech ends on a quiet note of sad longing; her second speech, by contrast, rises to a lengthy crescendo before she breaks off and abruptly leaves (*Aeneid* 4.381–89). She begins as before by calling Aeneas "traitor" (*Aeneid* 4.305, 366). This accusation is now embedded in a rhetorical denunciation of his coldheartedness. Once again there is a run of five questions, but each is now a rhetorical question, and the suggestion that she is thinking aloud is reinforced as she speaks of Aeneas in the third person in the middle three of these questions (*Aeneid* 4.365–71). These accumulated questions invite the reader to take the part of an imaginary audience and so to consider Dido's perception of Aeneas's refusal to engage with her emotionally.

The conclusion that Dido reaches is bleak and wide ranging. Neither mighty Juno nor Jupiter looks at these things with the eyes of justice: "'Nowhere is it safe to place your trust'" (*Aeneid* 4.373). At this point, embedded halfway through her speech, come two statements about herself and Aeneas (*Aeneid* 4.373–75). Now, however, these two statements cannot invite a charge of being one sided, since they relate deeds of kindness and generosity toward Aeneas and the Trojans, which the reader has seen Dido perform. Rather, they dismiss Aeneas's blanket acknowledgement of gratitude, with its renewed hint of hyperbole, and to the charge of coldheartedness they now add the further, telling charge of ingratitude. Aeneas's claims to be following divine orders she contemptuously rejects with a mixture of scorn and sarcasm, and now she loftily dismisses both Aeneas and his words (*Aeneid* 4.376–80). She expresses her fury in a seven-line tirade of rising emotional power. First she scornfully flings Aeneas's words back at him: "Go on then! Go after Italy on the winds, seek a kingdom through the waves!" (*Aeneid* 4.381). Then she paints a graphic picture of her hope of revenge: Aeneas will drown amid rocks while calling out the name "Dido," and she, even though distant, will hound him with fires. Her ghost will never leave him and the account of his punishment will reach her even in the Underworld (*Aeneid* 4.382–87). At this point Dido abruptly stops and departs, leaving Aeneas "delaying much through fear and preparing much to say" (*Aeneid* 4.390–91). After her departure, four lines concentrate the reader's attention once again on Aeneas's state of mind and quickly bring the passage to a close:

> But dutiful Aeneas, although wanting to soothe her pain
> with consolation and with his words to turn aside her cares,
> nevertheless with many a groan and a heart shaken by great love,
> followed the orders of the gods and went back to his fleet. (*Aeneid*
>   4.393–96)

It is the last time the two meet in life. Aeneas's subsequent meeting in the Underworld with the ghost of Dido is discussed in chapter 7.2.

Attention is drawn a number of times in this book to the self-consciously problematic nature of the *Aeneid*. This parting and Dido's subsequent suicide present the central, interpretative problem of its first half. This problem can be examined in two complementary ways. The first of these concerns the relationship between this sequence of events and the *Aeneid*'s grand narrative. Aeneas's separation from Dido is predetermined, not just within the *Aeneid* by Jupiter's unveiling to Venus of the destined role of Aeneas and his son in the construction of the future greatness of Rome (*Aeneid* 1.257–96), but also outside the *Aeneid*, by the sequence of historical events that have brought Rome and Carthage into bitter, protracted conflict and have ultimately led to the destruction of Carthage by Rome.[36] The reader is thus encouraged to see, within the *Aeneid*'s grand narrative, a close link between two different

---

36. Hardie (2014, 55) writes, "Carthage post-*Aeneid* 4 is the dangerous Other of Rome, as later still another North African kingdom, Cleopatra's Egypt, will be the enemy Other of Octavian's Rome."

forms of conflict: conflict between a woman and a man over the break-up of
their relationship, on the one hand, and war between two rival nations, on
the other. As the narrative of *Aeneid* 4 continues, this link is strengthened in
two further ways: first, by the words spoken to Aeneas by the dream figure of
Mercury, who urges instant flight in the face of danger from the enemy and
who ends by saying: "'Woman is something inconstant and forever changing'"
(*Aeneid* 4.569–70); and second, by the words Dido speaks at the end of her
soliloquy, shortly before she takes her own life, in which she calls with great
rhetorical power for a permanent state of war between the two nations (*Aeneid*
4.622–29). Since these two conflicts, one personal and the other national, are
so closely intertwined, each can be considered in terms of the other. Now the
distinction made along gender lines gains a new force. The foreign side in the
conflict between nations is doomed historically to lose. This side is typified
by the woman, and she in turn is typified by a set of characteristics that show
the passionate side of human nature, its changeable quality, and ultimately its
drive to self-destruction. The winning side in the conflict between nations is
the proto-Roman one. This side is typified by the *Aeneid*'s eponymous hero.
He in turn typifies a set of characteristics that show the triumph of duty over
emotion. Such, however, is the care with which the narrative is shaped that it
is also possible for the reader to question this construction, made along lines
of gender and race, and to reevaluate its constituent parts.

This reevaluation takes a different starting point, one that focuses on the
conflict between Aeneas and Dido in terms of a personal tragedy[37] rather than
in terms of national destinies and gender stereotypes. In this context, a further
examination can now be made of the range of significance given to certain
key words and ideas: love, marriage, trust, duty, and death. On either side of
this passage, Dido's love for Aeneas is shown as a destructive force. It is a trick
played on her by Venus to neutralize a potential enemy; it is a wound and it
burns her.[38] In her last words to Aeneas, Dido calls him "heartless brute"[39]
(*Aeneid* 4.386), and her undiminished love for him forces her to swallow her
pride and repeatedly to try tears and supplication. The narrator then uses
the same adjective to address Love in a brief aside: "'Relentless Love, is there

37. For this approach, see Hardie (1997b).

38. Cf. *Aeneid* 1.660, 673 (fire), 688 (fire and poison); 4.1–2 (wound and fire), 23, 54 (fire), 66–73 (fire,
wound, fire again, simile of the wounded deer).

39. The Latin word *improbus* is hard, if not impossible, to convey in one English word. R. G. Austin
(1955, 119–20) writes, "the basic sense of this adjective is persistent lack of regard for others in going beyond
the bounds of what is fair and right." Thus it includes the ideas "heartless" and "relentless."

nothing you do not force a human heart to do?'" (*Aeneid* 4.412). Yet when Dido has brought the confrontation to an end and Aeneas is left in a state of mental conflict, the narrator briefly but forcefully shows "a heart shaken by great love." As the word "love" is for once applied to Aeneas's feelings for Dido, who is now no longer present, it is stripped in part at least of its destructive associations in order to demonstrate the hard-won victory of duty over love.

Both Dido and Aeneas feel that their love makes them guilty of a betrayal, but here a crucial difference appears. Dido's sense of betraying her first love, the dead Sychaeus, is explored before she gives in to her desire for Aeneas. Aeneas's sense of betraying his duty is brought to him only after he has become Dido's lover. Any misgivings on his side about the affair are shown only retrospectively, after divine intervention has brought him a sudden moment of emotional crisis and an immediate change of course. Aeneas insists that he has taken no part in any marriage, nor does he acknowledge any fault on his side. Aeneas presents a strong case, and indeed the clipped, almost legalistic tone in which he opens his speech in reply to Dido—"'On the matter let me say a few things'"—helps color it as a defense speech in exactly these terms. Nevertheless, though his case may not be vulnerable in terms of law, it still raises a number of wider questions for the reader to consider.

The first of these questions concerns Juno and the wedding ritual. Juno emphatically expresses her intention that when Dido and Aeneas reach the cave, she will be present and will declare them man and wife: "'I will join them in a lasting marriage and will name her his own'" (*Aeneid* 4.126). The force of these words is strengthened by their previous use, when Juno promises a bride for Aeolus from among her Nymphs (*Aeneid* 1.73). Juno in her role as matron of honor does indeed officiate in the ritual, and the narrative of the ritual specifically includes the word "marriage": "the sky above was witness to their marriage" (*Aeneid* 4.167–68). In Venus's eyes, Juno may be playing a trick on Aeneas, just as Venus earlier plays a trick on Dido. But is the reader to set aside Juno's words as having no binding force? If so, this is something very different from the role Juno's words and actions are made to play elsewhere in the *Aeneid,* from beginning to end (*Aeneid* 1.23–52; 12.791–842). It may not be possible to call "the sky above" to appear as witness in a court of law, but are the carefully constructed, supernatural equivalences of the ritual of a Roman wedding ceremony similarly to be set aside? There is no suggestion that this ritual is going on only inside Dido's head. So, if it is not to be summarily dismissed, the reader is left to consider the significance of this divine intervention, despite the position Aeneas takes.

Then there are the wider questions of trust and duty. Venus is shown from the proto-Roman perspective as distrustful of the Carthaginians (*Aeneid* 1.661). Yet as seen through Dido's eyes, Aeneas is the one who has betrayed the trust placed in him (*Aeneid* 4.305, 366). Beyond stating categorically that he has not married her, Aeneas does not meet the charge of breach of trust. It seems then that the hard-won triumph of duty over love must also include the triumph of duty over another's trust. Here is a very big problem for the *Aeneid*'s reader to reflect on. Even duty itself cannot escape completely unquestioned. Aeneas is "dutiful," as the four-line description of him at the end of the encounter forcefully reminds the reader (cf. *Aeneid* 1.10, 220, 305, 378, 544–45). Devotion to duty places the individual in a special relationship with the divine (*Aeneid* 2.689–91). Prompted by gratitude to Dido for her help and generosity to his people, Aeneas says at their first meeting that he cannot thank her enough and continues:

> "May the gods give you a worthy reward, if any
> divine powers respect those who are dutiful,
> if there is any justice and a mind that knows what is right." (*Aeneid*
>   1.603–5)

Later, when she is prompted by the desire for revenge, Dido in her turn hopes that Aeneas will be rewarded for what he has done: "if the divine powers of duty have any strength" (*Aeneid* 4.382). Neither Aeneas's nor Dido's wish is fulfilled, and at the same time the terrible transformation shown to take place between both these appeals to "the divine powers of duty" comes about as a result of Aeneas's overriding devotion to his duty. Commentators are deeply divided here. R. G. Austin may be taken as representative of the mainstream, mid-twentieth-century, male view of Aeneas in *Aeneid* 4: "he has been true to himself, and done his duty at a dreadful cost; it is as if he has said, 'Get thee behind me, Satan'" (1955, 122). Perkell presents a view more likely to appeal to the modern reader when she notes that Aeneas's devotion to his sense of duty "is consonant with the loss of a female figure" (1981, 370). In her view, Aeneas is "irresponsible, even treacherous" toward Dido, and in his behavior he displays "an incomplete humanity." Oliensis gives new life to the issue of gender in this context by adopting a psychoanalytical reading of the *Aeneid*. She comes to a wide-ranging and controversial conclusion: "Virgil's epic regularly construes heterosexual desire as the enemy, never the support, of social order" (1997, 307). Here then a complex and disturbing paradox centers on the concept of duty in the *Aeneid*.

Lastly the reader is challenged to think about death. Here at once a gulf appears between Aeneas and Dido. Aeneas has himself escaped from a near-death experience, and Dido has some justification for her claim: "I brought your companions back from death" (*Aeneid* 4.375).[40] Aeneas does not speak of death in this context. Dido herself by contrast speaks repeatedly and with increasing emotional power of her own death (*Aeneid* 4.308, 323, 385–87), and once the encounter with Aeneas is over, the narrative of the remainder of *Aeneid* 4 is almost exclusively devoted to Dido and to her approaching suicide. Here then a final contrast can be drawn. The parting of Hektor and Andromache in *Iliad* 6 can be viewed both in an epic and in a tragic light. The parting of Aeneas and Dido, by contrast, suggests a pull between two different and, in part at least, competing readings: an epic reading and a tragic reading. While both readings can be accommodated, the slippage between the two is an important factor in creating the *Aeneid*'s complex and problematic nature.

---

40. Cf. *Aeneid* 1.522–29, 538–41, 561–64. For Calypso's angry reminder to Hermes that she saved Odysseus from death, cf. *Odyssey* 5.130–32.

7

Communicating with the Dead

7.1 ✒ Ghost Stories

Communication between the living and the dead—and among the dead themselves—greatly extends the scope of the *Odyssey*'s narrative. In the middle of his
account of his adventures since leaving Troy, Odysseus tells his Phaeacian audience how he both saw and talked with the ghosts of the dead. Odysseus's public
recall of this supernatural experience is told in two halves (*Odyssey* 11.51–332
and 385–640). Near the end of the *Odyssey*, the setting is once again transferred
from the world of the living to the world of the dead (*Odyssey* 24.1–204). Now the
reader can follow the progress of the ghosts of the dead suitors. Hermes leads
them to the Underworld, where they meet the ghosts of the great warriors of the
Trojan War. The ghosts of Achilleus and Agamemnon, with whom Odysseus
has already conversed in *Odyssey* 11, appear once more and now address one
another before the ghost of Agamemnon engages in conversation with one of the
newly dead suitors. He listens to the tale of events that have brought the suitors
to their untimely death, and the scene ends as the dead Agamemnon draws
an emotional contrast between the fortune of Odysseus and his faithful wife,
Penelope, and his own bitter fate of having been murdered by his wicked wife.[1]

As Odysseus's time with Circe comes to an end, she tells him that before
returning home he must make another journey—"into the house of Hades

---

1. In chapter 8.3, I discuss the long-standing doubts that have surrounded the conclusion of the *Odyssey*
from 23.297 to the end of Book 24.

and of dread Persephone" (*Odyssey* 10.491)—in order to consult the ghost of the blind Theban prophet, Teiresias. Odysseus and his crew sail until nightfall and reach an inhabited land at the limits of deep-flowing Ocean. This is a land of permanent darkness (*Odyssey* 11.1–19). They beach the ship and reach the place Circe has described. As instructed, Odysseus digs a trench in the ground with his sword. When the offerings and prayers to all the dead have been made, the dark blood from the slaughtered sheep pours into the trench. The ghosts of the dead come from below and gather around it. They include brides, unmarried young men, old men who have suffered much, tender young girls with fresh grief in their hearts, and many blood-stained warriors.[2] They roam in large numbers and in all directions around the ditch "with an eerie sound of wailing" (*Odyssey* 11.20–43). Reinhardt examines *Odyssey* 11, and of this first part of Odysseus's encounter he writes, "This turns out to be a meeting . . . with all of humanity that has gone before. . . . A concept of humanity seems to take shape only in the face of death" (1996, 117). Despite confessing that "pallid fear took hold of me," Odysseus does not lose his nerve. He tells his companions to sacrifice to the gods of the Underworld while he sits with drawn sword, keeping the insubstantial figures at a distance from the blood and waiting to learn from Teiresias (*Odyssey* 11.43–50).

Two ghosts, those of Elpenor and Antikleia, come before the ghost of Teiresias (*Odyssey* 11.51–89). The initial encounter with the ghost of Elpenor, the newly dead member of Odysseus's crew, creates a smooth transition between the record of events within the world of the living and the vast, timeless, and amorphous world of the dead. Since Odysseus has not yet had time to attend to Elpenor's funeral, here also is unfinished business for Odysseus to complete once his journey to Hades is over. Elpenor elicits the promise from Odysseus to cremate his body and to create a memorial to the part he played as a member of Odysseus's crew. The memorial is to take the form of a burial mound with his oar sticking out from the top of it. When a second ghost, the ghost of Odysseus's mother, Antikleia, appears, Odysseus grieves to see her but remembers Circe's instructions to keep the ghosts away from the blood until he has had time to learn from Teiresias about the completion of his homecoming (*Odyssey* 10.535–40).

Teiresias's ghost now comes and greets Odysseus. When Odysseus has stepped back and has put aside his sword so that the ghost can drink the blood and speak "infallible truths," he addresses Odysseus at length (*Odyssey* 11.98–137).

---

2. For a comparable division of the dead into various categories in the *Aeneid*, cf. *Aeneid* 6.305–8.

The words of the blind prophet demonstrate that even in death he has indeed, as Circe explained to Odysseus, retained "a mind to engage in thought" (*Odyssey* 10.493–95). He first tells Odysseus that a god will make the journey home a painful one, since he does not think Odysseus will escape from Poseidon's anger for the blinding of his dear son (the Cyclops, Polyphemos). Next Teiresias focuses on a specific time that is still to come for Odysseus and his companions, a time when their future will depend on their response to the situation that has arisen. If Odysseus can restrain himself and his companions on their arrival at the island of Thrinakie and leave the cattle and flocks of the Sun god unharmed, then despite their sufferings, they might still reach Ithaca. But if he harms them in any way, then Teiresias predicts destruction for Odysseus's ship and his companions. If Odysseus himself manages to escape, Teiresias tells him:

> "You will make a late and wretched return, having lost all your
>   companions,
> on someone else's ship, and in your home you will find miseries,
> arrogant men eating up your life's wealth,
> courting your godlike wife and offering her wedding gifts.
> But, once you return, you will pay them back for their violent
>   ways." (*Odyssey* 11.114–18)

Teiresias's ghost now looks further into the future, to more travel that Odysseus will undertake after the completion of the events narrated in the *Odyssey*, to the ritual he will perform in honor of Poseidon and all the immortal gods, to a return home and ultimately to a peaceful death in old age, surrounded by people enjoying prosperity (*Odyssey* 11.119–37). This final section of his prophecy is discussed in chapter 8.3.

Teiresias's speech plays a complex part in the unfolding narrative. In life the Theban prophet belonged to an earlier generation and to a homeland that, already before the Trojan War, had its own, separate stories of warfare and heroes alluded to from time to time in the *Iliad*.[3] Odysseus's meeting with the ghost of the blind prophet from this different and earlier epic world helps widen the context within which the narrative of the Odyssey unfolds. When he has been summoned up from the past, the ghost of Teiresias speaks to Odysseus, and in doing so, he gives the reader the big picture of Odysseus's place both within and beyond the narrative that bears his name and whose outline has first been sketched in its introduction (*Odyssey* 1.1–21). This big

3. Cf. *Iliad* 4.376–400; 5.801–8; 6.222–23; 10.284–90; 14.323–24; 19.96–99; 23.679–80.

picture is carefully embedded in the middle of the *Odyssey* and contributes to its intricate development. The words of Teiresias's ghost operate across the confines of time. They look toward the past and toward the future within the past as events unfold within Odysseus's own account of his adventures. The prophet's words look also outside that retrospective account and into the present, the future, and the future beyond the end of the narrative. This big picture is not cluttered with any further, specific detail about what still lies in the future, within the context of Odysseus's account of his past experiences. It is Circe who has enabled Odysseus to consult the dead Teiresias about his journey home, and it is from her that he subsequently learns how to respond to the further, supernatural dangers that lie ahead on the next leg of his journey (Odyssey 10.490–95, 535–40; 12.21–141). Odysseus acknowledges Teiresias's ability to reveal the threads of destiny spun by the gods, and he directs Teiresias's attention toward the ghost of his dead mother. When Teiresias has explained how contact can be made with her, he leaves, and when Odysseus's mother has come and has drunk some blood, she recognizes her son. With a cry of grief, she begins to speak to him (*Odyssey* 11.139–54).

As he looks back to this emotional reunion, Odysseus recalls two separate moments. The first moment comes when he recognizes his mother's ghost and sadly realizes that she has died since he left home for Troy (*Odyssey* 11.84–87). The second moment occurs when he subsequently enables her to recognize him. This allows him to focus separately on the sadness of the two of them, the living and the dead, before they engage in an extended dialogue (*Odyssey* 11.155–224). Odysseus's long absence from home and his mother's death during this time away leave both with pressing questions to ask. In her answer to her son's questions about his family, Antikleia supplements the big picture already given by Teiresias and focuses on Penelope's devotion to her long-absent husband:

> "Indeed she remains steadfast in her heart,
> inside the palace that belongs to you. Her days and nights
> waste away in tears of constant grief." (*Odyssey* 11.181–83)

Antikleia is like Teiresias in that both speak from the timeless world of the dead, but she is not gifted with the power to see into the future. Thus, in terms of strict chronology, the picture recorded by Odysseus that she gives of life in his home in Ithaca looks back to a time before his seven years of captivity on Calypso's island and before the arrival in the palace of Penelope's suitors.[4]

4. For the chronology of these events, cf. *Odyssey* 7.259; 2.89; 19.152–53.

The picture Antikleia gives of the other members of his family, his son and his old father, shows their dependence on Odysseus. As for Antikleia herself, whose cause of death was Odysseus's first concern, she could not endure the loss of her son, with all his gentle ways, but died of a broken heart.

Antikleia's words trouble Odysseus deeply, and he wants to take hold of the ghost of his dead mother:

> Three times I started forward and my heart told me to take hold of
>   her,
> and three times she flew from my hands, like a shadow
> or a dream. (*Odyssey* 11.206–8)[5]

Odysseus has been told by Circe that, with the exception of Teiresias, the ghosts of the dead are indeed no more than "darting shadows," but the emotional intensity of his encounter with his mother's ghost leads to this natural, wordless expression of human affection. His frustrated efforts to make physical contact with her add to his grief, and he addresses her "in winged words":

> "Why do you not wait for me, mother, when I long to take hold of
>   you,
> so that even in the house of Hades we may throw loving arms
> around one another and enjoy the bitterness of tears?
> What are you, a phantom that revered Persephone
> has sent, so that I may cry with yet more grief?"
>   (*Odyssey* 11.210–14)

Antikleia's reply combines tenderness toward her son for his suffering and a calmly expressed explanation of the gulf between the dead and the living (*Odyssey* 11.220–22). She ends by telling Odysseus to make all haste for the light, and to keep the knowledge of all that she has said, so that later he can tell his wife (*Odyssey* 11.223–24).

At line 225 Odysseus brings his account of his dialogue with his mother's ghost to an end, and he continues:

>   and the women
> came, for revered Persephone sent them,
> those who were the wives or daughters of the best of men.
>   (*Odyssey* 11.225–27)

---

5. Cf. *Aeneid* 2.792–94, repeated at 6.700–702.

In recording this experience (*Odyssey* 11.235–330), Odysseus names fourteen women. This list provides another example of the power of naming, since the names of the women whom Odysseus sees stand at the start of their entry in the list and act as headings for a series of miniature narratives. The first of these narratives opens with indirect speech attributed to the woman in the story, Tyro (*Odyssey* 11.235–36), but after this starting point, Odysseus himself takes over the role of narrator of her story, even enlivening his account by recording, in direct speech, the words spoken to her by the disguised figure of her divine lover, Poseidon, after he has made love to her (*Odyssey* 11.248–52). For most of the time after this, Odysseus's control of the various, comparatively short narratives is complete: he identifies the next woman whom he sees and tells his audience her story.[6]

Taken together, these accounts of distinguished women of the past have an effect that is similar to that of his meeting with the ghost of Teiresias. They help tie together various strands within the narrative of the *Odyssey* and widen the context within which it unfolds. The meeting with the ghost of his mother and the concern expressed about his wife shift the focus from the male to the female gender, and this prolonged change of focus may be felt to play a part in eliciting the enthusiastic response from Queen Arete (*Odyssey* 11.336–41). In the wider context, the stories add detail and variety to the background against which the narrative concerning Odysseus's own wife unfolds, while she remains out of the narrator's immediate focus, back home in Ithaca. The place names that occur in the course of these accounts evoke different regions within an identifiable, outside world: Thessaly, Messenia, Boeotia, Attica, Crete, and one of its offshore islands. This has two, complementary effects. On the one hand, it creates a sense of a familiar world that contrasts both with the distant land of Scherie and its Phaeacian inhabitants (*Odyssey* 6.8) and also with this part of Odysseus's own story, where he communicates with the world of the dead. On the other hand, it also creates a sense of geographical diversity[7] and so contributes to the range of people and places experienced in one form or another by Odysseus in the course of his long journey home.

6. This carefully controlled slippage from one overarching narrative to a series of comparatively small-scale narratives enclosed within it can be compared with the shift from the narrative of Hephaistos's creation of the scenes on Achilleus's shield to the narrative of the activities shown in those scenes at *Iliad* 18.490–606, discussed in chapter 2.3 of this volume.

7. In this sense, though on a more restricted scale, it can be compared with the list of Achaean fighting forces at *Iliad* 2.494–760.

As he tells of the genealogies of these women, the tone Odysseus adopts is neutral and free from disapproval. However, this neutrality disappears with the last entry: "and I saw hateful Eriphyle, / who accepted precious gold as the price for her dear husband's life" (*Odyssey* 11.326–27). This helps prepare the ground for the manner in which he later resumes his story. When Alkinöos asks whether Odysseus saw any of his companions who died at Troy, Odysseus speaks of even more pitiable sufferings, those of his comrades who escaped death at Troy only to die on their return home "through the will of a wicked woman" (*Odyssey* 11.384). This horrifying example of a woman's wickedness dominates the first encounter, with the ghost of Agamemnon, which Odysseus now recalls (*Odyssey* 11.385–466).

Persephone scatters the ghosts of the women and there comes on the scene the grieving ghost of Agamemnon. Just as in life he is seen surrounded by his followers, so now in death he is surrounded by the ghosts of those killed with him in Aegisthos's palace. As soon as the ghost drinks the blood, he recognizes Odysseus.[8] He utters a piercing wail and begins to cry, and now it is the turn of the ghost to try in vain to stretch out his hands to make contact with the living (*Odyssey* 11.385–94). Odysseus too begins to cry in pity at this sight. He asks Agamemnon how he met his death, and Agamemnon replies at length, describing in gruesome detail what happened (*Odyssey* 11.405–34). Agamemnon brings his speech to an end by assessing the effect of his wife's wickedness:

"By the outstanding wickedness in her mind,
she has brought disgrace both on herself and on future
    generations
of women, even on the one who acts well." (*Odyssey* 11.432–34)

Odysseus is sympathetic, and while not endorsing this blanket gender stereotyping, he sees "the designs of women" as the means chosen by Zeus to demonstrate his deep-seated hatred for the house of Atreus (*Odyssey* 11.438–39).

The narrative of events surrounding the homecoming of Agamemnon interrelates throughout the *Odyssey* with the narrative of Odysseus's own homecoming, both giving it shape and developing significance (*Odyssey* 1.28–47; 3.193–98; 4.512–37; 24.191–202). Here in the center of the *Odyssey*, as Agamemnon's thoughts turn to Odysseus and his wife, these thoughts sway

---

8. In the *Iliad*, Odysseus's relationship with Agamemnon is close, though at times stormy; cf. *Iliad* 4.329–63; 14.82–105. In the *Odyssey*, cf. *Odyssey* 3.162–64.

between advice to Odysseus not to be too trustful and open with Penelope about his plans, and happy memories of "prudent Penelope" and her little boy, left behind when the men went off to war (*Odyssey* 11.441–51). Odysseus has already recalled the reassurance about his wife brought to him by the ghost of his mother. Now, at the end of a harrowing account of his own murder, the ghost of his former commander-in-chief cautions Odysseus to return home in secret since "women are no longer to be trusted" (*Odyssey* 11.454–56). Here is a tension that will be resolved only at the end of the *Odyssey*. In the meantime, Agamemnon's ghost asks Odysseus for news of his son, Orestes, but Odysseus cannot tell him whether his son is alive or dead, and so the encounter draws to an end as the two exchange bleak words and weep together (*Odyssey* 11.457–61).

The ghosts of four more of Odysseus's companions from the Trojan War now arrive. "Achilleus, the son of Peleus" is the first to be named. With him are Patroklos, Antilochos, and Aias. The ghost of "swift-footed" Achilleus recognizes Odysseus and sadly addresses him "in winged words":

> "Offspring of Zeus, son of Laertes, Odysseus of many devices,
> Does nothing stop you? Whatever greater feat can you plan than
>   this?
> How have you endured to descend to Hades, where senseless
> corpses dwell, the phantoms of men who have died?" (*Odyssey*
>   11.473–76).

The tone of these words is complex: part banter, part irritation, part grudging admiration, and part sad acknowledgment of the gulf between the living and the dead. In his reply Odysseus first explains the reason for his visit and then attempts to draw a contrast between his own never-ending troubles and the unique good fortune of Achilleus, both in life, where the honor in which he was held put him on a par with the gods, and now in death, where he has great power among the dead. With these thoughts in mind, he concludes: "So do not agonize, Achilleus, over your death" (*Odyssey* 11.486).

Achilleus begins his reply with a powerful rejection of Odysseus's words:

> "Do not console me for my death, glorious Odysseus.
> I would rather be a hired laborer for another man,
> a man with no land or wealth of his own,
> than be lord of all the corpses of the dead." (*Odyssey* 11.488–91)

Nicolson discusses this famous encounter, focusing attention on the adjective "glorious," which the ghost of Achilleus uses in addressing Odysseus. He notes that the word conveys the sense of "shining" or "brilliance" and that while it is commonly applied to heroes, in this context it has a particular resonance. "As the dead Achilles speaks, it is the world of lightlessness addressing the world of light . . . the shining world from which Odysseus comes and from which Achilles is forever excluded" (2014, 125). This exclusion also has a special resonance in the case of Achilleus. As he hurtles toward Hektor to meet him in combat, Achilleus is "all-shining like a star, as he rushed over the plain" (*Iliad* 22.26), and this powerful simile is extended for a further six lines (*Iliad* 22.27–32). Richardson writes, "Priam sees Akhilleus shining in his armour like the Dog-Star, whose destructive character is described" (1993, 108). Achilleus asks whether Odysseus has any news of his son and of his father, Peleus. Odysseus has no news of Peleus but is able to give Achilleus a detailed, first-hand account of his son's glowing war record in the later stages of the Trojan War.[9] The ghost of Achilleus strides away "across the meadow of asphodel," rejoicing to hear of his son's fame (*Odyssey* 11.504–40).

Odysseus's encounter with the ghost of Agamemnon evokes the horrors of a violent, unheroic death. His meeting with the ghost of Achilleus, who died a hero's death on the battlefield, focuses not on the moment of death but on the state of being dead. An ironic contrast can be drawn here between Achilleus in life and Achilleus in death. Deprived of his honor, the living Achilleus can see no difference between dying a coward and dying a hero (*Iliad* 9.318–20). And at this point, when considering his two possible fates, he chooses long life rather than eternal glory (*Iliad* 9.406–19). Later, the moral imperative to gain revenge for the killing of Patroklos reverses that decision, and he can embrace his own forthcoming death as something logically to be wished for (*Iliad* 18.98–99). Now, with all the pathos of an unfulfillable wish, the dead Achilleus would rather choose once again his first fate and be alive at all costs, even if that life was the most humble and meagre imaginable. There is a further irony here since the reader of Homer in the modern world may feel that Achilleus's desire to be remembered is satisfied as much by his revisionism in the *Odyssey* as it is by his traditional role of short-lived epic hero in the *Iliad*. In this retrospective change of outlook there can also be sensed part of the *Odyssey*'s big picture. On the unexpected insistence of Achilleus's ghost, life itself, however lowly, is rated better than death with honor. Thus, by implication, the fate of the hero of the

9. For a different picture of the part played by Neoptolemus (Pyrrhus) in the sack of Troy, including his impious killing of Priam, cf. *Aeneid* 2.469–553.

Odyssey, who repeatedly faces violent death but each time somehow survives, is better than the fate of his dead, albeit famous, comrade, the hero of the *Iliad.*

Odysseus's third and final encounter with one of his dead comrades is with Aias, son of Telamon, the second best fighter after Achilleus (*Odyssey* 11.469–70, 550–51; *Iliad* 2.768–69). Death has not put an end to Aias's anger toward Odysseus, whose victory in successfully pleading his case to receive the arms of Achilleus over Aias himself led to the latter's suicide. Odysseus records the speech he makes in an unsuccessful attempt to pacify Aias's anger and make him come and listen (*Odyssey* 11.553–62). His speech is compassionate and regretful in its tone. Aias makes no reply and moves away to join the rest of the ghosts of the dead in Erebos. Odysseus's encounter with death here takes on a third form: the agonizing involvement of the living in a death by suicide. Odysseus does not persist in his attempts at communication with Aias since he is keen to see the ghosts "of the other dead."

The remainder of his account (*Odyssey* 11.566–640) takes the form of a list of six male figures. The first five of these Odysseus sees engaged in various activities. King Minos, the judge in the world of the dead, and the giant hunter, Orion, are described briefly. More details are given of the punishment that the next three figures, Tityos, Tantalos, and Sisyphos, are made to pay for their crimes. Here the proper names, standing at the head of each of the entries in this short list, introduce not a miniature narrative of events in a lifetime, but rather a specific scene of activity within the underworld. His account of the last figure, the mighty Herakles, is given in more detail (*Odyssey* 11.601–27), and on this occasion, the ghost sees Odysseus and addresses him. The phantom Herakles is surrounded by the dead, from whom there rises a confused din, like the sound of birds scattering in alarm. A tiny simile also opens the description of Herakles: "he is like black night." He holds his bow poised ready to shoot and casts terrifying glances around, but the object that most catches Odysseus's attention is the terrible, golden strap that he wears as a baldric across his chest and that wonderfully depicts fierce animals, fighting and battles, bloodshed, and killings. Herakles recognizes Odysseus and sadly addresses him. Odysseus, it seems, has to endure the same wretched fate that Herakles endured in life. The hardest of Herakles' labors was to be sent to Hades "to fetch a dog" (*Odyssey* 11.623–24), which he did successfully with the aid of Hermes and Athene.[10] With these words, the ghost goes back into the house of Hades.

---

10. Cf. *Iliad* 8.362–69. The dog's name "Cerberus" does not appear in Homer. For a vivid description of Cerberus, cf. *Aeneid* 6.417–25.

The encounter with Herakles helps bring closure to Odysseus's account of his communication with the ghosts of the dead. Even more than Teiresias, Herakles is marked out as a great hero of an earlier generation,[11] and his words show that in being sent to Hades in the course of his lifetime, Odysseus follows in the footsteps of a famous predecessor, Herakles, the son of Zeus. Even if Herakles himself is not among the dead but is now with the immortals, his phantom can bring Odysseus some sense of shared experience.[12] When the phantom Herakles returns inside the house of Hades, Odysseus waits for a time. His thoughts turn to other dead figures from the past, but now he is overwhelmed by the countless numbers of the dead who gather around with their unearthly sound. "Pallid fear" takes hold of him once again (*Odyssey* 11.633) as he worries that Persephone will send up the monstrous gorgon's head from Hades. So he hurries back to his ship. Thus the whole experience is quickly brought to an end, with no loss of tension, and Odysseus and his companions begin their return journey to Circe's island.

As *Odyssey* 24 opens, Hermes summons the souls of the suitors. They follow him, squeaking like bats flying around in the depth of a cave. Now the narrator focuses briefly on a new aspect of death: the journey to the Underworld (*Odyssey* 24.9–13). When they reach the meadow of asphodel, which is the dwelling place of the ghosts of the dead, they find the ghosts of Achilleus, Patroklos, Aias, and Antilochos together in a group, and the grieving ghost of Agamemnon comes close, surrounded by those who were killed with him. The ghost of Achilleus is the first to speak and addresses Agamemnon. Then Agamemnon's ghost addresses Achilleus in return and speaks at length (*Odyssey* 11.24–34, 36–97). This creates an unusual form of communication, in the second person and somewhere between narrative and dialogue. As ghosts, the two figures bear no rancor towards one another, but each looks back and speaks movingly of the other's death. The ghost of Achilleus contrasts Agamemnon's reputation in life as the leader of the Achaean forces at Troy and the wretched, untimely fate that was waiting to befall him (*Odyssey* 24.32–34). Agamemnon's ghost replies by addressing Achilleus with these words: "Blessed son of Peleus, godlike Achilleus, / who

11. Cf. *Iliad* 5.638–42 and 14.249–51 for a previous sacking of Troy by Herakles. As Hercules, the great hero from an earlier age, he also plays an important part in the *Aeneid*, as noted in chapter 2.1 of this volume.

12. In the *Iliad* Herakles is mortal (*Iliad* 18.117–19). The oddly double, posthumous existence that Herakles is given in *Odyssey* 11.602–4—as phantom in the Underworld but as "himself" among the immortal gods—has raised a long-standing suspicion about the authenticity of these three lines.

died at Troy, far from Argos" (*Odyssey* 24.36–37), and he gives a detailed account of the battle over his body, the magnificence of Achilleus's funeral rites and the display of grief both by his divine mother and her fellow sea-nymphs and by the Danaans (*Odyssey* 24.37–92). He continues:

> "for you were dearly loved by the gods.
> So even in death you have not lost your name, but for ever more
> among all mankind the fame of your greatness will live on, Achil-
> leus." (*Odyssey* 24.92–94)

He concludes by bitterly contrasting his own fate: to have come through the war only to find that Zeus had devised a wretched death for him on his return home at the hands of Aegisthos and his own, accursed wife (*Odyssey* 24.95–97).

As they are talking to one another in this way, Hermes approaches, leading the ghosts of the suitors. The two ghosts move quickly toward them in surprise, and Agamemnon's ghost recognizes Amphimedon and asks how they died. In reply Amphimedon gives a lengthy account of the circumstances that have led to their death (*Odyssey* 24.121–90). He concludes by telling Agamemnon that their loved ones do not yet know of the killings and that the suitors' bodies lie uncared for in Odysseus's palace.[13] Agamemnon does not reply to him but instead addresses the living Odysseus: "Blessed son of Laertes, Odysseus of many devices, / then you did indeed win a wife of great virtue" (*Odyssey* 24.192–93), and he eulogizes Penelope for the good sense she has shown in the faithful memory of her husband, Odysseus. The fame of her virtue will never die, but the gods will make for mortals "a pleasing song" in honor of "prudent Penelope." His own wicked wife, on the other hand, killed her husband. Hers will be "a hateful song" for people to hear, and she will bring a bad reputation on the female sex, even on those who act well (*Odyssey* 24.194–202, cf. 11.432–34).

These two hundred lines contribute in a complex way to a gathering sense of closure. Unlike the *Iliad* and the *Aeneid,* the *Odyssey* does not end with a death. Instead the reader is twice shown the world of the dead, once in the middle of the *Odyssey* and once as its last book begins. In each case the narrative then returns to the world of the living. The presence of the ghosts of the four warriors and of their leader helps link these two passages, but now

---

13. The ghosts of the suitors enter the Underworld, even though their bodies still lie unburied. In the *Iliad* (*Iliad* 23.71–74) and the *Aeneid* (*Aeneid* 6.373–75), by contrast, the dead cannot enter the Underworld if they have not been buried.

there is no internal audience. And whereas on the earlier occasion the ghosts of Agamemnon and Achilleus speak to the living Odysseus independently of one another, now they address each other. This helps create a sense of togetherness in death, something that in life was for the most part markedly absent (*Iliad* 1–19). Agamemnon's speech offers the reader a different viewpoint from the bleak rejection of posthumous honor made by the ghost of Achilleus himself in conversation with the living Odysseus. The last image of Achilleus, presented to him by the ghost of his one-time personal enemy, Agamemnon, is a consoling one: it is of the son of a goddess, "dearly loved by the gods," the subject of widespread, undying fame, and now there is no trauma of Aias, caused indirectly by Achilleus' death, to cast a cloud over this bright picture. Here then is something approaching closure for the pervasive part played by the Trojan War and its aftermath in the background of the *Odyssey*.

In their different and complementary ways, the two scenes in the world of the dead can now be seen as helping to tie together the *Odyssey*'s wide-ranging narrative. Now as the *Odyssey* nears its end, one of the dead suitors looks back and gives a representative account of events in the palace at Ithaca, as seen and interpreted by them. These events, over which the reader is long held in a state of suspense, are thus foretold in outline from within the world of the dead, narrated as happening within the world of the living, and finally revisited from within the world of the dead. Halfway through the *Odyssey*, the place of Penelope within the unfolding sequence of events at Ithaca has been shown to the reader but has not yet been made unambiguously clear to her husband. The terrible experiences recorded by the ghost of Agamemnon at the hands of his wicked wife color his outlook on women as a sex, and Penelope herself does not escape this. By *Odyssey* 23.300–43, however, Odysseus and Penelope have been reunited and have had time to regain each other's trust and to tell each other about their experiences during their long period of separation. Now, near the start of *Odyssey* 24, Penelope is the subject of glowing praise from the ghost of Agamemnon and is set in opposition to Agamemnon's own wife. First, Agamemnon's ghost addresses the dead Achilleus as "blessed" and speaks of his undying fame. Now he speaks to the living Odysseus and addresses him as "blessed," having won a wife of great virtue, "prudent Penelope," whose fame will never die. The context of Achilleus's undying fame is clear from the *Iliad*, and Agamemnon's ghost adds a pendant to that narrative: the glowing account of the honors shown to Achilleus at his death. Within the context of the *Odyssey*, Penelope wins undying fame, and both she and her antithesis, Agamemnon's wife, are accorded by Agamemnon's ghost their place in "song."

Communication with the dead begins in the *Odyssey* with the living in contact with the dead, recommences as the dead make contact with each other, and ends here as the dead Agamemnon speaks out to the living Odysseus.

7.2 ⚹ Messages from the Dead, Messages to the Dead

In the first half of the *Aeneid,* as in *Odyssey* 10 and 11, communication between the living and the dead takes place within the context of a long and hazardous journey. But in contrast to the *Odyssey*, such communication in the *Aeneid* is a recurring feature within the narrative rather than an isolated experience. Throughout the whole sequence, messages imparted from the dead to the living direct the path of the living toward a better future. Such communication reaches a climax in the culmination of Aeneas's journey through the Underworld and in his reunion with the spirit of his father, Anchises. Here the world of the dead is shown to be systematically involved with the world of the living and of those whose lives are still to come.

Twice within his account of his experiences on the night when Troy fell, Aeneas tells how he was ordered by the ghosts of the dead to leave the city. This message is reinforced by the final words of Venus, spoken to Aeneas in between these two encounters with the dead (*Aeneid* 2.268–97, 771–95, 619–20). When all are gently falling asleep, Hector appears to Aeneas in a nightmare. He is in tears and appears as he was when tied to the back of Achilles' chariot and dragged through the dust. As he recalls this vision, Aeneas exclaims on the terrible transformation of Hector from the figure who returns dressed in the spoils of Achilles or when he has cast fire on the Danaan ships.[14] In his nightmare Aeneas is also crying and is the first to speak. The ghost makes no reply to his string of uncomprehending questions but, groaning deeply, tells Aeneas to escape: "Alas! Escape, son of the goddess," he says. "Snatch yourself away from these flames. / The enemy holds the walls. From its high rooftops Troy is falling" (*Aeneid* 2.289–90). The ghost assures Aeneas in his dream that enough has been given to Troy and Priam, and that, if anyone, it was Hector himself who could have succeeded in defending the city. Troy, he tells Aeneas, entrusts its sacred household gods to his care (*Aeneid* 2.291–96).

Later, as Aeneas returns into the devastated city to search for his wife, Creusa appears before his eyes in the form of a greater-than-life-size phantom.

---

14. For the details of this dream, cf. *Iliad* 22.395–405; 17.183–214; 16.112–24.

Aeneas records his shock at this sight, but the ghost speaks words of comfort and reassurance, addressing him with the words "O sweet husband." It is, she tells him, all part of a divine plan. The ruler of the gods does not permit him to take Creusa from Troy as his companion, and her phantom gives Aeneas a clear prophecy of his future and shows that "happiness" is awaiting him at journey's end:

> "Long exile lies before you and you must plough the vast surface of
>   the sea,
> and you will come to the land of Hesperia, where the Lydian
>   Tiber[15]
> flows with gentle current through rich, cultivated fields.
> There happiness is in store for you, and a kingdom
> and a royal bride. Dispel the tears for your beloved Creusa."
>   (*Aeneid* 2.780–84)

Drawing attention to the ironic gap between prophecy and outcome, O'Hara writes, "She promises what will not yet be seen by the end of the poem . . . and makes no mention of wars that will have to be fought" (1990, 89). The ghost of Creusa accepts her fate (*Aeneid* 2.785–88). As she bids farewell, she tells Aeneas to maintain his love for their son (*Aeneid* 2.789). Then she disappears into thin air, leaving Aeneas in tears and with much that he wants to say. Aeneas recalls his frustrated attempts to take hold of her in three lines that the narrator later applies to Aeneas when he tries to embrace the spirit of his father, Anchises:

> Three times there I tried to put my arms around her neck.
> Three times the phantom eluded my grasp,
> as light as the winds, the very likeness of fleeting sleep. (*Aeneid*
>   2.792–94, repeated at *Aeneid* 6.700–702)[16]

Finally, when the night passes, Aeneas returns to his companions (*Aeneid* 2.795).

In these two encounters, the dead bring their message to the living in complementary ways. Both occur during the night, but the first of them, with the male figure, comes to the mind of the sleeping Aeneas. In Aeneas's recall

---

15. For Lydia as the traditional origin of the Etruscans, through whose land the Tiber flows, cf. *Aeneid* 8.479–80.

16. Jenkyns (1998, 402–9) gives a sensitive analysis of this scene.

of his sleeping state at the time, there is a subtle disconnection between this figure and Hector's recent, violent death and mutilation. Aeneas's dream is pervaded by the sense that Hector has been missing, but this absence appears as a delay in his long-awaited return rather than as the permanent absence caused by death. The ghost of Hector alerts the sleeping figure to the pressing danger from the outside world, and it justifies him in escaping rather than staying to fight in defense of his city. He gives the sleeping Aeneas a sacred mission, and this all-important event within the dream is described both in the words spoken by the dream-figure (*Aeneid* 2.293–95) and in Aeneas's account of seeing Hector's ghost bringing out "mighty Vesta," her "sacred head-bands" and her "eternal fire" (*Aeneid* 2.296–97).[17]

The second encounter, with the female figure, takes place while Aeneas is awake and on the move. Her calmly authoritative voice offers consolation to resolve Aeneas's emotional turmoil, directs his thoughts toward his own future rather than to the horrors of the past, and helps bring him an element of closure. By contrast, Hector's earlier message urging Aeneas to go against his instinct to fight rather than flee meets with considerable initial resistance (*Aeneid* 2.336–38, 431–34, 655, 668–70). The two messages can also be compared in terms of their imagined reception by the principal member of Aeneas's internal audience, Dido. Venus tells Aeneas of the dead Sychaeus's dream message to Dido urging her to escape (*Aeneid* 1.353–59), and Aeneas now tells Dido of a similar message spoken to him in a dream by the dead Hector. This suggests a shared experience in Dido's and Aeneas's past. On the other hand, a sense of emotional distance between them is reestablished when the phantom of Aeneas's dead wife directs his thoughts toward the future and speaks of his finding happiness, a kingdom, and a royal bride "there" (in Italy). These are words that both Aeneas and Dido may be imagined to have forgotten or overlooked, with tragic consequences, when they briefly became lovers.

At the start of Aeneas's account of his wanderings with his followers, he tells of a further, nightmarish experience (*Aeneid* 3.13–59). The Trojans have come first of all to Thrace, an ally of Troy before its fall (*Iliad* 2.844–45), but Aeneas's attempt to build a settlement here for his people is ill-fated. Aeneas is engaged in a preliminary religious ritual to secure the approval of his mother, Venus, and of the other gods. He tries to pull some tangled branches from a myrtle bush to lay on the altar, but blood appears on the ground and from the

---

17. For the close association between the household gods and Vesta, goddess of the hearth, cf. *Aeneid* 5.743–45.

bark of the bush. He prays to the local divinities for help, but when he pulls at the shoots with greater force, pitiful groaning can be heard, and a voice addresses Aeneas by name, telling him not to contaminate his hands but to leave the buried alone. The speaker, he tells Aeneas, was a fellow Trojan, and the flowing blood is his. He continues:

> "Alas! Escape from this cruel land, this greedy shore.
> For I am Polydorus. Here an iron crop of weapons struck me down
> and covered me and it has grown with its sharp spears." (*Aeneid*
>   3.44–46)

Aeneas explains the background to these events. When Troy came under siege, Priam sent his son, Polydorus, with a quantity of gold to be looked after by the Thracian king. But when Troy fell, the king chose to follow the winning side, killed Polydorus, and seized the gold.[18] When Aeneas seeks advice from his father and selected leaders of his people, the decision is unanimous: to leave the wicked land, where ties of friendship and hospitality were polluted, and to renew with solemn ritual the funeral rites for Polydorus before leaving (*Aeneid* 3.58–68).

This daytime encounter with the dead younger brother of Hector is even more horrific than the nightmare appearance of Hector himself. Now the boundaries between the living and the dead and between the human world and the world of vegetation are collapsed. The volley of spears that killed the victim has metamorphosed into the spearlike shoots of myrtle. Any attempt to remove them reveals the blood from his fatal wounds. Aeneas and his followers are still close to the horrors of the sack of their city and of its aftermath. Thrace, a former friend, is contaminated by this wicked murder, prompted by expediency and greed (a murder that once again chimes in with Dido's own experience). Now as they travel without a secure sense of direction, Aeneas and his followers are about to encounter horrors of a new form, heralded by this supernatural encounter with the world of the dead. Once again they must escape, but before they leave, they must renew their efforts to bury the dead past. The dead Polydorus calls from the ground to Aeneas, and Aeneas and his followers perform funeral rites for him and answer with the loud, final call once his spirit has been committed to its grave.

Toward the end of *Aeneid* 5, Aeneas faces another crisis. Aeneas and his followers have returned to Sicily, where Anchises died. Aeneas has performed

---

18. Cf. *Iliad* 20.407–18, where Polydoros, the youngest and much-loved son of Priam, is killed by Achilleus.

rites at his father's tomb, has addressed his "hallowed father," and has celebrated funeral games together with the friendly local Sicilians to mark the anniversary of his father's death (*Aeneid* 5.42–603). But a sudden change of fortune comes after the relaxation of tension and the sense of wellbeing generated within the games. Under Juno's influence, the women set fire to the ships, destroying a number of them (*Aeneid* 5.604–99). Aeneas is deeply worried by this fresh disaster and is unsure what to do. His old priest of Athena advises him, but as night falls, he is still a prey to anxiety. At this point, he has a vision of his father, Anchises, descending from the sky to speak to him (*Aeneid* 5.721–42). Anchises' first words to his son are full of love, sympathy, and reassurance. He has come on the command of Jupiter, who has put out the fire and who has at last felt pity for Aeneas. His son should follow the advice he has been given and take a select band of brave young men to Italy. Anchises continues:

> "In Latium you must conquer in war
> a people hard and rough in its ways. First, however, approach
> the underworld home of Dis, and over the depths of Avernus
> seek to meet me, my son." (*Aeneid* 5.730–33)

Anchises explains that he is now in Elysium and that the Sibyl will bring Aeneas there so that he may learn about his descendants and about his destined new home (*Aeneid* 5.737–38). Night is passing, and the figure vanishes like smoke.[19] Aeneas tries repeatedly to ask more questions, and he longs to embrace his father. As he speaks, he turns his attention to performing the correct, religious ritual (*Aeneid* 5.741–45).

Aeneas's experience of communication with the world of the dead in *Aeneid* 6 differs in various ways from that of Odysseus.[20] Aeneas hears of this forthcoming experience in a nighttime vision of his dead father, and it is at once made clear to him that the purpose of this journey into the Underworld is to meet his father once again. In both these ways, the experience is made more intimate than in the case of Odysseus. In the *Odyssey*, Odysseus and his crew travel to the edge of the world for Odysseus to summon the ghosts of the dead before returning to continue their homeward journey. In *Aeneid* 6, the experience of the world of the dead does not interrupt a journey. Rather, it marks its climax. The physical journey from the ruins of Troy to the shore of

---

19. Cf. *Iliad* 23.100–101.

20. Gransden (2004, 71–79) gives a concise introduction to the world of the dead in *Aeneid* 6. For further discussion, see Solmsen (1990).

the new home promised by fate is now completed, but before renewed fighting to secure that home takes place, the Trojan leader must set out on his own metaphysical journey. Odysseus, alone, conjures up the ghosts of the dead and has glimpses of scenes in the Underworld. Aeneas's whole experience of the Underworld takes the form of a journey, and just as he had a companion in his travels across the world, "faithful Achates," so now he has a spiritual companion and guide, the Sibyl, to lead him on his way through other worlds. Also, since the whole experience is conceived as a journey, the various encounters with the dead can be marked off from one another as stages along the way, and despite the emotions these encounters produce, the travelers are able to move on.

A further difference between the two experiences concerns how they are presented to the reader. As part of the account of his adventures, Odysseus tells his internal audience of Phaeacians of his communication with the dead. In doing this, he both answers Alkinöos's curiosity (*Odyssey* 8.572–76) and presents himself, for the most part, in a flattering light. In *Aeneid* 6, the role of the first person singular pronoun is given instead to the narrator:

> You gods who have command of the ghosts, you silent shades,
> and Chaos and Phlegethon, places stretching far and wide in the
> silence of the night,
> may it be granted me to speak what has been heard, and with your
> divine power
> to throw wide things plunged in darkness deep in the earth.
>   (*Aeneid* 6.264–67)

This multiple invocation to the gods of the Underworld, its inhabitants, its boundless empty space, and its river comes between the moment when Aeneas fearlessly follows the Sibyl into the open cave and the description of their journey through a shadow-land (*Aeneid* 6.262–63, 268–72). It differs from the invocations to the Muses discussed in chapter 1.1 in that it is a request for permission to speak rather than an appeal for help or a request that the Muses themselves should sing. It does, however, contain one feature that also occurs in the invocations to the Muses at *Aeneid* 7.641 and 10.163. This is the idea of "throwing wide," but in the present context this idea carries the sense of the revelation of arcane secrets. Hardie writes, "The epic Underworld, which stores the shades of all those who have ever lived, is a kind of time-free repository for memory and tradition" (2014, 25).

Before he meets the spirit of Anchises, Aeneas has three encounters with the dead in which some form of communication or attempted communication takes place. These meetings with his former helmsman Palinurus, Dido, and Deiphobus (*Aeneid* 6.337–83, 450–76, 494–547) take him back progressively through his past life. All have died violent deaths and all are introduced by name rather than as ghosts of their former lives, so that the communication between the living and the dead is given a sense of immediacy. As Hardie notes, it is possible to regard this series of encounters "as a psychotherapeutic working through of past trauma" before Aeneas "arrives finally at his own biological origin in the person of his father Anchises" (2014, 24). The account of the death of Palinurus brings *Aeneid* 5 to an end (*Aeneid* 5.833–71). Palinurus's fate suggests comparison with that of Elpenor: both fall to their deaths shortly before a journey to the Underworld; both are the first to speak from the world of the dead; and both are given a funeral mound and a means of being remembered after their deaths. Elpenor, however, is drunk when he falls to his death from a rooftop, whereas the dead Palinurus speaks of his selfless fears for those who might suffer from his falling asleep on duty and its tragic consequences (*Aeneid* 6.351–54). The death of Elpenor helps frame the journey to and from the Underworld, but the death of Palinurus is given a fuller part than this to play within the developing narrative. Here is a tragic story of an accidental near-drowning caused by the god of Sleep, and subsequently of a violent death, just when the longed-for new life is within the victim's grasp. It tells of a dutiful friend of Aeneas and how he becomes the victim of the greed and violence of a cruel people who wrongly think that, when he finally manages to swim ashore, he will have treasure to steal and who later make amends for their crime. Above all, it illustrates the intransigence of the divine order of life and death. Palinurus has not received burial, and so the ferryman Charon will not take him across the river of the Underworld. His heartfelt pleas to Aeneas are interrupted by the Sibyl and meet with a categorical rejection by her (*Aeneid* 6.362–76). Here also is a story that demonstrates another aspect of the power of naming. It explains the derivation of a place name in the geographical world of Italy, outside the immediate world of the text. When he hears from the Sibyl that the place where a funeral mound will be built and honor paid to him will forever be known by the name of Palinurus, just for a moment the pain in his heart is eased and he rejoices "in the land named after him" (*Aeneid* 6.377–83).[21]

---

21. Heinze (1993, 375–77) notes the *Aeneid*'s interest in the etymology of place names and comments, "Virgil was writing with a view to catching the interest . . . of the whole of Italy" (376).

On the other side of the river Styx, Aeneas and the Sibyl find the dead grouped together in categories: those who died in infancy, those falsely sentenced to death, those who died at their own hands, and those inhabiting the so-called "Mourning Plains," an area not far from where the suicides gather and stretching out in all directions (*Aeneid* 6.440–41). While Odysseus sees the ghosts of women who belong to noble families (*Odyssey* 11.227), those who inhabit the "Mourning Plains" are women whose unhappy love has led them to profound suffering that continues beyond death. A powerful image suggests the isolation of their suffering: they are hidden away on remote paths and covered in the midst of a forest of myrtle trees (*Aeneid* 6.442–44). Before Dido is mentioned, Aeneas sees five women from the world of Greek mythology, and they are accompanied by two further figures, one a woman, the other a transsexual. These figures exemplify women in whose lives love has been something abnormal, tragic, or guilt-laden, and so they create a complex and mixed association of ideas as a background before attention is focused on Dido: "Amongst them Phoenician Dido, fresh from her wound, / was wandering in a great forest" (*Aeneid* 6.450–51). At the moment when the "Trojan hero" stands beside her and recognizes her dark figure through the shadows, she is described in a powerful simile: "like the new moon at the start of the month, / which a man sees, or thinks that he has seen, rising through the clouds" (*Aeneid* 6.453–54). W. R. Johnson selects this simile as the epitome of Virgil's "mastery of this kind of controlled imprecision" (1976, 83) and analyses with great sensitivity what it might suggest about Aeneas's complex state of mind.

Aeneas sheds tears and speaks to her "with gentle love":

"Unhappy Dido, then was the message that came to me
true, that you had died, that you had put an end to your life with a
    sword?
Alas! Have I been the cause of your death?" (*Aeneid* 6.456–58)

Aeneas swears a great oath that he left her shores "unwillingly," under compulsion from the gods, just as now he is compelled by them to make this journey through the Underworld (Aeneid 6.458–63). He continues:

"nor could I believe
that my leaving you could bring you such great pain.
Do not go. Do not withdraw from my sight.
Who is it that you flee from? This is the last time fate grants me to
    speak to you." (*Aeneid* 6.463–66)

The look on Dido's face is one of wild rage as Aeneas tries tearfully to soothe her with these words. She keeps her back turned on him and her eyes fixed on the ground. As he starts to speak, her features are as hard as rock. Finally, she darts away from him and, "as his enemy," takes refuge in the shadowy grove, where her former husband, Sychaeus, responds to her sorrows and matches her love. Aeneas is deeply moved by the injustice of her fate, and he follows after her with his tears, pitying her as she goes (*Aeneid* 6.467–76).

Aeneas's meeting with the dead Dido is deeply embedded in the unfolding narrative of the first half of the *Aeneid,* and in this sense it differs from Odysseus's encounter with the ghost of Aias. Thus, although the meeting is the shortest of the three that precede Aeneas's reunion with his dead father, it carries the greatest emotional power. Here a distinction can be drawn between the first reactions of Odysseus on meeting the ghost of Aias and of Aeneas on meeting the ghost of Dido. Odysseus's first thought is the wish to go back and undo the past (*Odyssey* 11.548–51), whereas Aeneas asks a question: "then was the message that came to me true, that you had died?" This is a question that the reader may feel unnecessary or even inept. As Aeneas sails away from Carthage, he sees the walls of the city lit up by flames, which the narrator explains come from the burning of Dido's body. The cause of these flames is unclear to the Trojans, but they know what "a woman in a frenzy" is capable of doing when "a great love has been desecrated," and this fills their hearts with gloomy forebodings (*Aeneid* 5.1–7). The pressing question whether Aeneas can be held responsible for Dido's death is first posed and then answered by Aeneas himself. Despite the sadness he records in asking it, the situation is in some sense easier for Aeneas now that Dido is dead. The complexity of the moral issues raised during their separation is now reduced by the form Aeneas's response to his own question takes, and he is now the sole speaker.

Aeneas's attempt to reach out emotionally to the ghost of Dido is made clear throughout the description of their encounter (*Aeneid* 6.455, 467–68, 475–76), but his assurance to her that he could not believe that he was hurting her so much by leaving her raises a number of questions for the reader to consider. Is this deafness to Dido's anguish in their parting scene convenient self-deception on Aeneas's part, amounting to emotional cowardice? Is there perhaps a hint of remorse as he now confronts his own determination not to become emotionally engaged in her suffering? Can his much vaunted dutifulness accommodate such insensitivity (whether acknowledged or not) to the feelings of his former lover? Is there a universal issue here concerning the relationship between the two sexes? Dido's silence leaves these difficult questions hanging in the air. However, it is clear that she suddenly moves away from Aeneas when she hears these words (*Aeneid* 6.465), and this wordless response is enough to show the reader her reaction. Aeneas's last question, "Who is it that you flee from?" suggests a comparison with Dido's earlier question, "Is it me you flee from?" (*Aeneid* 4.314). While Dido's question seeks an answer, however painful, Aeneas's question may seem to the reader little more than a rhetorical flourish as part of his policy of self-defense, and his final words to her, "This is the last time fate grants me to speak to you," suggest that verbal explanation on his part is all that he considers required for a reconciliation. Commentators are divided in their response to this scene. R. Jenkyns (1998, 449) is uncharacteristically dismissive. Of Aeneas he writes that he is "left looking obscurely undignified: on some level this woman has got the better of him." Lyne, expressing a qualified sympathy for Aeneas, writes that "Aeneas therefore admits to a miscalculation at Carthage, a misjudgment of Dido's emotion . . . his departure could have been handled otherwise and perhaps better" (1987, 174). Eliot goes deeper still and writes of the scene that "it not only tells us about the attitude of Dido—what is still more important is what it tells us about the attitude of Aeneas. Dido's behaviour appears almost as a projection of Aeneas' own conscience" (1945, 20–21).

The further question of how far Aeneas's encounter with the ghost of Dido brings a sense of closure also remains unanswered. Now that Dido is dead, Aeneas's tears flow. He can address her in the Underworld "with gentle love" and can feel deeply moved by "her unjust fate." Gone is the vexed issue of a remarriage since Sychaeus is there for her, offering her in death his love and understanding. Aeneas has said what he could to soothe the dead Dido, and his attempt at achieving a posthumous reconciliation with her has been rebuffed by her. During their parting scene, Dido accuses him of being pitiless (*Aeneid* 4.365–70); now the final image is of Aeneas pitying her ghost as she goes from him. However, this comfortable sense of closure is undermined in a number of ways. Just as Dido dominated the scene of their separation with her two passionate speeches, now in death she dominates the scene with her silence and her wordless response. Throughout the encounter, the question subtly suggested is "how much has the tragedy of Dido's death cost Aeneas in emotional terms?" Nor does the scene dispel the charge that, from Dido's viewpoint, Aeneas is guilty at the very least both of betraying her trust and of displaying gross ingratitude (*Aeneid* 4.305–6, 366, 373–76). Finally, as Dido's ghost darts away from Aeneas, she is his "enemy," and this may remind the reader of the power with which, at the end of her life, she expressed her hatred of Aeneas and his descendants and of her call for revenge and undying hostility between the two nations (*Aeneid* 4.381–87, 584–629).

No such problems surround Aeneas's parting from the ghost of Deiphobus. When the Sibyl sternly interrupts their conversation, Deiphobus assures her that he is ready to return into the darkness and addresses a brief and rousing valediction to Aeneas: "Go forth, great glory of our people; enjoy a better fate!" (*Aeneid* 6.546), and so the journey through the Underworld continues. Following the instruction of the Sibyl, Aeneas purifies himself and places his holy gift, the Golden Bough, in front of a gateway.[22] With this ritual completed, Aeneas and the Sibyl enter Elysium. The Sibyl addresses "the blessed spirits" and in particular the towering figure of Musaeus, asking for help to find Anchises. Guided by Musaeus, they reach a hilltop and look down onto a shining plain. Deep in a green valley, father Anchises is engaged in reviewing the souls of his descendants and examining their fortunes and achievements. The Sibyl and Aeneas leave the high ground (*Aeneid* 6.628–78).

As he sees Aeneas coming toward him over the grass, "father Anchises" reaches out eager arms, and the tears flow down his cheeks as he addresses his son:

> "Have you come at last and has your sense of duty, expected of you
>   by your father,
> overcome the hard journey? Is it granted that I should see your
>   face,
> my son, and that we should hear and return the familiar voices?"
>   (*Aeneid* 6.687–89)

Despite the lack of fixity in Elysium (*Aeneid* 6.673), Anchises still has a sense of time and space. His calculation of the time of his son's coming has proved correct, and he exclaims on the distance that Aeneas has traveled to meet him and the dangers that have beset his son (*Aeneid* 6.690–93). One danger in particular he singles out: "How afraid I was that somehow the royal power of Libya would harm you!" (*Aeneid* 6.694). Aeneas replies to his father, before trying unsuccessfully to take hold of him and embrace him:

> "It was the image of you, father, your sad image,
> which kept coming to me and which drove me to reach this
>   threshold.

---

22. West (1990) examines the significance of the Golden Bough.

The fleet stands in Etruscan waters. Give me your hand, father,
give me your hand and do not withdraw from my embrace."
(*Aeneid* 6.695–98)

As he speaks, the tears roll down his face, but he is no more able to touch the
spirit of Anchises than he was able to touch the phantom of Creusa.

Aeneas receives an emotional welcome and a glowing acknowledgment
of his "sense of duty" from his father. Once again, as in Aeneas's encounter
with Dido's ghost (*Aeneid* 6.456–58), the first words to be spoken are two
tearful questions, but now these self-answering questions bring important
information to light, rather than hinting at other questions left hanging in the
air. Aeneas's ability to "overcome the hard journey" is a moral victory for him,
and his father had confidence that his son would succeed. Nevertheless, one
concern on his son's behalf has caused Anchises anxiety, and as he expresses
this anxiety, the process of redefining Aeneas's experience with Dido is completed. Seen through the eyes of Anchises in Elysium, Dido is not Aeneas's
victim but a worrying, potential source of harm to him. However, though
Anchises can hold out his hands eagerly to welcome his son, and father and
son can hear and return the old, familiar voices, he cannot give Aeneas the
emotional reassurance of physical contact. Feeney writes of Aeneas, "He moves
in solitude through a world which yields him no intimacy or comfort" (1990,
183). Anchises' tears of welcome (*Aeneid* 6.686) are now met with Aeneas's
tears of grief from the pain of thwarted physical contact, something he has
already experienced with the phantom of his wife and with his divine mother
(*Aeneid* 2.792–94; 1.408–9). When Odysseus has a similar experience with the
ghost of his mother, Antikleia, she responds to his anguish by explaining to
him that the cohesion of the physical body is destroyed by the fire of cremation,
but that the spirit flutters away like a dream (*Odyssey* 11.204–22). In *Aeneid*
6, the distinction between physical body and intangible spirit becomes the
centerpiece of a wide-ranging lecture from Anchises on reincarnation, the
universal life-spirit, the purification of the soul after death, and the life of
pure spirit in Elysium, attainable only by a select few (*Aeneid* 6.724–51).[23]

These ideas also provide a theoretical framework for the central tenet of
the *Aeneid*'s grand narrative, namely, that Troy is reborn as the imperial power
of Rome. They also prepare the way for Anchises' second and longer speech,

---

23. R. G. Austin (1977, 220) writes, "The passage is a poetic synthesis, blending the Stoic doctrine of
the *anima mundi* (world spirit) with Platonic and Orphic-Pythagorean teaching of rebirth."

in which he shows Aeneas and the Sibyl great figures from Rome's coming history (*Aeneid* 6.756–886). After kindling in his son a love of "the coming glory," Anchises tells him about the war he must fight, about the people of Laurentum and the city of their king Latinus, and he explains how to respond to the individual challenges he will face (*Aeneid* 6.886–92). Hardie gives a sense of the broad sweep of the journey through the Underworld. This journey first passes through a landscape of traditional mythology, with a series of Homeric-style encounters. The journey then comes to the age of philosophy in the Elysian fields as "Anchises delivers . . . a piece of philosophical didactic poetry, 'On the Nature of the Soul and the Nature of the World'" (2014, 24). The second and longer part of Anchises' speech moves the journey finally to the world of historical epic, which Virgil gives in the form of prophecy. This part of his speech is discussed in chapter 8.3.

Nine lines mark the return from Elysium and bring *Aeneid* 6 to a close:

> There are twin gates of Sleep, one of which is said to be of horn,
> and here true shades are granted an easy exit.
> The other is a shining gate, completed in gleaming ivory,
> but the Spirits of the Dead send false dreams up to the heavens.
> There it was that Anchises followed after his son and the Sibyl
> with these words, and sent them out through the ivory gate.
> Aeneas cuts his way to the ships and returns to his companions.
> Then he makes in a straight line for the harbor of Caieta.
> They throw the anchor from the prow; the ships stand on the
>   shoreline. (*Aeneid* 6.893–901)

Here right at the center of the *Aeneid* is a hard problem. The return from Elysium to the world of the living through one of the "twin gates of Sleep" raises two connected questions. In the first place, how does the introduction of "Sleep" at the moment of transition between the supernatural world and the everyday world bear on this journey, and in particular on the words of caution spoken to Aeneas by the Sibyl about the problem of returning (*Aeneid* 6.125–36)? In the second place, what is the significance of the choice of the second of the "twin gates of Sleep," where "false dreams" are sent "up to the heavens"?

Sleep and dreams are associated in a number of ways with death in the three poems. In the *Iliad*, Sleep and Death are twin brothers (*Iliad* 16.672), and at one point in the narrative a slain warrior is described with the words "he slept the sleep of bronze" (*Iliad* 11.241). In the *Odyssey*, both Odysseus and Penelope experience on occasion a deep, peaceful, death-like sleep (*Odyssey* 13.79–80; 18.199–205). Antikleia's soul flies from her son's attempt to embrace her "like a shadow or a dream," and on their journey to Hades, the souls of the suitors are led by Hermes past "the land of dreams" (*Odyssey* 11.206–8; 24.12–13). In the *Aeneid,* among the abstractions that Aeneas and the Sibyl pass in the entrance hall of Death is "Sleep, the brother of Death"; in the middle stands a tree, and it is said that "empty dreams" cling beneath its leaves (*Aeneid* 6.278, 282–84). When Charon challenges the armed figure of Aeneas to explain why he has come to the River Styx, he says: "This is a place of shadows, of sleep and of night and its slumber" (*Aeneid* 6.390). In the present context, at the end of *Aeneid* 6, a further association of ideas may be imagined. The description of Elysium as a place where "the plains are clothed in a richer air and in dazzling light," where its inhabitants have no fixed dwelling place but live in a beautiful countryside with the river Lethe flowing gently by, and where as-yet-unborn souls awaiting reincarnation flutter and hum like bees in a summer meadow (*Aeneid* 6.640–41, 673–75, 703–9) suggests a vision seen in the everyday world only as a dreamscape. Sleep and dreams thus provide in various ways an intermediate territory, somewhere between the land of the living, the land of the dead, and the blessed eternity of Elysium. Although the part played by Sleep at the end of their journey comes as a surprise, it provides a means of returning the travelers from their supernatural journey. The narrative tension is thereby preserved, a rich association of ideas is added, and a break is suggested between their experiences on that journey and those that follow their return to the everyday world.[24]

There remains the problem of the "twin gates of Sleep." This phrase and the association given to the two gates suggest comparison with a passage in *Odyssey* 19. There Penelope tells Odysseus, who is still unrecognized by her, of a vivid dream and asks him to interpret it. Odysseus confirms the interpretation already given to her within her dream, but Penelope remains unsure and tells him that dreams are hard to understand and do not always come true. She continues with these words:

"For there are two gates for fleeting dreams.
One is made of horn and the other of ivory.
Those dreams that come through the carved ivory gate

---

24. In a similar though less complex manner, Odysseus sleeps as the Phaeacian sailors bring him back from their world to his own land of Ithaca; cf. *Odyssey* 13.79–92.

deceive the dreamer, bringing words that do not come true,
but those that come out through the gate of polished horn
find true fulfilment, when the dreamer recognizes them." (*Odyssey*
    19.562–67)

Penelope still feels that her dream did not come from this second gate, the
gate "made of horn," much as it would please her and her son if it had done.
The distinction made here between two kinds of dreams is relatively straightforward,[25] though Penelope's response shows that in practice the distinction
may be less clear-cut for the dreamer. The distinction between "true shades"
and "false dreams" is much more difficult to understand, and the distinction
itself is made harder by the description of the gates, not as two, but as "twin
gates." In their journey through the Underworld, the two living figures of
Aeneas and the Sibyl are able to communicate with the spirits of the dead.
When they reach Elysium and listen to the words of Anchises, his account
of reincarnation, the purification of the spirit, and the life of pure and fiery
spirit attainable by a select few more systematically dissolves the distinction
between life and death. However, this blurring of the distinction is itself
challenged at the end of his speech by the extended lamentation for the young
Marcellus's premature death, foretold by Anchises. A different distinction, this
time between truth and falsity in the context of dreams and their significance
within the waking world, is hinted at by the description of the "twin gates
of Sleep." The blending together of these two separate distinctions, each of
which has been shown to be less than secure in itself, and the application of
this hybrid distinction to gates that are themselves twins of each other create
an insoluble puzzle.

As the narrator faces here the difficult task of bringing Aeneas and the
Sibyl back from their travels through eternity into the everyday world, he
himself adopts the form of communication that he has given to the Sibyl,
"wrapping the truth in obscurity" (*Aeneid* 6.100). It is possible for the reader to
respond in the following way: just as it is "easy" to descend to the Underworld
since people die all the time, so it is "easy" for "true shades" to come out of
one of the "twin gates of Sleep" (*Aeneid* 6.126, 893–94) since people dream
about the dead. But the other twin gate—the one that in its creation displays

---

25. For some examples of dreams that "find true fulfilment," cf. Dido's dream of Sychaeus and Aeneas's
dream of Hector (*Aeneid* 1.353–59; 2.289–97). For a dream "bringing words that do not come true," cf. the
destructive dream sent by Zeus to deceive Agamemnon, at *Iliad* 2.3–41.

the shining perfection of art and is the one through which Anchises sends Aeneas and the Sibyl back into the world after unfolding to them the *Aeneid*'s central message about Rome and Augustus—is also the one through which the "Spirits of the Dead" send "false dreams." Here, with the lightest of touches, the reader is offered the possibility of deconstructing the *Aeneid*'s grand narrative.[26] This opportunity is set right at the center of the *Aeneid* and is enclosed in mystery. For just as one mystery surrounds the entry of Aeneas and the Sibyl through the doorway into Elysium—the mystery of the ritual offering of the Golden Bough (*Aeneid* 6.136–48, 187–211, 628–39)—so another mystery surrounds the brief account of their departure and return home. And just as the Sibyl's songs of fate are thrown into perpetual disorder when the door of her cave is blown open (*Aeneid* 3.447–52), so the significance of the words spoken by Anchises in Elysium to Aeneas and the Sibyl is thrown into uncertainty when the gate is opened for them to return to the everyday world.

7.3 ⚔ Achilleus and the Dead Patroklos

Patroklos, the son of Menoitios, first appears near the start of the *Iliad*. After his public quarrel with Agamemnon, Achilleus returns to his tents and his ships, and Patroklos and his companions go with him (*Iliad* 1.306–7). A little later, it is Patroklos whom Achilleus asks to hand Briseïs over to Agamemnon's heralds, who have come to take her away (*Iliad* 1.337–38, 345–47). Two-thirds of the way through the *Iliad*, Achilleus allows Patroklos to impersonate him by donning his armor and leading the Myrmidon forces into battle against the Trojans. The ploy, suggested to Patroklos by Nestor (*Iliad* 11.796–804), is meant to bring much-needed relief to the exhausted Achaean forces (*Iliad* 16.38–45, 64–65). With careful instructions from Achilleus, Patroklos thus enters the battlefield, where he ultimately meets his death (*Iliad* 16.855–57). Between *Iliad* 1 and *Iliad* 16 a detailed and subtle picture emerges of the friendship between the two men, and this relationship, once Patroklos is dead, plays a central part in the remaining third of the *Iliad*.

At *Iliad* 18.231–38, the Achaeans finally retrieve Patroklos's body from the mêlée of battle. They place the body on a bier, and his dear companions

---

26. Outside the world of the *Aeneid*, cf. *Georgics* 2.493–98: among the distractions that do not divert the fortunate countryman, with his knowledge of the rural gods, are "the affairs of Rome and kingdoms destined to pass away."

stand around it grieving. Achilleus follows them, weeping as he sees the mangled remains of his "trusty companion," whom he sent out to war but was never to see return. There follows a night-long vigil of lamentation, which Achilleus himself leads, laying his "man-killing" hands on the chest of his dead friend (*Iliad* 18.314–55). Achilleus addresses the first half of his speech (*Iliad* 18.324–32) to his fellow Myrmidons, the remainder to the dead Patroklos:

> "But now, Patroklos, since I shall be coming after you beneath the
> ground,
> I will not give you burial honor, until I have brought here
> the armor and the head of Hektor, your mighty killer." (*Iliad*
> 18.333–35)

As he touches his dead friend, Achilleus addresses him as if he could still hear the words being spoken. He extends his promise of revenge to include cutting the throats of twelve noble Trojan children, a promise that is later carried out (*Iliad* 21.26–32; 23.22–23; 175–82). This act of savagery helps show the transformation brought about in Achilleus by the killing of Patroklos. However, he does not in the end behead Hektor's corpse, nor does he bring to Patroklos the armor worn by Hektor at the time of his death. This armor was in fact Achilleus's own, stripped from Patroklos's body and subsequently put on by Hektor (*Iliad* 17.183–214). For the present, Achilleus tells Patroklos that he will lie just as he is, beside the ships, and that he will be constantly mourned by the Trojan women whom the two men have captured in the course of fighting together (*Iliad* 18.338–42). In this way he both indirectly gives orders for the performance of the ritual lamentation for the dead and, in his mind, lets his dead friend hear these orders. The corpse is then washed and anointed with oil, the wounds are filled with ointment, the body is wrapped and placed on the bier, and the lamentation continues.

Before Achilleus returns to battle on the following day, the senior Achaean warriors try to persuade him to have something to eat, but the pain in his heart is too great for him to think of food and drink, and he resolutely refuses (*Iliad* 19.305–8). While a small group remains beside him and tries in vain to comfort him, he addresses the dead Patroklos intimately: "you, my ill-fated and dearest companion" (*Iliad* 19.315), and now the thought of food and drink takes his grief from the immediacy of the present to remembrance of the past, and to the bitter contrast between the care that Patroklos took over making his friend's meals and the current state of his body, now torn to pieces (*Iliad* 19.316–21). The reader can share in these memories since a detailed picture has been given of Patroklos preparing drink and hot food for Achilleus and his guests, in a context of warm hospitality and friendship even in the midst of war and bitter, personal animosity (*Iliad* 9.201–20).

The loss of Patroklos is more painful to Achilleus than would be the news of the death of his own father or son (*Iliad* 19.321–27), and this idea leads him to dwell with great sadness on these two absent family members. Achilleus had expected that Patroklos would survive him and would take responsibility for bringing Achilleus's son, Neoptolemos, if he were still living, to see all his father's property (*Iliad* 19.328–33). As for Peleus, Achilleus now imagines him either dead or an old man consumed with grief and anxiety for his son (*Iliad* 19.323–24, 334–37). Once again the reader can share in Achilleus's memories and recall an occasion of warmth and hospitality shown between family and friends. When Nestor asked Patroklos to try to persuade Achilleus to let him take Achilleus's place in battle, Nestor recalled the time when he arrived at Peleus's house with Odysseus in the course of raising troops. They found Achilleus and Patroklos and their two fathers together. The men share a meal together, and before the sons go off to war, their fathers give them parting advice. Peleus's advice to his son is always to be best, but Menoitios's vision is of the two men working together as a team: Achilleus has the edge in terms of birth and strength, but Patroklos has greater age and wisdom and should guide Achilleus and persuade him to do the right thing (*Iliad* 11.765–89). Here the supportive role that Patroklos played in his close friend's life takes on a deeper significance. The reader has also seen how Patroklos makes his request to Achilleus, combining a heartfelt appeal on behalf of his wounded companions with a denunciation of Achilleus's intransigent anger (*Iliad* 16.21–45). Here are moral strengths in Patroklos that have tragically contributed to his death. This death produces a wide-ranging response from those who knew him. Briseïs has spoken movingly of her sadness at his death, of all the other grief that she has had to bear, of Patroklos comforting her, and of his unfailing gentleness (*Iliad* 19.282–300). Now Achilleus's words move the hearts of the elders who remain with him, prompting each of them to recall the home he left behind (*Iliad* 19.338–39). Even Zeus feels pity at the sight of the tears of these warriors, and he sends Athene with divine food for Achilleus to prevent him from starving (*Iliad* 19.340–49).

Later, following the killing of Hektor, a respite from the fighting comes. Achilleus and the Myrmidons under his command drive their chariots three times around the body of Patroklos and lament for him. The occasion is one for a public display of tears, prompted by Thetis, and the promise made by Achilleus of a funeral feast (*Iliad* 23.1–16). Once again, as he leads the lament,

Achilleus lays his "man-killing" hands on the chest of his dead friend and addresses him: "Hail to you, Patroklos, even in the house of Hades" (*Iliad* 23.19). In this more formal context of lamentation (*Iliad* 23.9), the initial address to Patroklos now firmly acknowledges the gulf separating the living from the dead. Achilleus tells the dead Patroklos that he is carrying out his promise of revenge (*Iliad* 23.20–23). When the ritual acts are over and preparations have been made for the forthcoming cremation, Achilleus's men go to their tents for the night, while Achilleus himself lies down in the open air, beside the sea, still spattered with blood and still groaning deeply. He is physically exhausted from chasing Hektor, and sleep takes hold of him, bringing relief from his troubles (*Iliad* 23.24–64).

As Achilleus sleeps, the ghost of Patroklos comes to him. In all outward form the ghost resembles Patroklos: it has the same size, the same beautiful eyes, the same voice and clothes. It stands over Achilleus's head and speaks to him:[27]

> "You are sleeping and have forgotten me, Achilleus.
> You did not neglect me in life, but in death you neglect me.
> Bury me as quickly as you can, and I will pass through the gates of
>   Hades." (*Iliad* 23.69–71)

The ghost bears an uncanny physical resemblance to the living Patroklos. Sleep has at last brought rest to Achilleus's troubled heart, but in his sleeping state, the ghost finds him failing in his promise of eternal devotion to the memory of his dead friend (*Iliad* 22.387–90). Nevertheless, the ghost also holds out to Achilleus's sleeping mind two thoughts to bring him some comfort. The first of these suggests an emotional advance, which Achilleus was not able to make in his waking state. As he shared with his divine mother the trauma of the news of Patroklos's death, he tortured himself with the thought that he was not there when his friend needed him to save his life (*Iliad* 18.98–106). Now, however, the ghost absolves him from neglect in life. The ghost also holds out a way of escaping the charge of neglect in death, urging Achilleus to complete the funeral ceremony so that he may be free from his wandering and no longer be barred from the company of the other ghosts in Hades (*Iliad* 23.71–74).

But letting go of a dead loved one is not easy, even when sleep comes to the aid of the bereaved. Shortly before falling asleep, Achilleus confronts the

---

27. Cf. *Iliad* 2.20–22, 56–59; *Odyssey* 4.795–803; 6.21–24 for the position adopted by the dream figure. In these other contexts, the dream figure takes on the disguise of a living friend or relative.

idea of the final removal of Patroklos from the world of the living when he tells Agamemnon to give the orders for the construction of Patroklos's funeral pyre (*Iliad* 23.52–53). And yet Patroklos is still vividly present, in ghostly form, to Achilleus's sleeping mind. He sees Patroklos's "lovely eyes" looking at him and hears the sadness and reproach in the ghost's opening words, and as the ghost continues to speak, the moment of parting becomes more painful. The ghost now asks for a simple but profound gesture, something beyond words, as he makes the stark contrast between life, with its close companionship and its memories, and the obliteration of death:

> "And give me your hand, I beg you. For never more
> will I return from Hades, when you have consigned me to the fire.
> No more shall we in life sit apart from our dear companions,
> and talk over our plans together." (*Iliad* 23.75–78)

It is the destiny too of "godlike" Achilleus, the ghost tells him, to die on campaign in Troy, and now the ghost makes a further plea: just as the two of them were brought up together as children in Achilleus's home, so he begs that his bones should not be laid to rest apart from those of Achilleus, but that they should be put together in the same urn that Achilleus's "revered mother" gave to Achilleus, a request that Achilleus later takes care to see is carried out (*Iliad* 23.80–92; 23.236–54). In this flashback to the ghost's childhood, there are both painful and happy memories. In a fit of childish anger over a game, Patroklos unintentionally killed one of his playmates and had to leave his home. But this traumatic incident also brought him into the care of a kind, new father-figure, Peleus, who gave him a new identity, that of "attendant" to Achilleus. Now the two boys have grown into young adults. In their adult life as warriors, the battlefield rather than the playground has become the domain of anger. Although the two warriors are not shown fighting together at Troy, as Achilleus prepares to send Patroklos off into battle, he expresses a powerful vision of the two warriors as sole survivors on the battlefield, left to destroy Troy together (*Iliad* 16.97–100).

Achilleus promises that he will carry out everything that he is told to do. He tries in vain to reach out and take hold of the ghost (*Iliad* 23.93–100). This response is given in the narrative without reference to the fact that Achilleus is speaking and moving within his dream,[28] and so it hints for a moment at a fragment of everyday communication before the illusion is devastatingly broken:

---

28. Cf. *Odyssey* 4.808–9; *Aeneid* 2.279–96. In both of these cases, however, the narrative shows that the sleeping figure is speaking within the dream.

"But stand closer to me. Though only for a moment, let us throw
 our
arms around each other and take pleasure in weeping bitterly."
So saying, he stretched out with loving hands,
but could not hold him. The ghost went away like smoke,
under the earth, squeaking. (*Iliad* 23.97–101)

At the moment of frustrated physical contact with the dead figure in his dream, Achilleus springs out of sleep, and the movement of his hands within the dream is transformed in the waking world into another simple but profound gesture, a loud clap:

In amazement Achilleus sprang up
and loudly clapped his hands and spoke words of mourning:
"Oh! Then there does remain, even in the halls of Hades,
a ghost and an image, but it has no living substance.
For all night long the ghost of poor Patroklos
has stood over me, crying and lamenting,
and has given me all his instructions, and it seemed marvelously
 like him."
So he spoke and in all of them he aroused the longing to cry,
and as they lamented, rosy-fingered Dawn appeared
around the pitiful corpse. (*Iliad* 23.101–10)

An instantaneous, double transition takes place here between Achilleus's sleeping state and his waking state and between communication with the dead and communication with the living. Such a jolt goes for an instant beyond the power of words. Achilleus springs up, claps his hands loudly, and his first utterance is a cry. The vividness with which in his sleeping state he has experienced the presence of the ghost of Patroklos and has communicated with him, as well as his sense of the duration of this experience on waking, convince Achilleus that there is some kind of continuing existence after death, albeit one that lacks any "living substance." His relaying of this experience to those around him has an immediate emotional effect on them. When the night comes to an end, the dawn enables them to see once again, not the image of the living man, but "the pitiful corpse."

When the preparations have been made, a great military procession escorts the body to the place on the shore where the funeral pyre is to be constructed and where the burial mound for the two warriors is destined to be built. The body is carried by Patroklos's companions and is covered in locks of hair, cut off by them in his honor. Achilleus comes behind, holding the body by the head, and he is the last to make the gift of a lock of his hair, which he places in the hands of his "dear companion."[29] In the course of this solemn, public ritual, Achilleus again looks forward to his own, impending death, but now he does not address Patroklos but speaks of him in the third person: "And now, since I am not returning to my dear native land, / I should like to give a lock of my hair to the hero, Patroklos, for him to bear" (*Iliad* 23.150–51). This gesture moves the attending crowd to tears, but after a while Achilleus asks Agamemnon to tell the crowd to leave so that only those who have close ties with the dead man, together with the commanders, should remain (*Iliad* 23.152–60).

A huge funeral pyre is now built, and "grieving in their heart" they place the body on top of the pyre, and Achilleus prepares it for burning, together with the bodies of numerous animals and other gifts. Finally, Achilleus slaughters the twelve Trojan children. As he starts to light Patroklos's funeral pyre, he groans aloud and once again calls on his beloved companion by name: "Hail to you, Patroklos, even in the house of Hades" (*Iliad* 23.179). Achilleus is keen to emphasize the completion of all his obligations to Patroklos, but now, as the absence of his beloved friend is on the point of being made complete by the cremation of his body, this complementary sense of completion within the world of the living is at once undermined. Divine intervention will thwart the accomplishment of Achilleus's renewed threat to give Hektor's body to the dogs, preserving it from decomposition (*Iliad* 23.184–91). Even the moment at which the funeral pyre is set alight by human hand is delayed until Achilleus has made a further prayer and asked for the divine help of the winds to kindle the wood and the bodies on the pyre (*Iliad* 23.177, 192–216).

As the flames roar throughout the night, Achilleus pours wine on the ground, "calling the soul of wretched Patroklos" (*Iliad* 23.221). He is compared with a father grieving for the death of his newly married son, and he walks slowly beside the pyre, crying all the time in grief. By dawn, the fire is burning low, and Achilleus falls into a "sweet sleep" before being aroused by the arrival of Agamemnon and the other leaders. At once he sits up and starts talking to them, giving his instructions for the retrieval and safekeeping of Patroklos's

---

29. Richardson (1993, 182–83) discusses the custom of cutting one's hair in mourning and offering a lock of hair to the dead.

bones and the preliminary work on the grave mound (*Iliad* 23.226–48). All these plans and the bustle of activity for the funeral games, arranged by Achilleus in commemoration of Patroklos, provide plenty of mental and physical activity for the day after the funeral, but when night comes, Achilleus cannot recapture the enjoyment of "sweet sleep." From now on, night for him is a time for restless movement and anguished memories of Patroklos's physical presence and of all the experiences they shared, and dawn is a time to renew his violent revenge on Hektor's body (*Iliad* 24.1–18), until divine intervention brings about the crucial change of heart in Achilleus.

Later, in the course of Achilleus's nighttime meeting in his tent with Priam, Achilleus himself helps make Hektor's body ready to be taken back to Troy. As he does so, he utters a cry and, for the last time, calls on Patroklos:

> "Do not be angry with me, Patroklos, if you find out,
> even where you are in Hades, that I have released godlike Hektor
> to his dear father, since it was no unworthy ransom that he gave
>   me,
> and to you in turn I shall give a fitting portion of it." (*Iliad*
>   24.592–95)

The vivid experience of his communication with Patroklos's ghost in his dream now lies in the past, and the continuation of communication between the world of the dead and the world of the living is now, in his mind, no more than a possibility: "if you find out."[30] Schein writes, "Homer suppresses all mention of any continued or posthumous existence for mortal warrior-heroes" (1984, 69). Achilleus's words create a strong sense of closure. In place of his own, all-consuming anger, there has now come a heartfelt request to his dead friend not to be angry with him at this crucial moment. Achilleus's acceptance of a ransom, guaranteed by Zeus both to honor him and to cheer his heart (*Iliad* 24.110, 119), makes a sharp contrast with Agamemnon's angry rejection of a ransom at the start of the narrative (*Iliad* 1.12–33). In his final promise to his dead friend to share the ransom with him, Achilleus ends by focusing on what is "fitting," in contrast with the three-times-unfulfilled promise of further mutilating Hektor's body.

---

30. King Evander, by contrast, has no such doubts that pleasure can be brought to his dead son, Pallas, by the rightful killing of his son's killer, *Turnus* (*Aeneid* 11.181).

8

Deaths and Endings

8.1 🖋 The Burial of Hektor, Tamer of Horses

At *Iliad* 24.777–803 Priam gives orders to his people to make the preparations for Hektor's cremation. With tears they bring out "bold Hektor" and place him on the funeral pyre, setting it alight. At dawn they gather around the funeral pyre "of famous Hektor," extinguish it with wine, and his brothers and companions, their cheeks wet with tears, collect his bones, drape them in soft purple cloth, and place them in a golden chest. Then they put this in a hollow grave, heap stones over it, and build a grave mound on top. This last part of his burial they carry out in a hurry, with lookouts posted all around to warn of an early attack by their enemy, "the Achaeans with their fine greaves." When they have completed the grave mound, they go back and duly assemble for a "splendid feast" in the palace of Priam, their king "nurtured by Zeus." Then comes the final line: "So they went about the burial of Hektor, tamer of horses" (*Iliad* 24.804). After the monumental narrative that has preceded it, the last line of the *Iliad* creates a deep and complex sense of finality, inviting the reader to consider the burial of Hektor from a number of different viewpoints and hence to reflect in various ways on its links with what has gone before.

Hektor plays a central and evolving role in the account of "the anger of Achilleus" (*Iliad* 1.1). As Schein notes (1984, 179–80), the actions, words, and descriptions of the two warriors dominate the *Iliad*, which reaches its climax when one kills the other. When Hektor is first mentioned, he is used by Achilleus as his chief weapon in his public battle of words with Agamemnon.

Without Achilleus, Agamemnon will have no power to stop "man-killing Hektor" from inflicting numerous fatalities on the sons of the Achaeans, and he will tear his heart out in anger against himself for not showing honor to the "best of the Achaeans" (*Iliad* 1.240–44).[1] Achilleus withdraws both physically and emotionally from the action on the battlefield, and as his prediction starts to be fulfilled with divine assistance, his position hardens. In a sensitive analysis of Achilleus's preoccupation with his honor, Graziosi and Haubold write, "In the course of the poem, Achilles' honour is in fact gradually restored, but only at the cost of social catastrophe" (2005, 130). When the embassy from Agamemnon arrives to negotiate with him, Odysseus makes a strong case for Achilleus to lay aside his anger and to rejoin his companions on the battlefield (*Iliad* 9.225–306), but his argument fails. However, when all the talking comes to an end, Achilleus modifies his out-and-out refusal to fight. His interest in his own safety and that of his forces and their ships both sets a limit on Hektor's usefulness to him in his private battle with Agamemnon and reengages his desire to demonstrate his superiority over Hektor on the battlefield (*Iliad* 9.650–55).

The course of events, however, turns out to be more complex than Achilleus's oversimplified prediction. The news that Patroklos is dead[2] and that Hektor has stripped him of his armor (*Iliad* 18.15–21) changes everything for Achilleus. With the death of Patroklos, the significance Achilleus ascribes to the quarrel with Agamemnon dies too. Now Achilleus can take a further step and see this quarrel and the fatalities on the Achaean side to which it has led as benefiting their enemies, Hektor and the Trojans, and so he pledges his return to the battlefield (*Iliad* 19.55–73). Hektor is no longer a weapon in the private world of Achilleus's mind, nor an acknowledged danger to be stopped by a pretense that Achilleus is back in action. Now Hektor has become his archenemy, out in the public world of the battlefield, and as this change takes place, Hektor is endowed in Achilleus's mind with an emotional significance both simple and complex. Hektor must die, even though Achilleus's own life will, in the near future, be the price for taking Hektor's life. Grief, anger, shame, and concern for his own legacy create in Achilleus an unstoppable drive for revenge. Schein (1984, 181–83) draws a contrast here between the two men. From the start of the *Iliad*, Achilleus knows that his own death is near (*Iliad* 1.352, 505–6). On the other

---

1. G. Nagy (1999, 26) writes, "It is an overall Iliadic theme that Achilles is the 'best of the Achaeans.'"
2. For the dying Patroklos's assessment of the part played by Hektor in his death, cf. Patroklos's words to Hektor at *Iliad* 16.843–50.

hand, though Hektor may on occasion imagine dying,[3] he does not share with the reader the foreknowledge of his approaching death (*Iliad* 6.497–502; 15.68, 612–14; 17.201–8). Nevertheless, "both are mortal, and both move inescapably in the course of the poem towards their deaths" (Schein 1984, 181).

In the final, climactic battle of the *Iliad*, Achilleus kills Hektor in single combat and strips the bloody armor from his shoulders (*Iliad* 22.92–369). As the two close in on each other, Hektor addresses Achilleus and Achilleus replies. Richardson notes that the number of speeches that punctuate the duel and the extent of divine intervention "together . . . raise the whole scene to a different plane from that of the other duels" (1993, 132).[4] Now Hektor is resolved to stand up to him and either to kill or be killed, but first he calls for a solemn agreement between them:

> "But come now and let us make an exchange of our gods, for they will be
> the best witnesses and overseers of agreements.
> I will commit no extreme outrage on you, if it is I whom Zeus
> grants to endure to the end and I take away your life.
> But when I have stripped you of your famous armor, Achilleus,
> I will give back your corpse to the Achaeans, and you do likewise."
>   (*Iliad* 22.254–59)

Achilleus angrily rejects any such talk of an agreement, and likens his relationship with Hektor to that of predator and prey:

> "Just as there are no trusted oaths between lions and men,
> nor do wolves and lambs have a united heart,
> but bear constant hostility toward each other,
> so between you and me there is no friendship, nor will there be
> any oaths between us, before one of us falls
> and gives his fill of blood to Ares, the warrior with the bull's-hide
>   shield." (*Iliad* 22.262–67)

The position that Achilleus adopts here, driven by his overwhelming desire for revenge, specifically rejects the formulation of agreements between people at war, which carry the authority of shared, religious sanction, and therefore

---

3. Cf. *Iliad* 6.464–65, 487–89; 7.77–80.

4. Barker and Christensen (2013, 8) note that over forty percent of the *Iliad* is made up of direct speech, and that this opens up the tale "to different perspectives." For further discussion, see Griffin (2004).

the all-important application of such an agreement to the treatment of war dead. In adopting this position, he puts himself at variance with the practice of both sides shown at an earlier stage in the conflict (*Iliad* 7.323–37, 375–78, 408–13), and once again, in this earlier context, it is Hektor who gives a clear formulation of this principle (*Iliad* 7.76–86). A comparison with these earlier passages helps show all that Achilleus rejects in his reduction of his relationship with his enemy to that of predator and prey, while Hektor is shown to speak with the voice of reason in emphasizing the importance of agreeing not to inflict "extreme outrage" on the body of a dead adversary, but rather of allowing its repatriation.

Achilleus is now intent on gaining revenge for all his companions killed in battle by Hektor, but for all its emotional power, Achilleus's retrospective concern for his dead companions is deeply compromised by his earlier request that Zeus should help the Trojans kill them (*Iliad* 1.408–12). Here is a fundamental problem for Achilleus. He has proudly told his fellow warriors that "As much an enemy to me as the gates of Hades / is the man who hides one thing in his mind and says something else" (*Iliad* 9.312–13), and yet the concealment of his change of heart is essential for the claim he now makes to Hektor: "You will pay the price in full / for the sufferings of my companions, whom you killed, as you raged with your spear" (*Iliad* 22.271–72). And moments later, as he triumphs over the dying Hektor (*Iliad* 22.331–36), Achilleus adds to this concealment in glossing over the reason for his earlier absence from the battlefield, though ironically Hektor already knows, from Aias, that this was caused by Achilleus's anger toward Agamemnon (*Iliad* 7.229–30).

In the final exchanges (*Iliad* 22.337–66), the language reaches an emotional climax. With his strength failing, Hektor makes a last appeal to Achilleus. He no longer speaks in terms of an abstract agreement, witnessed by the gods, but rather in the language of a direct, physical act of supplication. Here he invokes not only Achilleus but also Achilleus's parents, and he speaks of the willingness of his own father and mother to pay the ransom for his body. His words are met once again with angry rejection:

> "Make no appeal to me by my knees or by my parents, you dog!
> If only somehow my heart would let me
> cut your flesh up and eat it raw, for what you have done." (*Iliad*
>   22.345–47)

And Achilleus ends: "But the dogs and birds will eat you, every part of you" (*Iliad* 22.354).

Achilleus's rhetoric collapses the distinction between human and animal—"you dog!"[5]—and in his fantasy world, he himself becomes the predator, eating strips of Hektor's raw flesh in revenge rather than granting him his request.[6] By contrast, even with his dying words, Hektor speaks with a clear vision. He can see Achilleus for what he is and knows his own fate. In his last words, he speaks ominously and with great precision, linking Achilleus's threatened treatment of him in death with Achilleus's own forthcoming death:

> "Think now, lest I become the cause of the gods' anger toward you,
> on that day when, brave warrior though you are,
> Paris and Phoibos Apollo destroy you at the Skaian gates." (*Iliad*
>   22.358–60)[7]

At this point Hektor dies, but even though he is now dead, Achilleus still addresses him: "Die! As for my fate I will take it whenever / Zeus and all the other immortal gods wish it to happen" (*Iliad* 22.365–66).

Achilleus's obsessive and constantly thwarted attempts to inflict posthumous damage and dishonor on Hektor's corpse have already been examined in chapters 4.1 and 7.3. As the *Iliad* nears its end, a scene of great emotional profundity takes place at night in Achilleus's tent. Achilleus yields to the request, which Priam himself has come to him to make, to accept a ransom and to return Hektor's body. Just before Priam meets Achilleus, Hermes tells Priam to appeal to him in the name of his father, his mother, and his child, in order to move his heart (*Iliad* 24.465–67). And now, before he makes his supplication, Priam's body language goes far beyond words or ritual gestures: "He took Achilleus's knees in his hands and kissed his hands, / those terrible, man-killing hands, which had killed many of his sons" (*Iliad* 24.478–79).

This amazing act of Priam's crosses the divisions brought about by war and killing. Macleod writes of Priam that "he becomes a new kind of hero who shows endurance (24.505–6) and evokes wonder (480–4) not merely by facing

---

5. For Achilleus's earlier use of this and related terms of abuse, cf. *Iliad* 1.159, 225; 9.373; 20.449. For the different connotations when such language is used of herself by Helen, cf. the discussion in chapter 5.1 of this volume.

6. Violent feminine hatred is expressed elsewhere in the form of the desire to eat the raw flesh of enemies; cf. *Iliad* 4.34–36; 24.212–14.

7. B. Graziosi and J. Haubold (2005, 128) note "the deep-seated antagonism between Achilles and Apollo throughout the *Iliad*." They explain that a central reason for this is "that Apollo is the Homeric god most concerned with upholding the divide between gods and humans, whereas Achilles is the human being who most consistently challenges that divide."

death but by humbling himself and curbing his hatred before his greatest enemy" (1982, 22).When he speaks, Priam succeeds in making Achilleus think of his own father's troubles and so enables him to make the imaginative leap needed to see the present situation from Priam's own point of view as Hektor's father. In Priam's eyes, Hektor was Troy's sole hope against the Achaeans and died a hero's death at Achilleus's hands (*Iliad* 24.499–501). Achilleus and Priam share their grief at the loss of their loved ones and at the thought of the sadness that old age brings. In the context of this shared, emotional release, Achilleus once again displays some of the key characteristics that set the human world of the *Iliad* apart from the rest of the animal kingdom. These include pity, respect for the gods and for human endurance, and a profoundly articulated acceptance of the human condition and rejection of the excesses of grief (*Iliad* 24.507–51). Even so, the release of Hektor's body remains charged with emotion for Achilleus (*Iliad* 24.559–601). By the end of the *Iliad*, however, Achilleus's change of heart is no longer a private matter between himself and Priam. The final reference to Achilleus comes when Priam, speaking to the Trojans, quotes Achilleus's authority to guarantee on behalf of the Achaean army a truce of sufficient length to attend to Hektor's burial *(Iliad* 24.656–72). The contingencies of war may end by showing the fragility of such an undertaking. Nevertheless, for "the anger of Achilleus," which the *Iliad* introduces in its opening words and subsequently explores in great detail and with great attention to the changing relationship between Achilleus and Hektor, the burial of Hektor can be felt to bring closure.

Hektor's death and eventual burial, however, are linked with more than "the anger of Achilleus."[8] Amid the carnage on the battlefield, the focus on the killing of Sarpedon by Patroklos, of Patroklos by Hektor, and of Hektor by Achilleus, and on the aftermath of these deaths (*Iliad* 16–22) creates a powerful model of the domino effect of such killings in war. This focus also provides a sense of growing momentum as the narrative moves through its last third and toward its close. Patroklos and Hektor, though on opposite sides, have a number of features in common. Both are shown as unstoppable by their human enemies when at the height of their destructive power. Both fight and die in a conflict that is not of their making (doubly so in the case of Patroklos), and both die in part at least from failing to take notice of good, strategic advice

---

8. Graziosi and Haubold see the extreme anger of Achilleus and the cunning and adaptable nature of Odysseus as part of a bigger picture, writing that "their character traits speak . . . of their place within the unfolding history of the universe" (2005, 122).

(*Iliad* 16.80–96, 684–91, and 18.249–313; 22.99–108). The two deaths also invite the reader to consider the ironic gap between outcomes in war and the words and plans of war leaders. "Wide-ruling Agamemnon" plays no direct part in this crucial development in the realization of his dream of victory over the Trojans. Hektor's death comes to him as a fortuitous consequence of the death of one of his own side. Achilleus, "the best of the Achaeans," knows that there was a time, while Patroklos was still alive, when he might have killed Hektor (*Iliad* 9.304–6) and that, albeit unintentionally, he has sent his beloved companion out to his death. As for "bold Hektor," although he feels that he retrieves his reputation in the eyes of posterity after his initial moment of panic (*Iliad* 22.304–5), he also knows, as he faces death at Achilleus's hands, that as a result of his own folly he has already destroyed his own people (*Iliad* 22.104).[9]

Off the battlefield, Patroklos and Hektor have both been presented as sympathetic characters, but here once again an important difference emerges and contributes to the sense of a carefully modulated crescendo. Although Patroklos's death brings great pain to Briseïs (*Iliad* 19.282–300), Patroklos, both in life and in death, is shown in a male context. Hektor's life and death, by contrast, are intimately connected with the lives of his family and with the lives of the wider Trojan community. The Achaeans have brought war to the previously peaceful city of Troy, and both in life and in death it is Hektor who takes the reader inside Troy to show the effects of the war on family life inside the beleaguered city. With great emotional power, Priam and Hekabe plead with their son not to maintain his lone stand against the onslaught of Achilleus. But their pleading is to no avail, and they have to endure the agony of seeing their newly dead son's corpse tied by its feet to the back of Achilleus's chariot and dragged at speed through the dust (*Iliad* 22.25–92, 405–36). Andromache's first experience of her husband's death takes her from a scene of domestic tranquility, through terrible forebodings and an anguished rush to the scene, to a collapse from shock and an agonized outpouring of her grief both for herself and more particularly for the fate of her baby son (*Iliad* 22.437–515). As the *Iliad* draws to its close with formal lamentation, the speeches of the women close to Hektor—his wife, his mother, and his brother's wife—commemorate from three complementary viewpoints the life of Hektor and assess what his death

---

9. For the debate in which Poulydamas urges retreat into Troy and Hektor rejects his advice, see *Iliad* 18.243–313.

means, both to his family and to his city.[10] Andromache addresses a husband whose protective power extended to include the whole city with its "beloved wives and little children." But at the same time this husband was a warrior whose ferocity has left many a bereaved enemy eager for revenge, and who, by his premature death, has brought a future of destruction, death, and slavery. Hekabe addresses the dearest of all her sons, who in life was loved by the gods and who in death, despite all that Achilleus could do, was preserved without disfiguration and is now laid out at home. Finally, Helen addresses the dearest of her brothers-in-law, who was unfailingly kind to her (*Iliad* 24.723–76).

Hektor's death and the subsequent treatment of his corpse are also matters of great concern to the gods, and in this respect too, they can be seen as the climax in a sequence of ideas that gathers momentum across the final third of the *Iliad*. At *Iliad* 16.431–61, Zeus laments to Hera that it is the fate of his son, Sarpedon, "the dearest of men," to be brought down by Patroklos. The possibility of Zeus overriding the preordained time set for a human to die is raised and immediately dismissed at this point because of the divisive and destabilizing effect such an action would have on the gods. But this sequence also underlines a hard but basic truth that the *Iliad* does not shy from presenting to the reader: a time comes when human beings must die. When that time comes, it brings great grief to their fathers, and Zeus himself, "the father of men and of gods" (*Iliad* 16.458), is no exception. Nevertheless, as Hera makes clear, some comfort can be found when death is associated with the idea of painless sleep, when the body can be brought home and be given due funeral rites by those who were close to the deceased, and when the death can be marked by a place of burial and a gravestone (*Iliad* 16.453–57). These, at least, are circumstances over which the gods have the power to exercise control, and they are all the more valuable in Hektor's case after the violent and protracted human action taken to deny them.

When Hektor's own death is approaching and all the gods are looking on, Zeus again initially expresses indecision (*Iliad* 22.166–76). This time Zeus asks the other gods whether they should save Hektor from death or let him be killed by Achilleus despite his good qualities. Athene responds, and her words repeat the first part of Hera's earlier reaction to the question of Sarpedon's fate (*Iliad* 22.179–81, repeating 16.441–43). But there she stops and Zeus reassures her that he was not speaking in earnest. There is a chilling irony here. Zeus speaks

---

10. Alexiou (1974) examines the place of ritual lamentation in Greek culture from Homeric times to the folk tradition of the modern world.

lightly and tenderly to his divine daughter and gives her a father's support, while at the same time dismissing his moment's sadness at the thought that a human should in his hour of need fail to find divine recompense for his attentiveness. Divine involvement in the approaching moment of human death now reaches a climax. First comes the visually arresting image of the golden scales:

> Then the Father held out the golden scales,
> and on them he placed two fates of death, the bringer of long woes.
> The one was of Achilleus, the other of Hektor, tamer of horses,
> and he held them up by the center, and Hektor's fated day sank
>   down
> and went to the house of Hades. (*Iliad* 22.209–13)[11]

Richardson writes, "Hektor's fate is already decided . . . and this is a visual or symbolic representation of the crucial moment at which the decision becomes irrevocable" (1993, 129). On the battleground this at once brings the vital change in the divine support for the two warriors: Apollo, Hektor's divine protector, now leaves him and Athene stands beside Achilleus, aiding and encouraging him and deceiving his enemy. Nevertheless, although Zeus's love of Hektor does not override Hektor's appointed fate, Hektor continues to occupy Zeus's thoughts after his death and ultimately Zeus finds the way to release his body (*Iliad* 24.22–30, 55–76).

The related killings of Sarpedon, Patroklos, and above all Hektor also create an arena in which to explore the limits of behavior in war that are acceptable in the eyes of the watching figures of Zeus and the other gods. The victor may take the armor of the vanquished as a legitimate trophy and give it to his companions, as Patroklos does with Sarpedon's armor (*Iliad* 16.663–65), but when Hektor takes off his own helmet and armor and replaces them with the immortal armor of Achilleus, stripped from Achilleus's beloved Patroklos, this action provokes divine disapproval and so contributes to Hektor's coming death (*Iliad* 16.799–800; 17.183–209). The maltreatment of the body of the fallen foe after death is also increasingly shown as provoking divine disapproval, as discussed in chapter 2.2. When Patroklos dies, his body repeatedly faces the threat of being eaten by dogs and even of being decapitated until Zeus himself intervenes to prevent this and the body is eventually retrieved by the Achaeans. The emotional power of the image of corpses being eaten by animals reaches a climax when it is expressed by the anguished members of

---

11. For earlier references to Zeus's scales, cf. *Iliad* 8.68–74; 16.658; 19.223–24.

Hektor's family: his father, his mother, and his wife (*Iliad* 22.41–43, 66–71, 88–89, 508–10).[12] Later, Apollo makes a strong attack on the gods for refusing to save Hektor's body and restore it to his own people. Instead, they wish to support the deadly Achilleus:

> "whose mind will not see reason and whose heart
> cannot be made to move, but knows only one idea, savagery, like a
>   lion,
> when he gives way to his great might and his proud spirit
> and goes after the flocks of men to take his meal.
> Just so has Achilleus destroyed pity, and has no respect." (*Iliad*
>   24.40–45)

Here the simile returns to focus on what Achilleus has rejected: the ability to think rationally and to respond to moral argument, the very characteristics that set human experience apart from the lives of predator and prey. The point is made explicit with great metaphorical force. Apollo's words give a final, complex, and authoritative rebuttal of the position stated by Achilleus as he kills Hektor, and so they add to the gathering sense of closure.

The description of Hektor as "tamer of horses" ends the *Iliad*. In so doing, it reunites the leader with his forces, "the Trojans, tamers of horses," and reminds the reader of the close association between man and horse throughout the poem and the wide, emotional range of that association. Horses are a mark of their owners' status and confer glory on them, sometimes even a godlike glory. Hektor himself is shown, earlier in the conflict, boasting of the power of his horses to breach the Achaean defenses and calling on them by name to repay him for the tender care lavished on them by his wife, Andromache (*Iliad* 8.179, 184–90). Later, however, as the moment of his death approaches, horses take on a terrifying significance for him. As Achilleus rushes toward Hektor, who is standing outside the gate of Troy waiting for him, his speed is likened to that of a prize-winning horse pulling a chariot effortlessly over the plain (*Iliad* 22.21–24), and as Achilleus chases "Hektor, tamer of horses" around the city walls, intent on killing him, a similar image recurs within a more extended and ironic comparison with the world of funeral games (*Iliad* 22.162–66). After Hektor's death, such nightmarish imagery is transformed into action as Hektor's body is tied by its ankles to the back of Achilleus's chariot and driven first around the city walls of Troy and later around Patroklos's tomb. But in the end,

---

12. See Segal (1971).

whereas other warriors, such as Kebriones at *Iliad* 16.776 and Achilleus himself at *Odyssey* 24.40, are shown at death "to have forgotten their horsemanship," this is not the case with Hektor. The recent, painful images are dispelled and Hektor is finally remembered as having the power to tame wild horses.

This leads to a last thought. The poem ends with the line "So they went about the burial of Hektor, tamer of horses" (*Iliad* 24.804). As that line's opening word "So " sums up the description of Hektor's burial, it also draws attention to the poem's descriptive power. The narrative has evoked a world rich in descriptive detail, whose recurrence across its vast tract gives the reader reassuring, fixed points of reference—"Achaeans with their fine greaves," "Trojans, tamers of horses," and so forth. But that detail also constantly challenges the reader to see new associations of ideas and hence to be aware of change and complexity as the narrative unfolds. Now, in death, Hektor is shown both in a heroic light, as "bold" and "famous," and also in a context suggestive of peacetime activity, as a "tamer of horses." His father, Priam, is fated to watch the killing in battle of his beloved son and heir and is shown with animal dung piled on his head and neck from wallowing on the ground in his grief (*Iliad* 24.163–65). And yet now, even as his city teeters on the edge of destruction, he is still "a king nurtured by Zeus." Eating in the presence of death, which in the violence of his emotion became impossible for Achilleus and which has been sullied for the reader from the start of the *Iliad* by the recurring image of dogs and other scavengers mauling unburied corpses on the battlefield, is now reinstated as something right and proper, "a splendid feast" to bring the people together in the king's palace after the funeral. So the final line acts as a farewell in three complementary ways: in it the narrator bids farewell to Hektor, to the reader, and to his creation, with all its descriptive power.

8.2 ⚔ The Killing of Turnus

The long-awaited duel between Aeneas and Turnus, which forms the climax of the fighting between Trojans and Italians in the second half of the *Aeneid*, is narrated in two halves, the second of which brings the *Aeneid* to an end (*Aeneid* 12.710–90, 887–952). This end, as Tarrant writes, "has long been a site of controversy" (2012, 16).[13] As the pressure on King Latinus and his city

---

13. In his introduction, Tarrant gives a detailed discussion of Turnus and Aeneas and of The Final Scene (2012, 9–30). He notes that the critical response to Aeneas's killing of Turnus ranges from unconditional acceptance to outright abhorrence.

grows, Turnus tells his divine sister, Juturna, that he is resolved to meet Aeneas in single combat and to face death rather than dishonor. "Father Aeneas" is overjoyed when he hears the name "Turnus," since he has long wanted this resolution of the conflict. Everyone, King Latinus included, fixes their eyes on the two men (*Aeneid* 12.704–9). As Tarrant notes, "The duel between A. and T. has some of the character of a gladiatorial combat" (331). They throw their spears, charge at one another, and lock their shields together in battle. In a powerful, extended simile the two men are likened to a pair of bulls fighting on an Italian mountain top (*Aeneid* 12.715–24).[14] As the two men fight, Jupiter places their fates in the scales to see which one is doomed to die (*Aeneid* 12.725–27). This detail occurs early in the conflict and, unlike the comparable moment at *Iliad* 22.208–13, does no more than hint at the eventual outcome.

Turnus springs out and strikes, bringing the full force of his body down on his raised sword. A cry goes up from the crowd, but "the treacherous sword" breaks in mid-stroke and Turnus takes to his heels. Aeneas chases him around and around in the confined space. Now they are competing for no trivial, athletic prize but for the lifeblood of Turnus (*Aeneid* 12.728–65). At *Iliad* 3.361–68, Menelaos lifts high his sword and strikes the ridge on Paris's helmet, but his sword shatters. At the other end of the *Iliad*, at *Iliad* 22.136–66, fear takes hold of Hektor and he runs away. As Achilleus chases him, a comparison is made between competition for prizes in sport and the present race "for the life of Hektor, tamer of horses." The combining of these two moments in the context of *Aeneid* 12 dissolves the initial image of an epic conflict between two, evenly matched warriors. In the simile that now describes the two men, Turnus is like a deer and Aeneas in full pursuit of him is like an eager, Italian hunting dog (cf. *Iliad* 22.188–93). The duel itself has already been long delayed, and now a further delay postpones its outcome. Aeneas's spear sticks fast in the stump of a tree, sacred to the god Faunus, which the Trojans cut down in readiness for the duel. Faunus and Mother Earth respond to Turnus's agonized prayer and resist Aeneas's efforts to pull the spear free. Seizing her opportunity, Turnus's divine sister brings him his sword. Venus is enraged to see this action on the part of "the bold nymph" and in return pulls the spear free. Thus the two great warriors resume their battle (*Aeneid* 12.766–90).

---

14. Much of the detail in this simile also occurs in the description of two bulls fighting over a mate; see *Georgics* 3.209–41. For a conflict between two animals of the same kind in a simile, cf. *Iliad* 16.428–30, where Sarpedon and Patroklos are likened to a pair of vultures fighting on a high rock.

The scene switches to the divine world with the connector "meanwhile," and Jupiter and his wife/sister are shown talking together (*Aeneid* 12.791–842). Hardie writes, "We have to do with alternative endings, one on earth and one in heaven. These are alternative ways of ending the wrath theme" (1997a, 148). Jupiter tells Juno that she must go no further in her efforts to thwart Fate. Juno submits and withdraws her support from Turnus, albeit reluctantly (*Aeneid* 12.791–818). The switch of attention to the gods on Olympos in the middle of the *Iliad*'s final duel is shorter than the corresponding scene in the *Aeneid*, and there all the gods are watching the duel (*Iliad* 22.166–87). In the *Iliad*, it is "the father of men and of gods" who wishes to save the human who is doomed to die in the duel, and it is the goddess Athene who reminds him of the concerted opposition that such action would meet from the other gods. In the *Aeneid* "the almighty king of Olympus" speaks solely to Juno as she watches the fighting from a cloud, and now it is the god who expresses the inevitability of fate and makes clear to the goddess that she cannot go any further in her efforts to thwart the inevitable. Cumulatively, Jupiter's words suggest not only that the end has come for Turnus but also that the end is coming for the *Aeneid*. Juno has done all in her power to oppose the fulfilment of the *Aeneid*'s grand narrative, and her efforts have from the start done much to help drive the *Aeneid*'s narrative forward, but now she must stop her attempts to block what is inevitable. Juno herself knows that immortality is owed to Aeneas (*Aeneid* 12.794–95); he cannot die.

The conversation between Jupiter and Juno is a complex blend of the formal and the informal. Two speeches by Jupiter enclose a single speech by Juno. Thus together they form the inverse configuration of the speeches of Dido and Aeneas at *Aeneid* 4.305–87. These three speeches give time for the *Aeneid*'s grand narrative to reach its final unfolding, and this conclusion is reached through dialogue that takes the form of divine compromise and in a tone of voice that is in part bantering, with a hint of domestic comedy, and in part a joint, solemn declaration of national destiny. A deeper irony underlies this surface blending of widely differing registers. In terms of an individual's life, Turnus is the one who is about to die, but the opposite is the case in terms of the big picture encompassing Troy and Italy. Troy, her name, her language, and her costume are destined to die, whereas Italy is promised a glowing future. Juno proposes this future—"Let there be Roman offspring, made mighty by the brave manhood of Italy. / Troy has died, allow that Troy and its name are dead" (*Aeneid* 12.827–28)—and Jupiter smiles at her, as earlier he has smiled at Venus (*Aeneid* 12.829; 1.254). After calling a halt to her frenzied but ultimately ineffectual anger, Jupiter willingly concedes to Juno's request and elaborates in diplomatic terms the nature of the blending of the two peoples. The Latin people will keep their own language, their way of life, and their name. Here the wide-ranging power of naming is brought within the *Aeneid*'s grand narrative. The Trojans, on the other hand, will bring no more than a subsidiary, physical addition to the common stock. Jupiter himself will add religious rituals and will make all the Latin people speak "with one voice," and the resulting, mixed race will display in unrivalled measure the characteristic of the Trojan leader, "dutifulness." In addition, no race will celebrate Juno with more honor. Juno nods in agreement, and her mood as she is last seen is for once happy rather than angry (*Aeneid* 12.830–42).[15]

After telling Juno all this with a smile,[16] Jupiter displays a very different side as he intervenes in the duel in order to drive Juturna away from her brother. He sends a Dread Monster down from the sky, a winged creature of the night, which keeps screeching as it flies into Turnus's face and knocks against his shield. Turnus is reduced to a state of numb terror, and Juturna, unable to withstand this portent of doom and forced to leave him to his death, expresses the agonizing sense of her powerlessness to save her mortal brother (*Aeneid* 12.843–86). A form of ring composition here joins together the early and closing stages of the second half of the *Aeneid*. Just as Juno employs the infernal Fury, Allecto, to arouse first a passion in Amata and then the frenzied lust for war in Turnus (*Aeneid* 7.323–462), so Jupiter now brings the final duel to its conclusion by sending one of a pair of dreadful monsters from his throne in the sky, first to create panic in Turnus and then to force Juturna to abandon her brother and to utter her anguished farewell to him. This raises a difficult and far-reaching question: how far are these divine enforcers, used by Juno and by Jupiter, alike in what they bring about and how far are they different? Tarrant writes, "It would seem that in Virgil's world madness and disorder . . . are not overcome by their opposites, but by like forces" (2012, 16). W. R. Johnson writes of Jupiter's Dread Monster, "It is this sudden chilling embodiment of the powers of darkness and the forces of unreason that makes the final intervention of the divine in the *Aeneid* as sinister as it is original" (1976, 128).[17] Tarrant's conclusion is to

15. For further discussion of the complexities of this scene, see W. R. Johnson (1976, 123–27), Lyne (1987, 95–99), Feeney (1991, 147–51), and Tarrant (2012, 290–91).

16. Cf. *Iliad* 15.47. The reader can interpret these divine smiles in various ways. The light-hearted manner in which divine conflict is resolved, in contrast to the continuation of violent conflict in the mortal world, suggests comparison with *Iliad* 1.595–600.

17. Feeney (1991, 151) sides with Tarrant, while Lyne (1987, 93) comes closer to W. R. Johnson's position.

adopt an "ambivalent reading," which he defines as "a continuing tension of opposites" (2012, 17).

Now the narrative of the duel resumes. Aeneas presses forward his attack and angrily taunts Turnus for delaying the outcome of the combat. Turnus shakes his head and replies in brief and measured terms (*Aeneid* 12.887–95). Turnus's sense that Jupiter is his enemy is an even more horrific realization than Hektor's sense that the gods are calling him to his death (*Iliad* 22.297, 300–303). He thereby equates Jupiter with his human enemy, Aeneas. Then, as Turnus catches sight of a huge rock that has acted as a boundary marker, "the hero" (*Aeneid* 12.902) lifts it up and hurls it, but now he cannot recognize his own actions. His knees give way and his blood runs cold. The rock fails to reach its target. A powerful simile draws attention to Turnus's state at this point:

> And as in our sleep, when the languid quiet of the night lies heavy
> on our eyes, we seem to be trying in vain to run forward eagerly,
> and in the middle of our attempts we fall exhausted,
> our tongue has no power, the familiar strength has gone
> from our body, and neither voice nor words will come,
> so it was with Turnus: wherever he sought a path for his bravery,
> the dread goddess denies him success. (*Aeneid* 12.908–14)

W. R. Johnson calls Turnus's dream "one of the great nightmares of poetry" (1976, 98). This description of Turnus's psychological state suggests comparison with two passages in the *Iliad*. Turnus's inability to recognize himself in his actions invites comparison with the sense of the loss of bodily strength experienced by Patroklos when Apollo has struck him (*Iliad* 16.805–6), and the extended nightmare simile can also be compared with *Iliad* 22.199–201, where the fruitless attempts of Achilleus to pursue Hektor and of Hektor to escape from him are likened to a nightmare. In one sense, the simile in *Aeneid* 12 is more specific in that it applies to Turnus alone and his losing battle against "the dread goddess." In another sense, it is more general and more inclusive in that it describes a wider range of frustrated activity and embraces both narrator and reader in its use of the word "we."

Attention now turns to Aeneas. As Turnus falters, Aeneas carefully aims his spear and releases it with enormous force. It pierces Turnus's shield, strikes him in the thigh, and brings "huge Turnus" to the ground (*Aeneid* 12.919–27). At the climax of the duel in *Iliad* 22, Hektor is fatally wounded and crashes to the dust, but with his dying breath he is able to reply to Achilleus before he dies (*Iliad* 22.306–63). At the climax of the duel in *Aeneid* 12, by contrast,

Turnus's energies have already been fatally weakened by the winged monster
sent against him by Jupiter, and for all its godlike power, Aeneas's spear does
not threaten Turnus's life. Turnus is the first to speak. His eyes, his hand
outstretched in entreaty, and his words all have the humility of a suppliant.
He admits that he deserves to die and that Aeneas can take advantage of his
fate. He continues:

> "If some care for a wretched father
> can touch your heart, I beg you (and such was once your own
>   father,
> Anchises) have pity on Daunus in his old age,
> and send me, or, if you prefer, my body bereft of its life
> back to my people. You have won, and the people of Ausonia have
>   seen me
> defeated and holding out my hands to you. Lavinia is yours to be
>   your wife.
> Do not press your hatred any further." (*Aeneid* 12.932–38)[18]

Turnus's short, powerful speech makes a strong contrast with the loss
of the power of speech imagined in lines 911–12. It suggests that sparing
his life, in addition to showing pity for Turnus's father, would be reasonable.
Aeneas's winning of the duel is incontrovertible, as is its consequence. Though
still the fierce warrior standing over his fallen enemy, Aeneas hesitates while
Turnus's words are beginning to take effect on him. But then he catches sight
of the "ill-starred baldric" that Turnus stripped from the body of young Pallas
after killing him and wore as a mark of triumph over the enemy (*Aeneid*
10.495–505). The following lines bring the *Aeneid* to an end:

> After he had let his eyes dwell on this plunder, this memorial
> to his violent grief, fury blazed up in him and, terrible
> in his anger, he said: "Are you to escape from me here, wearing
>   the spoils
> of my people? It is Pallas who inflicts this wound, Pallas
> who makes sacrifice of you and exacts punishment on your wicked
>   blood."
> Raging as he spoke these words, he buried his sword deep in the
>   heart

18. The word "hatred" is nowhere else associated with Aeneas. For Juno's hatred of the Trojans, cf.
Aeneid 1.667–69; 5.785–87; 7.297–98.

of Turnus. His limbs dissolved in coldness
and with a groan his indignant life fled down to the shadows.
    (*Aeneid* 12.945–52)

Here is a busy narrative that carries the reader along relentlessly to the sudden, violent, and thought-provoking ending. The *Aeneid* opens with the narrator presenting his subject ("I sing of arms and the man") and closes by demonstrating the ultimate exercise of one man's armed supremacy over another. At stake in the outcome of the duel are two separate issues: the choice between Aeneas and Turnus as a husband for King Latinus's daughter, Lavinia; and Aeneas's exacting of revenge for Turnus's killing of King Evander's son, Pallas. This process of amalgamating and re-forming details suggestive of the duels at either end of the fighting in the *Iliad* to form a single, complex climax, enriched with further reminiscences of the fighting in the *Iliad*, creates a sense of completion for the *Aeneid*'s second, "Iliadic" half. Thus, for all its abruptness and for all the questions it leaves the reader to ponder, the ending of the *Aeneid* at some level brings closure both to the work as a whole and also, more specifically, to its second half.

A comparison with the duel between Menelaos and Paris suggests a wide-ranging contrast. There the roles of the figures involved in the triangle are fixed: deserted husband, runaway wife, and wife's seducer who becomes her second husband. In the *Aeneid* the roles are more fluid. Lavinia is not married but is awaiting marriage, and Turnus has the prior claim on her and enjoys strong, emotional support from Lavinia's mother (*Aeneid* 7.55–57). Here, however, Turnus comes into conflict with a central detail in the *Aeneid*'s grand narrative since Lavinia is destined to be Aeneas's wife (*Aeneid* 2.783–84; 6.763–65; 7.314). Beyond this, through the association of her name with "the Lavinian shore," "the kingdom of Lavinium," and through Aeneas's choice that Lavinia should give her name to his new city, she is embedded in geographical terms in its grand narrative at the start, the middle, and toward the end of the *Aeneid* (*Aeneid* 1.2–3; 6.84–85; 12.193–94). Lavinia's father, King Latinus, is quick to see in Aeneas the prophesied son-in-law from overseas who will bring future glory to his people (*Aeneid* 7.251–73). In the eyes of Turnus, on the other hand, Aeneas appears as a second Paris, coming to steal another man's wife and tainting his followers with this crime (*Aeneid* 9.136–39). By the early stages of *Aeneid* 11, Turnus still has his supporters, but public opinion among the Latin people is beginning to turn against him (*Aeneid* 11.215–19). Here, as seen through the eyes of those of his own side who have lost loved ones in the war, it is Turnus who is now made to resemble Paris.[19] This process of isolating Turnus from his own people is hastened by his old, personal enemy, Drances (*Aeneid* 11.336–75). Conversely, in the course of his reply to Drances and in the interests of Latinus and his people, Turnus formally dedicates his life to single combat with Aeneas (*Aeneid* 11.440–44).[20]

Turnus is increasingly colored as the figure who claims for himself the woman who rightfully belongs to another man, and his confidence that Lavinia is his wavers as he comes under pressure from Latinus and even from Amata to give up his claim. First he speaks of Lavinia as a wife whose loss he will not tolerate, then as a wife whom he may concede to another, and finally as a wife to be won on the field of battle (*Aeneid* 9.136–39; 12.17, 80). Of the two men, however, it is Turnus whom the narrative makes the more interesting in emotional terms (and once again this aligns him with Paris). Aeneas and Lavinia do not meet in the course of the narrative, while there is no doubting that love plays an important part in the turmoil of Turnus's emotions, both in her presence and when he is away from her on the battlefield (*Aeneid* 12.70, 666–68). When the delayed duel finally takes place, it leads, unlike the duel between Menelaos and Paris, to an indisputable result: a publicly witnessed conceding of defeat on the part of Turnus and the relinquishing of his right to Lavinia as his wife. It is a mark of the *Aeneid*'s complex and problematic nature that the grand narrative of the birth of a nation in accordance with divine destiny is also a human narrative of fatal family division between father and mother over the marriage of their daughter, and fatal conflict between two male rivals over one girl. Perhaps most paradoxical of all is the fact that the outcome of the duel over Lavinia does not provide a closing point for the narrative but instead offers a tantalizing glimpse of the avoidance of a final killing, which is then summarily rejected.

The second issue for resolution, the exacting of revenge for Turnus's killing of Pallas, raises more complex problems, and these include a more far-reaching realignment of the suggested equivalence between the central characters of the *Iliad* and the central characters of the second half of the *Aeneid*. As part of her prophecy, the Sibyl tells Aeneas that he will find "another Achilles, already born in Latium" (*Aeneid* 6.89–90). In broad terms, Achilles' name stands here, heralding an epic narrative of war, just as it stands at the

---

19. Cf. the Trojans' universal loathing for Paris at *Iliad* 3.453–54.
20. The significance of Turnus's devoting his life to the coming combat is discussed by W. R. Johnson (1976, 117–19).

opening of the *Iliad*. In a narrower sense, Achilles' name recalls the earlier duel on the plains of Troy between the Iliadic Achilleus and the Iliadic Aineias (*Iliad* 20.79–350) and now, in the form of "another Achilles," suggests unfinished business that waits for completion in this new theater of war. In the gradual process of realignment, the difference between the two narratives becomes something more complex than that of location, strategy, or personnel involved, something closer to a process of revision and reattribution of identity within the new context.

In broad terms, Turnus is initially "another Achilles"—he is a terrifying enemy leader who inflicts heavy losses on Aeneas's followers and who is at times unstoppable on the battlefield. At one point, Turnus himself makes this identification when he challenges the Trojan giant, Pandarus, and anticipates Pandarus's death: "here too you will tell Priam that an Achilles has been found" (*Aeneid* 9.742). Nevertheless, despite being "another Achilles" in the prophetic words of the Sibyl and in his own estimation made halfway through the fighting, Turnus is unlike the Achilleus of the *Iliad* in that, by the end of the narrative, he has lost everything: the war, the duel, his bride-to-be, and ultimately his own life. The difference between the two figures, the Achilleus of the *Iliad* and this new Italian Achilles, becomes more apparent as the battle narrative develops. Turnus is shown making a number of mistakes as a result of frenzied or impetuous action, mistakes that damage both his chances of winning the war and ultimately of saving his own life (*Aeneid* 9.756–61; 11.901–5; 12.735–41). In fact, from the time when Turnus leads an attack on the Trojan settlement and attempts to set fire to their ships, he comes to resemble not so much Achilleus as Hektor. It is Aeneas himself who—at broadly the same point in the narrative, when he returns from Pallanteum to assist his beleaguered companions—begins to play in many ways the role of "another Achilles." This process accelerates with the death of Pallas at Turnus's hands, after Pallas's moment of glory on the battlefield (*Aeneid* 10.362–509). Aeneas's response to the news of Pallas's death is like that of Achilleus to the news of Patroklos's death at Hektor's hands: he engages in retaliatory killings on a massive scale, shows no mercy to his victims, and commits himself to finding Turnus and avenging Pallas's death (*Aeneid* 10.510–605). Nevertheless, this commitment on the part of Aeneas to gaining revenge does not bring on him the subsequent certainty of imminent death.

The relationship between Aeneas and Pallas, moreover, belongs in a different world from that of Achilleus and Patroklos, and hence so too does the imperative that drives Aeneas ultimately to take Turnus's life. Aeneas's first meeting with Pallas and his father, Evander, is prompted by strategic considerations (*Aeneid* 8.51–56, 146–49). His appeal to the common origins of the Arcadian and the Trojan peoples strengthens the alliance, as does Evander's enthusiastic memories of meeting Aeneas's father and his assurance of a friendship already cemented by the presents Anchises left for Evander and his son, Pallas (*Aeneid* 8.131–42, 155–69). For the reader, Pallas's name, no less than Lavinia's, ties him into the *Aeneid*'s grand narrative since he shares his name with the founder of the Arcadian people, and hence is linked with the name of their dwelling place, Pallanteum, itself the site of the future city of Rome (*Aeneid* 8.51–54, 97–100). Beyond all this, a strong tie combining emotion and duty is created between Aeneas, on the one side, and Evander and his son, Pallas, on the other. When they meet, Aeneas is already a hardened warrior and leader of his people, and Evander hands his son over into Aeneas's care so that Aeneas can set an example for Pallas to follow as he embarks on his rite of passage and assumes the status of a full-fledged warrior. In an emotional parting scene, his father bids him farewell and prays that he may never live to hear that his beloved son has been killed (*Aeneid* 8.514–17, 572–84). To Aeneas, the man of duty, all this gives a deeply ingrained imperative to avenge the death of Pallas, who dies a hero's death on the battlefield. There is no hint of failure on Aeneas's part to save the life of his young protégé, and a grief-stricken Evander later absolves the Trojans from any blame for Pallas's death, and he is proud of the circumstances in which his son's funeral is now taking place (*Aeneid* 11.42–58, 164–72). The message, which Evander wishes to be carried to Aeneas, is this:

> "The reason why I let my hated life linger on, with Pallas taken
>   from me,
> is this: your right hand. You see that it owes Turnus
> to a son and to his father. This is the one place remaining for your
>   services
> and for your fortune. I seek no pleasure in life—
> I have not the right—but to bring pleasure to my son down among
>   the dead." (*Aeneid* 11.177–81)

The duel between Turnus and Pallas is no evenly matched fight but a battle between a seasoned war leader and a youth new to the perils of war. The words spoken by Turnus in this context add a sense of brutality to the forthcoming killing: "I and I alone have Pallas / owed to me. I wish that his father were present in person to watch" (*Aeneid* 10.442–43). For a moment, a comparison between Turnus and Achilleus is again suggested: if this wish had been fulfilled, then Turnus's killing of Pallas would have resembled Achilleus's killing of Hektor before his father's eyes (*Iliad* 22.25–78, 408–9). As it is, this expression of gratuitous cruelty places Turnus alongside Achilles' son, Pyrrhus, who is cursed by Priam for forcing on a father the polluting sight of his own son's violent death (*Aeneid* 2.538–39). As he stands over Pallas's fallen body, Turnus speaks again of Pallas's father: "Remember these words of mine, you Arcadians, and take them / to Evander: I send him back the Pallas that he has deserved" (*Aeneid* 10.491–92). Turnus's callousness in victory toward the bond between father and son undermines his own, subsequent appeal to his victor, Aeneas, to show pity for Turnus's aged father, Daunus, and in so doing, to think of Aeneas's own father, Anchises. Thus a fleeting resemblance between the *Aeneid*'s closing scene and Priam's appeal to Achilleus at *Iliad* 24.486–506 is both suggested and at the same time countered. Any sympathetic feeling that Aeneas may have for a father has already been appropriated by the words of Evander.

This last point can be felt to be part of a wide-ranging and profound difference between the portrayal of the two losing figures in the final duels of the *Iliad* and the *Aeneid*. Hektor, as already noted, is shown at the center of a number of crisscrossing relationships. Turnus, by contrast, is shown more and more in isolation, and this makes the divinely enforced abandonment of him by Juturna the more telling. Turnus too, the Sibyl tells Aeneas, is the son of a goddess (*Aeneid* 6.90), but his mother, Venilia (*Aeneid* 10.76), makes no appearance in the narrative. In this way, she is unlike both Thetis and Venus and also unlike Hekabe, Hektor's mortal mother. Turnus's father, Daunus, is a shadowy figure, whose name appears in various forms a number of times before the *Aeneid*'s final scene,[21] but he does not appear in person. In his case too, a number of contrasts can be drawn: with the physically distant figure of Peleus, who nevertheless remains in his son's thoughts; with Anchises, who both in life and in death plays a dominant part in his son's life and to whom Turnus refers in his last words; and with Priam, who with his wife witnesses his son's death and whose appearances in *Iliad* 3 and 24 frame the narrative of war. Since Turnus is not seen with a mother or a father of his own, his association with the couple whose daughter he wants to marry can be felt to take on an additional importance. Similarly, the early condemnation of him

---

21. Cf. *Aeneid* 8.146–47; 10.616, 688; 12.22, 90–91, 723–24, 785. At *Aeneid* 12.43–45, Latinus begs Turnus in vain to pity his old father and to give up his claim on Lavinia.

by his hoped-for father-in-law, Latinus, for dragging his people into an unholy war, and Latinus's conviction that Turnus will incur divine punishment, have an added sting (*Aeneid* 7.595–97).

Here then is the second issue for resolution in the duel. Though it does not have a direct bearing on the *Aeneid*'s grand narrative, the resolution of this issue brings the *Aeneid* to its close. Once again the *Aeneid*'s problematic nature appears here. It does not end with a confident foreshadowing of the birth of the Roman nation as the ultimate consequence of the Trojan hero's victory in single combat over the enemy leader, nor does it end with a scene of reconciliation between enemies made possible by the shared sense of suffering. Rather, it looks back, both painfully and violently, to the sufferings of the past and to the legacy of revenge killing. A further comparison can be made here with the *Iliad*. In the *Iliad*, conflict between two men over one girl is eventually laid aside (*Iliad* 19.63–68) and replaced by a climactic conflict between two men over the killing of a close comrade on the battlefield. In the final lines of *Aeneid* 12, a comparable switch takes on an additional intensity. Now one man's anger remains focused on the same person rather than moving from one person (Agamemnon) to another (Hektor), and now attention is drawn to the moment's pause when anger is beginning to give way to persuasion before flaring up again and leading to the killing with which the *Aeneid* ends.

On the battlefield in the *Iliad*, Trojan warriors who fall into the hands of their Achaean enemies plead unsuccessfully for their lives (*Iliad* 6.45–65; 11.126–47; 20.463–72; 21.64–119, and 10.446–57 for Diomedes' killing of the Trojan spy, Dolon). The first in this sequence of supplications has some similarity with the present situation in that it too contains a moment's uncertainty about the fate of the victim. Menelaos is about to accept Adrestos's offer of a rich ransom for his life, but Agamemnon appears on the scene and forcefully reminds his brother of the need to exact blanket revenge on the Trojan community. When Aeneas himself carries out a frenzied slaughter of the enemy in revenge for Turnus's killing of Pallas, he too bitterly rejects pleas to be spared (*Aeneid* 10.521–36, 550–56, 595–601). The situation with Turnus and Aeneas, however, is more complex. Turnus does not make a direct plea for his life; instead he asks Aeneas to set a limit to his "hatred." At this moment Aeneas wavers and is beginning to be won over by Turnus's words (*Aeneid* 12.940–41). Then Turnus's request is rejected, not by the force of argument but by a sudden surge of emotion on the part of Aeneas. The trigger for this sudden, lethal combination of grief and anger is the sight of the "ill-starred baldric." Smith memorably characterizes this moment as "vision's dominance over rhetoric" (2011, 142).

The ending of the *Aeneid* is like that of the *Iliad* in that it is rich in its association of ideas. Now, however, these ideas take on an added complexity in that they involve both the *Aeneid* and the *Iliad,* and there is no corresponding sense of final resolution. Three issues can now be explored. First is the question of where the reader is placed in relation to the death with which the narrative ends. In the *Iliad* the final image is that of the arrangements made by the living for the commemoration and burial of the defeated leader. In the *Aeneid* the final image is of the killing of the defeated leader after a tantalizing moment when it seemed as if his life might be spared. After the wealth and intricacy of the points of comparison between the two final duels in the *Iliad* and in the *Aeneid,* and after the moments when the *Aeneid*'s narrator has portrayed Turnus and his plight with a degree of sympathy, the absence of any lamentation, funeral rites, or obituary for the fallen suggests the sense of something missing. Hardie writes, "the *Iliad* ends with ritual after death, the funeral of Hector, and the *Odyssey* with ritual designed to prevent further killing" (1997a, 143–44). By contrast, he notes that the solemn ritual recorded near the beginning of *Aeneid* 12 to regulate the forthcoming duel (*Aeneid* 12.161–215) is all to no avail. "Thus the killing of Turnus inverts the expected sequence of violence followed by ritual" (Hardie 1997a, 144). W. R. Johnson writes in more general terms, contrasting the paradoxical sense of calm "issued as it is from such rage and destruction" in the *Iliad* with "the degree to which calm of any kind has been consciously excluded from the *Aeneid*" (1976, 120). In a word, Turnus's death does not receive closure, and this may leave a subliminal sense of anxiety in the reader's mind.[22]

A second issue is how to place the killing of Turnus in the wider context of the unfolding narrative. The line with which the *Aeneid* ends has already been used as the climax of a longer description of a death in battle, that of the maiden warrior, Camilla (*Aeneid* 11.831, repeated at 12.952), but in her case, and unlike that of Turnus, her killing is avenged by divine intervention. A repetition of lines on a slightly more extended scale occurs in a similar context in the *Iliad.* Among the common features of the description of the deaths of Patroklos and Hektor are the following two lines: "The soul flying away from the limbs came to Hades, / lamenting its fate, having left young manhood" (*Iliad* 16.856–57, repeated at 22.362–63).

All four passages share the viewpoint of the dying warrior, but sadness in the Homeric contexts becomes the different emotion of indignation in the

22. For further discussion of closure, see D. Fowler (1997).

Virgilian contexts. And while the two deaths in the *Iliad* are linked in a cycle of revenge killing, the two deaths in the *Aeneid* occur on the same, ultimately losing, side. A further detail links Turnus specifically with Hektor: both warriors take equipment from the body of their victim and wear it themselves, and in both cases this act is linked with their own approaching death (*Iliad* 16.799–800; 17.183–209; *Aeneid* 10.500–505). Turnus's death can thus be placed as the last in a sequence of premature deaths on the battlefield, a sequence that stretches back to the *Iliad* and includes, within the *Aeneid* and in addition to the death of Camilla, the much lamented deaths of Pallas, Lausus, Nisus, and Euryalus (*Aeneid* 11.26–99; 10.819–30; 9.446–49). Nor is the battlefield the only context in which tragically premature deaths occur in the *Aeneid*. One of the most abiding images of its first half is Dido's death, which Aeneas is directly involved in, as he is in Turnus's.[23] There is another, broader sense in which Turnus's death acts as the last in a sequence of deaths. In a variety of different contexts, a death occurs at or near the ending of eight of the eleven books that precede the final book of the *Aeneid*.[24] Thus, death features regularly in the construction of an intermediate sense of closure. As *Aeneid* 12 comes to an end, this juxtaposition of deaths and endings takes on an increased significance since both the narrative and the life of one of the two individuals on whom it has recently focused come to an end at the same time.[25]

A third and final issue is how to place Aeneas as he appears in the closing lines of the narrative that bears his name. Aeneas has already cited the judgment of his dead father, Anchises (together with that of his son, Iulus), in support of his killing a suppliant in the heat of battle and in revenge for Turnus's killing of Pallas (*Aeneid* 10.532–34). Now he goes further and twice names the dead Pallas as the one who inflicts the fatal wound on Turnus. In doing this, Aeneas sidesteps the issue of his own responsibility for killing Turnus. The terms in which he describes this posthumous killing make uncomfortable reading, since Pallas is given a combination of three distinct

---

23. Pöschl gives a detailed discussion of the roles of Dido and Turnus in the *Aeneid*. He compares *Aeneid* 4.1–2 with the simile describing Turnus at *Aeneid* 12.4–9 and writes, "The warrior's passion is similar to the queen's, appearing as a festering wound which tragically destroys the victim" (1970, 110).

24. Cf. the confirmation of the death of Creusa at *Aeneid* 2.771–95; the account of the death of Anchises at *Aeneid* 3.708–15; the death of Dido at *Aeneid* 4.642–705; the loss overboard of Palinurus at *Aeneid* 5.854–71; the anticipation of the death of Marcellus at *Aeneid* 6.860–86; the anticipation of the death of Cleopatra among the scenes depicted on Aeneas's shield at *Aeneid* 8.709–13; Aeneas's killing of Mezentius at *Aeneid* 10.870–908; and the death of Camilla and the divine killing of Arruns in revenge at *Aeneid* 11.827–67.

25. This concentration on earlier deaths is only part of a network of allusions that can be sensed to earlier points in the *Aeneid*'s narrative; cf. Hardie (1997a, 150–51).

and ill-matched roles: priest officiating at a human sacrifice,[26] recipient of that sacrifice, and executioner exacting the ultimate punishment for a crime. As the power of persuasion gives way to the greater power of homicidal fury in the *Aeneid*'s closing lines, this explosive moment brings with it the collapse of a number of the *Aeneid*'s hitherto fixed points. Throughout the *Aeneid*, Aeneas and Juno have been set in opposition to one another. But now they are shown to be alike: each acts in violent rage based on a memory of the past (*Aeneid* 1.4, 23–28; 12.945–47). Central to the depiction of Aeneas is his dutifulness, and this has been shown, in particular in his association with Dido, to require the suppression of his emotion. Yet now his final recorded act is one of unbridled emotion, the emotion of blazing fury. At the *Aeneid*'s halfway point, the spirit of Anchises spells out the Roman mission statement. It ends with these words: "to spare those who submit and crush the proud in war" (*Aeneid* 6.853). This confidently expressed distinction between those who are to be spared and those who are to be crushed collapses when it is put to the test in the *Aeneid*'s closing lines. Turnus has submitted. He has been proud (*Aeneid* 10.445–46, 514–15; 12.326–27), but now he is humble (*Aeneid* 12.930–31). At Aeneas's final appearance, the realignment that places him rather than Turnus in the role of Achilleus is complete, and the *Aeneid* ends just as the *Iliad* begins, with the terrible anger of its eponymous hero. With such a complex relationship between the *Aeneid* and the *Iliad*, with such shifting characterization, and with such difficult questions raised both directly and indirectly within the text, "an attitude of genuine ambivalence" (Tarrant 2012, 24), though difficult to maintain, seems a convincing response.

8.3 🕊 Still to Come

The *Iliad*, the *Odyssey*, and the *Aeneid* differ from each other in the nature of the future they look forward to after the completion of their narrated events. Such foreshadowing of things still to come occurs across each of the three poems and plays a part in the construction of their endings. In the first three-quarters of the *Iliad*, such moments offer the reader a glimpse of the war continuing, after the truce for the burial of Hektor, toward its eventual outcome. Thus Odysseus relates Kalchas's prophecy that Troy will be taken in the tenth year of the war (*Iliad* 2.299–330), and both Agamemnon and Hektor

---

26. For the preparations made earlier by Aeneas for human sacrifice to the dead Pallas, cf. *Aeneid* 10.517–20; 11.81–82.

express the conviction that the day will come when Troy will be destroyed, together with its king and its people (*Iliad* 4.163–68; 6.447–65). The prediction that Hektor expresses to Andromache leads him to an agonized vision of the miseries of enslavement that will then await her, and after her husband's death, Andromache herself imagines the sufferings that now lie ahead for their orphaned baby son, for herself, and for their city (*Iliad* 22.477–507; 24.723–45).[27] The human conviction that Troy will fall is confirmed by Zeus at the start of *Iliad* 15, when he tells Hera of the sequence of events that lie ahead on the battlefield and looks beyond the killing of Hektor to its sequel:

> "From that point on, I will turn the flight of the Achaeans around,
> away from their ships, into a constant, unbroken advance,
> until they take steep Troy, through the designs of Athene." (*Iliad*
>   15.69–71)

However, set against this unfolding vision of ultimate success for the Achaean war effort and destruction and misery for their enemies, the reader is also shown midway through the *Iliad* that once the fighting is over, the gods have the power to erase all trace of the Achaean military presence left by them on a foreign land. At *Iliad* 7.436–63, the Achaeans construct a wall and dig a ditch to defend their camp and ships from attack, but they fail to make the proper sacrifice to the gods for such a great undertaking, and Zeus tells Poseidon to break down and destroy all trace of the wall once the Achaeans have returned home. As the fighting around the ditch and the wall intensifies, the narrative moves quickly forward in order to detail these changes (*Iliad* 12.3–35):

> But when all the best men of Troy had died,
> and some of the many Argives had been brought down and others
>   were left,
> and the city of Priam was sacked in the tenth year,
> and the Argives went in their ships to their own dear land,
> then it was that Poseidon and Apollo devised a way
> to destroy the wall, driving the force of rivers against it. (*Iliad*
>   12.13–18)

A short list follows of the eight rivers that run down from the mountains of Ida to the sea and whose mouths are made by Apollo to converge and pour their waters on the wall for a nine-day period. Zeus adds constant rain to the process

---

27. For two other ways in which this future is foreshadowed, cf. *Iliad* 9.590–94; 22.410–11.

of destruction, and Poseidon with his trident sweeps the remains of the wall away into the sea and covers its site on the shore with sand before redirecting the rivers to flow in their original courses once again (*Iliad* 12.19–35). Here in the midst of intense fighting halfway through the narrative, the reader is given for a short time a change of perspective and taken forward in time. Now the human forces both of construction and of destruction are set against the scale of destruction and geographical change that the gods are able to cause, and an ironic contrast emerges between what eight rivers described in 6 lines achieve in nine days, on the one hand, and what twenty-nine contingents of warriors described in 292 lines (*Iliad* 2.494–785) achieve in ten years, on the other.

The anticipation of the imminent death of Achilleus after the completion of the narrative is introduced early in the Iliad (*Iliad* 1.352–54, 415–18), but it is then modified a third of the way through to appear as one of two possibilities rather than as a certainty (*Iliad* 9.410–16). It reappears as a certainty deeply embedded in the final quarter of the *Iliad,* where it contributes in a subtle way to the ending of the poem by suggesting both the potential for the continuation of the narrative beyond its end and also an end point for that hypothetical continuation. Achilleus is variously told of his coming death by his mother Thetis, by his horse Xanthos, by the dying Hektor, who gives the most detailed account of it, and by the dream figure of Patroklos's ghost.[28] Achilleus himself speaks of it in a variety of contexts.[29] Thetis too expresses her grief at the thought of her son's approaching death, and she receives a sympathetic response from her fellow Nereids, from Hephaistos, and from Hera and Zeus.[30] Achilleus is unique in the *Iliad* in knowing of his own imminent death, and the foreshadowing of this event throughout the last quarter of the *Iliad* is conveyed to the reader through accounts of a wide range of communication shown taking place within and across different worlds. Here is a final, profound paradox: the *Iliad*'s narrative of individuals and communities at war with one another is of monumental length and intricacy, and yet the life of its central hero is painfully short, and his death is not part of that narrative but is forever left rapidly approaching as the narrative comes to an end.[31]

---

28. *Iliad* 18.95–96 and 24.131–32; 19.408–17; 22.359–60; 23.80–81.

29. *Iliad* 18.98–99, 329–35; 19.328–37; 21.108–13; 21.273–83; 23.150–51.

30. *Iliad* 18.35–67 and 24.83–86; 18.462–67; 24.101–5.

31. Schein writes of the *Iliad,* "to think about war in the poem is to hold a kind of ethical mirror up to our own practices and values" (2016, 165). Among the works that, in various ways, present a large-scale view of the Homeric poems are Kirk (1962), Camps (1980), Griffin (2001), Graziosi and Haubold (2005), Barker and Christensen (2013), and Nicolson (2014). Jones (2003) and (1988) give the reader of the *Iliad* and the *Odyssey* in English a useful book-by-book commentary.

The eventual return home from war of "a man of many ways"—after wandering far and wide and after many encounters with new places and new people and much suffering on the high seas (*Odyssey* 1.1–5)—suggests a sequence of events that already contains its own movement toward completion and hence toward an ending. Nevertheless, from the outset the *Odyssey* warns the reader against making too simple an identification between journey's end for the characters within its narrative and journey's end for the narrative itself. The *Odyssey* is like its eponymous hero in that it wanders far and wide, displaying great ingenuity in doing so. N. Austin (1975, 81–253) discusses the *Odyssey*'s breadth and complex structure.[32] In its first hundred lines, its main characters and main concerns are introduced, and as the narrative moves toward its close, these concerns are gradually resolved. Athene and Zeus once again discuss the situation, and now their concern is how best to resolve it without further conflict. Zeus puts forward a peace plan, whose wording suggests a sense of closure:

> "Since the godlike Odysseus has gained his revenge on the suitors,
> by making a treaty on oath, let him be king for ever more
> and let us bring forgetfulness of the killing of their sons
> and their brothers and let them be friends with one another
> as before, and let there be wealth and peace in abundance." (*Odyssey* 24.482–86)

The narrative, however, has not quite reached its close. A set battle with those of the suitors' kinsmen who are intent on seeking revenge for the killings is stopped by divine intervention, but not before the three generations, Odysseus, Telemachos, and old Laertes, have proudly taken their stand in battle together with the disguised Athene by their side. Divine intervention halts the Ithacans from shedding blood, prevents Odysseus's enemies from being utterly destroyed and "deprived of their homecoming," and forcefully cautions a still belligerent Odysseus against arousing the anger of Zeus by prolonging the conflict. And so the narrative comes to a close:

> So spoke Athene and he obeyed and his heart was glad.
> Thereafter a solemn treaty was made between the two sides
> by Pallas Athene, daughter of Zeus who bears the aegis,
> in the appearance of Mentor, both in body and in voice. (*Odyssey* 24.545–48)

---

32. For the enduring appeal of the *Odyssey*, see Hall (2008).

After the horrific massacre of the suitors and their accomplices, the *Odyssey* does much to suggest the sense of a happy ending. The ruling family of Ithaca is reunited and is strong and happy. The people lay aside their quarrel and all are friends again "as before." The intervention of Zeus and Athene makes this possible and so completes the process of Odysseus's homecoming begun by them in the first hundred lines of the poem. It also guarantees the stability of this homecoming beyond the end of the narrative. Odysseus will be undisputed king "for ever more," and his people will enjoy peace and prosperity. The Trojan War and its aftermath cast a long shadow over the *Odyssey*, but the shadow does not darken the *Odyssey*'s ending. Odysseus himself is a survivor, and he has the support of Athene, who in her disguises transcends the basic distinctions between god and human and between female and male, and who helps him through his many crises, all the way to the *Odyssey*'s closing lines.

The *Odyssey* opens by proclaiming itself to be a sequel to events that took place earlier in its hero's life: "Tell me, Muse, of a man of many ways, who wandered / far and wide, when he had sacked the sacred city of Troy" (*Odyssey* 1.1–2).[33] The sense of taking up and continuing a narrative of earlier events that the reader may be expected to be familiar with, at least in outline, is an effective opening gambit, but it raises a problem for bringing the narrative to a close since a sequel by its very nature suggests the possibility of further expansion. This problem goes back to classical times, when the suggestion was made that the *Odyssey*'s proper ending should be considered to come at *Odyssey* 23.296, where the reunited couple are shown going happily to bed together. De Jong (2001, 561–62, 565–66) makes a strong case for the inclusion of the remainder of the *Odyssey* within its overall structure. But doubts about its authenticity remain, and in particular about the often-rushed nature of the narrative, as Rutherford (2013, 97–102) shows.[34]

The *Odyssey* skillfully solves the problem of how to close and, in so doing, creates the additional advantage of drawing together its middle and its end. In *Odyssey* 11.121–37, Odysseus recounts the prophecy Teiresias's ghost gives him of a further journey he must make after completing his homecoming and exacting revenge on his wife's suitors. Odysseus also relates the vision given to him of the circumstances in which he will come to the end of his life. When he is reunited with Penelope, Odysseus unfolds both parts of this

---

33. Rutherford (2013, 76–81) gives a concise discussion of this point.

34. Barker and Christensen discuss this part of the *Odyssey*, noting that "the poem explicitly sets up its ending as a problem" (2013, 182).

prophecy before they go to bed together (*Odyssey* 23.247–87). Thus to the question, "What did Odysseus do next?" the *Odyssey* has embedded within it a ready and satisfying answer. His journey home, itself a sequel to his earlier life as a champion warrior, is itself destined to have a further sequel, another journey, whose details are surrounded by an intriguing sense of mystery. After that further journey is completed, he will return home once more, fulfil his obligations to the gods, and die a painless death, leaving his people in the midst of prosperity.

The key feature of this projected travel in the future is its complete difference from the experiences of his journey home, as recorded in the *Odyssey*. Here he suffers repeatedly on the high seas (*Odyssey* 1.4), but in that future journey, the sea will be conspicuously absent:

> "Then you will go, taking your well-poised oar,
> until you come to people, who know nothing of the sea
> and do not eat their food mixed with salt.
> They know nothing of boats with their crimson cheeks
> or of well-poised oars, which act as wings for boats." (*Odyssey*
> 11.121–25)

In the course of his wanderings, Odysseus sees the homes of many different people and learns of their way of thinking (*Odyssey* 1.3). This process of discovery is projected into the journey in the future, but now at the end of this further wandering, the links with features of the familiar world, such as its food and transport, will no longer apply. Here even the most familiar object will be redefined:

> "And now I will tell you a clear sign, one which you will not miss:
> when another traveler falls in with you,
> and says that you have a winnowing-fan on your fine shoulder,
> then will be the time for you to fix your well-poised oar in the
> ground,
> and to perform a splendid sacrifice to lord Poseidon." (*Odyssey*
> 11.126–30)

The limit to Odysseus's future wandering is thus set in terms both geographical and conceptual. When he meets "another traveler" who says that the "well-poised oar" on his shoulder is a "winnowing-fan," his days of using what the narrator reassures the reader is in fact still his "well-poised oar," to wing his way across the sea as he has done in the course of the *Odyssey*, will have come to an end. The point that he will have reached here at journey's end also addresses unfinished business. The anger of Poseidon toward Odysseus (*Odyssey* 1.20–21; 11.100–103) will be appeased, as Zeus predicted at the start (*Odyssey* 1.77–79), and Odysseus will come safely home again, where his death will be "easy" and will resemble his subsequent journeying in being "away from the sea" (*Odyssey* 11.134).[35]

In one sense, the *Aeneid*'s grand narrative creates a much fuller future waiting to unfold than the future shown in outline either by the *Iliad* or by the *Odyssey*, and it is a future that the reader's attention is confidently drawn to from the outset and that colors the whole narrative. However, this is also a future restricted in terms of time and space. Here, projected into the future, is a version of events that have already happened in Italy, long before the time of the present day reader and outside the world created by the narrative. This double time frame poses a problem for the creation of the sense of an ending. Thus it can be argued, as Hardie (1997a, 142) notes, that the problematic killing of Turnus that concludes *Aeneid* 12 is not the end of the story of "the founding of the Roman nation" (*Aeneid* 1.33). Rather, that ending is brought up to the time of the *Aeneid*'s composition and shown in the triumphal celebrations of Augustus depicted in the culmination of scenes shown on the shield of Aeneas (*Aeneid* 8.626–728). This adds to the range of multiple endings that the *Aeneid* offers the reader to consider.

In the heralding of what is still to come, a sharp contrast emerges between the *Iliad* and the *Aeneid*. The *Iliad* looks forward to destruction brought about by human and divine hands and to the approaching death of its central character, despite his divine origin on his mother's side. The *Aeneid* looks forward to the exact opposite of this. Fate has in store for the Trojans' descendants the building first of a great city and then of an "empire without end" (*Aeneid* 1.279), and Venus's son, the *Aeneid*'s eponymous hero, will not die but will become a god (*Aeneid* 1.259–60; 12.793–95). Initially the reader shares with Venus the privilege of foreknowledge granted by Jupiter, from which Aeneas himself is excluded (*Aeneid* 1.257–96).[36] Once Aeneas reaches Italy, however, two extensive passages, one in *Aeneid* 6 and one in *Aeneid* 8, give him a detailed

---

35. The words translated here as "away from the sea," however, are the subject of a long-standing controversy since they can also be understood to mean that Odysseus's death will come "from the sea." For further discussion see Stanford (1959, 387).

36. Here Jupiter creates a smooth transition between his foreshadowing of events to be narrated in the second half of the *Aeneid* and what is still to come beyond its end; cf. *Iliad* 15.53–71.

account of what lies in the future, after his own lifetime. From a vantage point in Elysium, the spirit of Anchises speaks of the glory that lies ahead for the Trojans in Italy, and he picks out and identifies each of a crowd of as yet unborn spirits as they pass in front of him (*Aeneid* 6.752–846, 855–59). The emperor Augustus comes in the middle of this parade of the spirits of the future. Here is a different trajectory from the one used in *Aeneid* 1 and later in *Aeneid* 8. Jupiter's unfolding of the future ends with a vision of Augustus, of his expansion of the empire, and of peace and justice, while the scenes shown on Aeneas's shield culminate in a lengthy picture of Augustus as the triumphant victor in war (*Aeneid* 1.286–96; 8.675–728). Now, by contrast, a third of the way through Anchises' speech, Aeneas sees the whole Roman nation with Augustus at the center of its history.

As well as foregrounding Augustus and keeping him at a distance from any mention of civil war, the configuration of Anchises' speech has two further advantages. The first is that it allows him to come to a rousing conclusion twice. As he finishes describing the unparalleled mark that Augustus will make on the world, Anchises pauses briefly to ask a rhetorical question: "And do we still shrink from extending our bravery in action, / or does fear prevent us from settling in the land of Italy?" (*Aeneid* 6. 806–7). The conclusion to the second half of his speech is longer and takes the form of a confident mission statement:

> "You, Roman, remember this: to rule with your empire the peo-
> ples on earth,
> (these will be your arts), and make peace their custom,
> to spare those who submit and crush the proud in war." (*Aeneid*
> 6.851–53).

Already Aeneas has been urged to look at "your Romans" (*Aeneid* 6.788–89). Now the identity of Anchises' addressee becomes a generalized "You, Roman," but at the same time as it bridges a gap between different worlds, this address also creates a fresh gap since it distances the reader of the modern world from this world shared by Aeneas and "You, Roman." A moment before, a more bellicose Anchises was celebrating how later generations of Romans will avenge their Trojan ancestors on the Greeks (*Aeneid* 6.836–39). Now in more magnanimous mood, he accords the Greeks, thinly disguised behind the generalizing term "others," their place as world leaders in the plastic arts, forensic oratory, and in science (*Aeneid* 6.847–50). The Roman's arts, by contrast, belong in the practical world. They are the arts of ruling an empire, and here the Roman has a solemn duty, which he must not forget. It is to impose peace as a way of life on the peoples brought within her empire and, in war, to combine clemency and toughness.

The second advantage that comes from the configuration of Anchises' speech is more complex. If Anchises' review of the unborn spirits of great figures of Roman history had taken a strictly chronological form and had ended, in the time of the poem's composition, with the figure of Augustus Caesar, it might have prompted the question "And what happens after Augustus?" Rather than introduce an air of uncertainty about what the future may hold at the time of the poem's composition, the final section of Anchises' vision turns the reader's attention to an acknowledged certainty in the recent past and brings a radical change of mood. It focuses attention on the premature death of Marcellus, who as both nephew and son-in-law of Augustus was for a time regarded as a possible heir to the ailing emperor.[37] Aeneas asks Anchises who the outstandingly handsome but sad-faced young warrior is, whom he can see walking beside the triumphant figure of an older Marcellus, and his question prompts an outpouring of emotion from Anchises (*Aeneid* 6.860–86). These are Anchises' last recorded words.

In their different ways, both the *Iliad* and the *Odyssey* incorporate the foreshadowed death of their central hero as part of their sense of an ending. In the *Odyssey* this foreshadowing takes place halfway through the narrative in the course of the hero's encounter with the Underworld, and it comes from the mouth of a spirit gifted with the ability to see into the future. Here near the end of *Aeneid* 6, in a similar context, it is not the death of Aeneas that is foreshadowed (the reader already knows that Aeneas will become immortal); instead the foreshadowed death is that of the historical figure of a possible successor to the emperor Augustus. Here is an opportunity for Anchises to express patriotic, Augustan fervor in a different context: in a funeral eulogy in which the incomparable virtues of Augustus's close relation are celebrated both by Anchises' tribute to him and by the splendor of the state funeral he describes. The expression of grief spans the double gap between the spirit of Anchises and Aeneas and between the world of Aeneas and the world of the Roman reader: "Alas for the sense of duty! Alas for old-fashioned reliability and a right hand / unconquered in war!" (*Aeneid* 6.878–79). A moment later, Anchises addresses Marcellus himself: "Alas wretched boy, if somehow you

37. Glei (2009) discusses the historical figure of the young Marcellus and his place in *Aeneid* 6.

were to break harsh fate, / you will be Marcellus" (*Aeneid* 6.882–83).[38] Here, at the *Aeneid*'s halfway point as at its ending, attention is focused on the premature death of young men (Marcellus, Pallas, Turnus), and the fact that the first of these three is a public figure in the historical world of the *Aeneid*'s composition, a figure on whom the highest of hopes were fixed (*Aeneid* 6.875–77), gives an added power to this sequence of early deaths.

The third foreshadowing of the future history of Rome is expressed in visual, rather than oral terms. In a detailed discussion of the shield of Aeneas, Hardie states that it displays a "blend of cosmic allegory and political ideology," and he characterizes the shield's description as the "climax of the *Aeneid*" (1986, 342, 362–64). The description of the scenes created by Vulcan on the shield is a little shorter than that of the scenes created by Hephaistos on the shield of Achilleus (*Aeneid* 8.626–728; *Iliad* 18.481–608). Aeneas's shield has no preliminary scene of earth, sea, and sky, nor is there a final scene of the Ocean river running around its edge, and there is no hint of a world or of a cycle of life. In place of the *Iliad*'s nonlocalized and contrasting scenes of peace and war, of cooperation and conflict, and of interplay between the sexes, the subjects shown on Aeneas's shield are both more limited and more specific:

> There the god of fire, with knowledge of the prophets and of the
>   time to come,
> had made the history of Italy and the triumphs
> of the Romans. There he had made the whole family of the future
> line of Ascanius and wars and the order in which they were
>   fought. (*Aeneid* 8.626–29)

The result is a wealth of specific detail and of proper names set within a context of national, predominantly military, history. These details are shown not in the process of being created by the god but as they appear to the wondering eyes of Aeneas (*Aeneid* 8.617–25, 729–30). Aeneas has just been taken on a tour of the sites that will one day be a familiar part of the city of Rome; now he is shown traditional scenes from the tales of Rome's early history, scenes that are necessarily outside the scope of the *Aeneid*'s main narrative (the twins being suckled by a she-wolf, freedom fighters in their struggle against Lars

---

38. The punctuation and interpretation of this sentence is disputed. The reading here follows the punctuation of the Oxford Classical Text. Page (1894, 502–4), and R. G. Austin (1977, 272) argues for an exclamation mark, rather than a comma, at the end of line 882. This produces the sense, "Alas, wretched boy, if only in some way you could break harsh fate! You will be Marcellus."

Porsenna and Tarquin, the goose that saved the day by singing out to alert Manlius to the imminent Gallic attack, and suchlike).

These and the two culminating scenes differ in construction from the scenes on Achilleus's shield. Comparatively small vignettes follow one another quickly in the first half of the description of Aeneas's shield, and the second half is taken up entirely by a long description of the battle of Actium and a shorter description of the triumphal celebrations following it (*Aeneid* 8.675–713, 714–28). Emotive coloring is stronger than in the scenes on Achilleus's shield: the snippets of Rome's early history have a homely quality and an underlying sense of right and wrong that reaches a climax in readiness for the portrayal of the two sides in the battle of Actium. While the scenes of war on the shield of Achilleus are stripped of any sense of glory, the central place on Aeneas's shield is taken by the figure of Augustus in all his glory (*Aeneid* 8.678–81). Here is a battle depicted as a titanic struggle between civilization and barbarism. The Olympian gods, Neptune, Venus, Minerva, and Actian Apollo, are ranged against the outlandish gods of Egypt. The fighting begins, and in the presence of all the divinities of war, the forces of the East collapse in terror and they and their queen flee. Even here, however, where distinctions are at their most clear cut, there is a brief change of tone as the figure of the grieving Nile is shown opening his clothes to offer the shelter of his "sea-blue bosom and his secret waterways to the defeated" (*Aeneid* 8.711–13). Then the triumph of Augustus brings the description of the scenes shown on the shield to a rousing conclusion (*Aeneid* 8.714–28). Now there is no complex and ambivalent relationship between shield and its owner, as in the *Iliad*, but a piece of comparatively straightforward symbolism. Aeneas may be ignorant of the things shown on the shield, but he rejoices at the representation of them "as he lifts onto his shoulders the fame and the fate of his children's children" (*Aeneid* 8.730, the last line of the book). Once before he lifted his father onto his shoulders to protect him from destruction at Troy (*Aeneid* 2.721–23); now he happily shoulders the future of his people, with its culmination in the triumph of Augustus. Hardie writes, "In lifting the Shield Aeneas thus becomes the guarantor of the future emergence of the order of the Roman universe" (1986, 374–75).

Both the *Aeneid*'s account of its eponymous hero and its grand narrative of the birth and growth of the Roman nation toward its current position as world ruler under its glorious leader are sequences of narrative that allow the reader to ask what remains untold. The *Aeneid* does not offer the reader blanket reassurance in answer to this question. In the first foreshadowing of the future, Jupiter tells Venus that after crushing the ferocious peoples of Italy, Aeneas will have a three-year reign and will build walls and bring to the people "a civilized way of life" (*Aeneid* 1.263–66). As *Aeneid* 2 draws to a close, the phantom Creusa tells Aeneas that he will find in his new land "happiness, royal power, and a royal wife" (*Aeneid* 2.783–84). These predictions do not sit comfortably alongside the *Aeneid*'s closing image of the sudden welling up of homicidal fury in Aeneas. The reader is left to wonder how Aeneas will manage his first meeting with his young bride, his renewed meeting with her father, now a widower, and his meeting with the people of Latinus's city, whom he has threatened to annihilate (*Aeneid* 12.554–73), and how far these experiences will bring "happiness." Then there is still Carthage to consider. Immediately after its opening, the *Aeneid* draws attention to Juno's fear that her beloved Carthage will be destroyed by the Trojans' descendants (*Aeneid* 1.12–22), and this fear adds to her already deep-seated hatred of the Trojans. Two stark reminders of the coming conflict between Carthage and Rome come between this point and Juno's ultimate willingness to sever the connection between Trojan and Roman, a willingness that is accompanied by Juno's "happy state of mind" at hearing from Jupiter about the future people of Italy (*Aeneid* 12.820–42). The first reminder comes from Dido, and the second from Jupiter himself (*Aeneid* 4.622–29; 10.11–14). Here is an aspect of Rome's place in the world, and specifically of her continuing relationship with Juno, that is almost completely edited out of the *Aeneid*'s grand narrative.[39]

---

39. For the *Aeneid*'s enduring appeal, see Farrell and Putnam (2010) and Hardie (2014).

Bibliography

Alexiou, M. 1974. *The Ritual Lament in Greek Tradition*. Cambridge University Press.

Allen, T. W., and Monro, D. B., eds. 1902–1917. *Homeri Opera Tomi I–IV*. Oxford Classical Texts. Oxford University Press.

Austin, N. 1975. *Archery at the Dark of the Moon: Poetic Problems in Homer's Odyssey*. University of California Press.

————. 1994. *Helen of Troy and Her Shameless Phantom*. Cornell University Press.

Austin, R. G., ed. 1955. *P. Vergili Maronis Liber Quartus*. Oxford University Press.

————, ed. 1964. *P. Vergili Maronis Liber Secundus*. Oxford University Press.

————, ed. 1971. *P. Vergili Maronis Liber Primus*. Oxford University Press.

————, ed. 1977. *P. Vergili Maronis Liber Sextus*. Oxford University Press.

Barker, E., and Christensen, J. 2013. *Homer: A Beginner's Guide*. Oneworld.

Bergren, A. L. T. 2009. "Helen's 'Good Drug'." In *Oxford Readings in Classical Studies: Homer's Odyssey*, edited by L. E. Doherty, 314–55. Oxford University Press.

Bespaloff, R. 1962. "Helen." In *Homer: A Collection of Critical Essays*, edited by G. Steiner and R. Fagles, 100–104. Prentice-Hall.

Burkert, W. 2009. "The Song of Ares and Aphrodite: On the Relationship between the *Odyssey* and the *Iliad*," translated by G. M. Wright and P. V. Jones. In *Oxford Readings in Classical Studies: Homer's Odyssey*, edited by L. E. Doherty, 29–43. Oxford University Press.

Buxton, R. 2004. "Similes and other Likenesses." In *The Cambridge Companion to Homer*, edited by R. Fowler, 139–55. Cambridge University Press.

Camps, W. A. 1969. *An Introduction to Virgil's Aeneid*. Oxford University Press.

————. 1980. *An Introduction to Homer*. Oxford University Press.

de Jong, I. J. F. 2001. *A Narratological Commentary on the Odyssey*. Cambridge University Press.

Dodds, E. R. 1951. *The Greeks and The Irrational.* University of California Press.

Doherty, L. E. 1995. "Sirens, Muses and Female Narrators in the Odyssey." In *The Distaff Side: Representing the Female in Homer's Odyssey*, edited by B. Cohen, 81–92. Oxford University Press.

———. 2009. "Introduction," and "Gender and Internal Audiences in the *Odyssey*." In *Oxford Readings in Classical Studies: Homer's Odyssey*, edited by L. E. Doherty. 1–17, 247–64. Oxford University Press.

Edwards, M. W. 1987. *Homer Poet of the Iliad.* The John Hopkins University Press.

———, ed. 1991. *The Iliad: A Commentary.* Vol. 5, *Books 17–20.* Cambridge University Press.

Eliot, T. S. 1945. *What Is a Classic?* Faber and Faber Ltd.

Emlyn-Jones, C. 2009. "The Reunion of Penelope and Odysseus" In *Oxford Readings in Classical Studies: Homer's Odyssey*, edited by L. E. Doherty, 208–30. Oxford University Press.

Farrell, J., and Putnam, M. C. J., eds. 2010. *A Companion to Vergil's Aeneid and its Tradition.* Chichester and Malden.

Feeney, D. C. 1990. "The Taciturnity of Aeneas." In *Oxford Readings in Vergil's Aeneid*, edited by S. J. Harrison. 167–90. Oxford University Press.

———. 1991. *The Gods in Epic: Poets and Critics of the Classical Tradition.* Clarendon Press, Oxford.

Felson-Rubin, N. 1996. "Penelope's Perspective: Character from Plot." In *Reading the Odyssey: Selected Interpretive Essays*, edited with an introduction by S. L. Schein, 163–83. Princeton University Press.

Foley, H. P. 1995. "Penelope as Moral Agent." In *The Distaff Side: Representing the Female in Homer's Odyssey*, edited by B. Cohen, 93–115. Oxford University Press.

———. 2009. "'Reverse Similes' and Sex Roles in the *Odyssey*." In *Oxford Readings in Classical Studies: Homer's Odyssey*, edited by L. E. Doherty, 189–207. Oxford University Press.

Fowler, D. 1997. "Second Thoughts on Closure." In *Classical Closure: Reading the End in Greek and Latin Literature*, edited by D. H. Roberts, F. M. Dunn, and D. Fowler, 3–22. Princeton University Press.

Fowler, R. 2004. "The Homeric Question." In *The Cambridge Companion to Homer*, edited by R. Fowler, 220–32. Cambridge University Press.

Galinsky, G. K. 1990. "Hercules in the Aeneid." In *Oxford Readings in Vergil's Aeneid*, edited by S. J. Harrison, 277–94. Oxford University Press.

Gei, R. H. 1998. "The Show Must Go On: The Death of Marcellus and the Future of the Augustan Principate (*Aeneid* 6.608–27)." In *Vergil's Aeneid: Augustan Epic and Political Context*, edited by H-P. Stahl, 119–34. The Classical Press of Wales.

Goldhill, S. 1991. *The Poet's Voice: Essays on Poetics and Greek Literature.* Cambridge University Press.

Goold, G. P. 1990. "Servius and the Helen Episode." In *Oxford Readings in Vergil's Aeneid*, edited by S. J. Harrison, 60–126. Oxford University Press.

Gould, J. 1985. "On Making Sense of Greek Religion." In *Greek Religion and Society*, edited by P. E. Easterling and J. V. Muir, 1–33. Cambridge University Press.

Gransden, K. W. 1976. *Virgil Aeneid Book VIII*. Cambridge University Press.

———. 1984. *Virgil's Iliad: An Essay on Epic Narrative*. Cambridge University Press.

———. 2004. *Virgil, The Aeneid: A Student Guide*. 2nd ed., by S. J. Harrison. Cambridge University Press.

Graziosi, B., and Haubold, J. 2005. *Homer: The Resonance of Epic*. Classical Literature and Society. Duckworth.

———, eds. 2010. *Homer: Iliad Book VI*. Cambridge University Press.

Griffin, J. 1980. *Homer on Life and Death*. Oxford University Press.

———. 2001. "The Epic Cycle and the Uniqueness of Homer." In *Oxford Readings in Homer's Iliad*, edited by D. L. Cairns, 365–84. Oxford University Press.

———. 2004. "The Speeches." In *The Cambridge Companion to Homer*, edited by R. Fowler, 156–67. Cambridge University Press.

Guillermo, J. 2013. *Sibyls: Prophecy and Power in the Ancient World*. Overlook Duckworth.

Hall, E. 2008. *The Return of Ulysses: A Cultural History of Homer's Odyssey*. I. B. Tauris.

Hardie, P. 1986. *Virgil's Aeneid: Cosmos and Imperium*. Oxford University Press.

———, ed. 1994. *Virgil Aeneid Book IX*. Cambridge Greek and Latin Classics. Cambridge University Press.

———. 1997a. "Closure in Latin Epic." In *Classical Closure: Reading the End in Greek and Latin Literature*, edited by D. H. Roberts, F. M. Dunn, and D. Fowler, 139–62. Princeton University Press.

———. 1997b. "Virgil and Tragedy." In *The Cambridge Companion to Virgil*, edited by C. Martindale, 312–25. Cambridge University Press.

———. 1998. *Virgil*. Greece and Rome New Surveys in the Classics, No. 28. Oxford University Press.

———. 2014. *The Last Trojan Hero: A Cultural History of Virgil's Aeneid*. I. B. Tauris.

Harrison, E. L. 1990. "Divine Action in *Aeneid* Book Two." In *Oxford Readings in Vergil's Aeneid*, edited by S. J. Harrison, 46–59. Oxford University Press.

Harrison, S. J. 1990. "Some Views of the *Aeneid* in the Twentieth Century." In *Oxford Readings in Vergil's Aeneid*, edited by S. J. Harrison, 1–20. Oxford University Press.

———. 1991. *Vergil Aeneid 10 with Introduction, Translation, and Commentary*. Oxford University Press.

Heinze, R. 1993. *Virgil's Epic Technique*, translated by H. Harvey, D. Harvey, and F. Robertson. Bristol Classical Press.

Heubeck, A., and Hoekstra, A. 1989. *A Commentary on Homer's Odyssey*. Vol. 2, *Books 9–16*. Oxford, Clarendon Press.

Highet, G. 1972. *The Speeches in Vergil's Aeneid*. Princeton University Press.

Hooker, J. T. 1998. "Homeric Society: A Shame-Culture?" In *Homer*. Greece and

Rome Studies, Vol. 4, edited by I. McAuslan and P. Walcot, 14–18. Oxford University Press.

Hughes, B. 2005. *Helen of Troy—Goddess, Princess, Whore.* Jonathan Cape.

Jenkyns, R. 1998. *Virgil's Experience: Nature and History: Times, Names, and Places.* Oxford, Clarendon Press.

Johnson, J. F. 2016. *Acts of Compassion in Greek Tragic Drama.* University of Oklahoma Press.

Johnson, W. R. 1976. *Darkness Visible: A Study of Vergil's Aeneid.* University of Chicago Press.

Jones, P. V. 1988. *Homer's Odyssey: A Companion to the English Translation of Richard Lattimore.* Bristol Classical Press.

———. 2003. *Homer's Iliad: A Commentary on Three Translations.* Bristol Classical Press.

Kearns, E. 2004. "The Gods in the Homeric Epics." In *The Cambridge Companion to Homer,* edited by R. Fowler, 59–73. Cambridge University Press.

Kirk, G. S. 1962. *The Songs of Homer.* Cambridge University Press.

———. 1985. *The Iliad: A Commentary.* Vol. 1, *Books 1–4.* Cambridge University Press.

Knauer, G. N. 1990. "Vergil's *Aeneid* and Homer." In *Oxford Readings in Vergil's Aeneid,* edited by S. J. Harrison, 390–412. Oxford University Press.

Laird, A. 1997. "Approaching Characterization in Virgil." In *The Cambridge Companion to Virgil,* edited by C. Martindale, 282–93. Cambridge University Press.

Leaf, W., and Bayfield, M. A., eds. 1895–1898. *The Iliad of Homer.* 2 vols. Macmillan.

Lee, M. O. 1979. *Fathers and Sons in Virgil's Aeneid.* State University of New York Press.

Lyne, R. O. A. M. 1987. *Further Voices in Vergil's Aeneid.* Oxford Clarendon Press.

Macleod, C. W., ed. 1982. *Homer Iliad Book XXIV.* Cambridge University Press.

———. 2001. "Homer on Poetry and the Poetry of Homer." In *Oxford Readings in Homer's Iliad,* edited by D. L. Cairns, 294–310. Oxford University Press.

McAuslan, I., and Walcot, P., eds. 1998. *Homer.* Greece and Rome Studies, Vol. 4. Oxford University Press.

Murnaghan, S. 1995. "The Plan of Athena." In *The Distaff Side: Representing the Female in Homer's Odyssey,* edited by B. Cohen, 61–80. Oxford University Press.

———. 2009. "Penelope's Agnoia: Knowledge, Power and Gender in the *Odyssey.*" In *Oxford Readings in Classical Studies: Homer's Odyssey,* edited by L. E. Doherty, 231–46. Oxford University Press.

Mynors, R., ed. 1972. *P. Vergili Maronis Opera.* Oxford Classical Texts. Oxford University Press.

Nagy, G. 1999. *The Best of the Achaeans: Concepts of the Hero in Archaic Greek Poetry.* Revised Edition. The John Hopkins University Press.

Nicolson, A. 2014. *The Mighty Dead: Why Homer Matters.* William Collins.

O'Hara, J. J. 1990. *Death and the Optimistic Prophecy in Vergil's Aeneid.* Princeton University Press.

Oliensis, E. 1997. "Sons and Lovers: Sexuality and Gender in Virgil's Poetry." In *The Cambridge Companion to Virgil,* edited by C. Martindale, 294–311. Cambridge University Press.

———. 2009. *Freud's Rome: Psychoanalysis and Latin Poetry.* Cambridge University Press.

Osborne, R. 2004. "Homer's Society." In *The Cambridge Companion to Homer,* edited by R. Fowler, 206–19. Cambridge University Press.

Page. T. E. 1894. *Virgil Aeneid I–VI.* Macmillan and Co. Ltd.

Parry, A. 1966. "The Two Voices of Virgil's Aeneid." In *Virgil: A Collection of Critical Essays,* edited by S. Commager, 107–23. Prentice-Hall.

Perkell, C. P. 1981. "On Creusa, Dido and the Quality of Victory in Virgil's *Aeneid.*" In *Refexions of Women in Antiquity,* edited by H. P. Foley, 365–77. Gordon and Breach Science Publishers.

Pöschl, V. 1970. *The Art of Vergil: Image and Symbol in the Aeneid,* translated by G. Seligson. The University of Michigan Press.

Pucci, P. 1995. *Odysseus Polutropos: Intertextual Readings in the Odyssey and the Iliad, with a New Afterword.* Cornell University Press.

———. 1996. "The Song of the Sirens." In *Reading the Odyssey: Selected Interpretive Essays,* edited with an introduction by S. L. Schein, 191–99. Princeton University Press.

Redfield, J. M. 1994. *Nature and Culture in the Iliad: The Tragedy of Hector.* New Edition with Additional Chapter on the Gods. Duke University Press.

Reinhardt, K. 1996. "The Adventures in the *Odyssey.*" Translated by H. I. Flower. In *Reading The Odyssey: Selected Interpretive Essays,* edited with an introduction by S. L. Schein, 63–132. Princeton University Press.

Richardson, N. J. 1993. *The Iliad: A Commentary.* Vol. 6, *Books 21–24.* Cambridge University Press.

Rudd, N. 1990. "Dido's *Culpa.*" In *Oxford Readings in Vergil's Aeneid,* edited by S. J. Harrison, 145–66. Oxford University Press.

Russo, J., Fernandez-Galiano, M., and Heubeck, A. 1992. *A Commentary on Homer's Odyssey.* Vol. 3, *Books 17–24.* Oxford University Press.

Rutherford, R. B. 2001. "From the *Iliad* to the *Odyssey.*" In *Oxford Readings in Homer's Iliad,* edited by D. L. Cairns, 117–46. Oxford University Press.

———. 2013. *Homer.* Greece and Rome New Surveys in the Classics, No. 41. Cambridge University Press.

Schein, S. L. 1984. *The Mortal Hero: An Introduction to Homer's Iliad.* University of California Press.

———. 1995. "Female Representations and Interpreting the *Odyssey.*" In *The Distaff Side: Representing the Female in Homer's Odyssey,* edited by B. Cohen, 17–27. Oxford University Press.

———. 2016. *Homeric Epic and Its Reception: Interpretive Essays.* Oxford University Press.

Segal, C. 1971. *The Theme of the Mutilation of the Corpse in the Iliad*. Mnemosyne, Supplement 17. Brill.

———. 1994. *Singers, Heroes, and Gods in the Odyssey*. Cornell University Press.

Slatkin, L. 2001. "The Wrath of Thetis." In *Oxford Readings in Homer's Iliad*, edited by D. L. Cairns, 409–34. Oxford University Press.

Smith, R. Alden. 2011. *Virgil*. Wiley-Blackwell.

Solmsen, F. 1990. "The World of the Dead in Book 6 of the *Aeneid*." In *Oxford Readings in Vergil's Aeneid*, edited by S. J. Harrison, 208–23. Oxford University Press.

Stanford, W. B., ed. 1958–1959. Homer *Odyssey*. 2 vols. Second Edition. Macmillan.

———. 1963. *The Ulysses Theme*. Second Edition. Oxford, Blackwell.

Taplin, O. 1992. *Homeric Soundings: The Shaping of the Iliad*. Oxford, Clarendon Press.

———. 2001. "The Shield of Achilles within the *Iliad*." In *Oxford Readings in Homer's Iliad*, edited by D. L. Cairns, 342–64. Oxford University Press.

Tarrant, R. J. 1997. "Poetry and Power: Virgil's Poetry in Contemporary Context." In *The Cambridge Companion to Virgil*, edited by C. Martindale, 169–87. Cambridge University Press.

———, ed. 2012. *Virgil Aeneid Book XII*. Cambridge University Press.

Walcot, P. 2009. "Odysseus and the Art of Lying." In *Oxford Readings in Classical Studies: Homer*, edited by L. E. Doherty, 135–54. Oxford University Press.

West, D. A. 1990. "The Bough and the Gate." In *Oxford Readings in Vergil's Aeneid*, edited by S. J. Harrison, 224–38. Oxford University Press.

Williams, R. D. 1962. *P. Vergili Maronis Liber Tertius*. Oxford University Press.

———. 1990a. "The Purpose of the *Aeneid*." In *Oxford Readings in Vergil's Aeneid*, edited by S. J. Harrison, 21–36. Oxford University Press.

———. 1990b. "The Sixth Book of the *Aeneid*." In *Oxford Readings in Vergil's Aeneid*, edited by S. J. Harrison, 191–207. Oxford University Press.

Zeitlin, F. I. 1995. "Figuring Fidelity in Homer's *Odyssey*." In *The Distaff Side: Representing the Female in Homer's Odyssey*, edited by B. Cohen, 117–52. Oxford University Press.

Index

Lightning Source UK Ltd.
Milton Keynes UK
UKHW01f1817290518

323416UK00001B/83/P